Understanding Attention Deficit Disorder

Ground-breaking Methods of Diagnosis and Treatment

HAROLD N. LEVINSON, M.D.

This book has also been published as
Total Concentration

MJF BOOKS
NEW YORK

Published by MJF Books
Fine Communications
Two Lincoln Square
60 West 66th Street
New York, NY 10023

Understanding Attention Deficit Disorder
LC Control Number 01-130244
ISBN 1-56731-396-5

10   9   8   7   6   5   4   3   2   1

Dedication

This work is dedicated:

- ☐ To Diggy, Laura, and Joy, who taught me love, affection, and parenthood
- ☐ To my many suffering patients and their boundless courage and endurance, their determination to overcome, no matter what, their steadfast loved ones, and their desperate need for understanding and treatment
- ☐ To *all* who need and seek help, for themselves and others
- ☐ To *all* clinicians and researchers whose efforts have enabled the vital separation of scientific fact from fiction and chaos

Contents

Contents

A Personal Note To Readers

Total Concentration is about people—for people! Those who've *lost and found* this vital force. And those who desire nothing more than to regain it.

- ☐ Some with impaired concentration or attention deficits are very young, others much older.
- ☐ Some suffer directly, others indirectly (parents, wives, husbands, friends. . . .)
- ☐ Some "merely" require an enhancement in otherwise normal powers of concentration so as to survive and succeed in the *overload* characterizing the 1990's.

All are bonded by common aims:

- ☐ to understand and overcome concentration-related symptoms and their underlying disorders
- ☐ to achieve and even enhance Total Concentration

To date, most *everything* my colleagues and I have learned about the many and varied functions comprising and implementing *Total Concentration* have come from listening to and observing people describe their problems and/or struggling to cope and/or compensate—even overcompensate.

As a result, I have chosen to teach you about *Total Concentration* in a similar manner—by letting scores of suffering and successfully treated people share their amazing insights and experiences with you.

Since the best studied and researched concentration symptoms stem from a dysfunction of previously unknown physiological origin called Attention Deficit Disorder or ADD, the content described and presented in *Total Concentration* will primarily emphasize and highlight this impairment. Eventually, the patients you listen to will enable you to completely understand and solve the scientific riddles previously characterizing this heretofore puzzling problem.

So listen and read carefully! You will also learn about the various types of physiologically and psychologically determined concentration symptoms and how they may also be successfully overcome. And you will be introduced to methods which facilitate the development of exceptional powers of concentration. All these contrasting studies are crucial for ultimately understanding concentration-related functioning and dysfunctioning.

In the final analysis, you will clearly understand the commonly used and practiced dictum: Sound body, sound mind! Indeed, discovering the physiological basis responsible for this intuitively derived dictum led:

☐ to a solution of the riddle characterizing Attention Deficit Disorder or ADD.
☐ to an understanding of the momentary "supernormal" concentration and coordination phenomena called by athletes "in the zone."
☐ to the means and methods needed to attain and even surpass *Total Concentration.*

P.S. With only partial tongue-in-cheek, I might add that it is anticipated that eradication of Attention Deficit Disorders would more than eradicate the national deficit disorder.

Preface

Have you ever wondered:

- [ ] Why you can't stick to a task for more than a few seconds or minutes?
- [ ] Why you are so easily distracted?
- [ ] Why your eyes wander across the page, focusing on everything . . . and nothing?
- [ ] Why reading—or writing—exhausts you?
- [ ] Why you can't seem to concentrate while in a car? Why you always get lost?
- [ ] Why your child has trouble staying seated at his desk?
- [ ] Why your child tends to be moody or impulsive?
- [ ] Why your child seems to have a low frustration tolerance or temper tantrums?
- [ ] Why you have difficulty paying attention to a speaker?
- [ ] Why you have to procrastinate endlessly?
- [ ] Why you can't remember exactly what it is that must be done *right now*?

If you've searched for answers to questions like these, you are not alone. In fact, as this book will show you, the problems that may be plaguing you or your child now—difficulties with concentration, distractibility, hyper- or overactivity, impulsivity, and related memory and learning symptoms—occur ithin the general population *far more frequently* and impair academic, behavioral, emotional, and occupational functioning *far more often* and in many more ways than anyone ever imagined!

Inside the pages of *Total Concentration*, you'll find descriptions and holistic explanations of these symptoms in their many and varied shapes and disguises. You'll also meet scores of individuals who will tell you of the devastating impact these obstacles have had on their personal, academic, and occupational lives. Most important, you'll learn everything you need to know about the comprehensive treatment that has already enabled thousands to compensate for this seemingly "invisible" disorder. By providing this information to the general public, it is my hope that millions more will learn of the crucial, life-enhancing techniques that can minimize or *eliminate* the concentration and related problems that permeate—and often destroy—the fundamental ability to survive successfully and happily in everyday life.

By the time you finish *Total Concentration*, I think you'll understand why this book *had* to be written. Although many sophisticated research articles and books have attempted to describe this concentration and distractibility disorder in its purest form—now called Attention Deficit Disorder, or ADD—such works have barely scratched the surface in terms of its description, understanding, and treatment. How can that be? Unfortunately, when members of the medical community first identify a disorder, they often describe it in terms of the most obvious or dramatic symptoms—those of greatest severity or intensity. For example, when diabetes was first recognized, clinicians simply viewed it as a comatose state. Yet we now know that many other symptoms are part and parcel of this pancreatic disorder and that mild and compensated forms far exceed those with severe and obviously recognizable problems. In fact, many parallels can be drawn between the capability of diagnosing diabetes and ADD. Thus, there are two distinct forms of diabetes, called Type I (the severest) and Type II (a milder form), each characterized by *similar* symptoms. (And as noted, there are five types of concentration disorders.) To complicate diagnostic matters further, the degree and onset of symptoms within each type is different: Type I symptoms are dramatic and appear suddenly, while those of Type II are less severe and develop slowly. But if you think even these distinctions have made diagnosis of diabetes a clear-cut matter, think again: signs of the disease, not always what we think of as "logical clues," include frequent urination; unquenchable thirst;

ravenous appetite; weight loss; weakness and fatigue; irritability; nausea and vomiting; tingling, numbness, or pain in the hands or feet; blurred vision; itchy genitals; recurring gum or bladder infections; and cuts and scratches that heal slowly! Doesn't it seem incredible that our initial definition of this disorder as a "comatose state" could have been so vague and imprecise?

Until now, Attention Deficit Disorder—a physiologically determined impairment of concentration—has been described in both a highly restrictive and broad-brush fashion. Its current description—found in textbooks, in psychiatric diagnostic manuals, and in the minds of many a well-meaning clinician—recognizes only the tip or "comatose" part of the total disorder. According to my research, current definitions ignore the facts that there are five basic *types* of concentration disorders (CD); that there are two physiologically based types, referred to as ADD; that Type IV is more severe than Type III; that each type may share characteristics of similar *quality*; and that there are myriad symptoms—mild, moderate, and severe—that may stand alone or overlap with others for each of these types. Some occur suddenly, others more slowly and insidiously. And like diabetes, the numbers with mild and compensated symptoms far outnumber those with severe forms.

Moreover, by considering only the severest and most obvious cases in their studies, those who have devised the current description of ADD have also minimized its prevalence. According to published statistics, roughly 3 to 10 percent of the population is affected. Yet in my opinion, based on twenty-five years of research, it's more likely that over *three times* this number suffer from varying degrees and intensities of this disorder!

Of course, because researchers and clinicians have concerned themselves only with the most obvious symptoms of ADD, they also have tended to investigate the most obvious sources for its cause(s). According to some scientists, chromosomal disorders are at the root of the problem. Others believe perinatal stresses such as low birth weight, maternal alcoholism, or difficulties during pregnancy and delivery may increase one's chances of developing ADD. Still others have suggested that poor nutrition, allergies, unsatisfactory living conditions, or the psychological trauma brought about by critical life events—death of a family member or parents' divorce—may trigger ADD. While these and scores of other current theories are certainly plausible explanations for why a person might be predisposed to ADD, none has been clinically proven. In my practice I have not found significant numbers of patients with any of these problems or histories, genetic possibilities aside. What I *have* discovered, however, is that roughly 90 percent of all my ADD patients suffer from balance and coordination problems—diagnostic signs of an inner-ear-system dysfunction. And over 90 percent also complain of one or more academic and related symptoms characterizing dyslexia or learning disabilities. When treated with proper medication and behavioral techniques, more than 80 percent of patients are relieved of their symptoms!

In *Total Concentration,* I hope to expand our present knowledge of Attention Deficit Disorder and to add a logical, new dimension to this elusive problem. I believe that my research moves our understanding of ADD a giant step forward. By sharing my findings—and the experiences and insights of thousands of patients who have already been helped—I truly hope that this book will enable countless children, adolescents, and adults to better understand their disorder and its seemingly infinite variations and complexities, and to overcome it! Furthermore, the study of ADD sheds significant light on the "normal" ADD-like symptoms that affect us all—albeit in a temporary and reversible way.

CHAPTER I

Introduction

Sometimes the most complex problems have the simplest solutions. An overwhelming amount of medical evidence now suggests that disordered concentration is one such problem.

The physiological basis of impaired concentration—Attention Deficit Disorder, or ADD—has been significantly researched and described.[1] However, the specific neurophysiological origins and mechanisms responsible for symptom formation have until now defied detection and clarification. Yet once this physiological basis was recognized, it was immediately obvious that clinical researchers had overlooked the most important piece of the puzzle. Today, having treated more than twenty thousand patients, and having analyzed the appearance and disappearance of a vast array of concentration-related symptoms, I can share this crucial missing piece with you.

In the pages that follow, you will learn the differences between *realistic* concentration disorders (Type I), *neurotic* concentration disorders (Type II), *physiologically* determined concentration disorders, or ADD (Types III and IV), and *secondary* concentration disorders (Type V^2) resulting from the mental energy drain of a variety of conditions such as anemia or metabolic disturbances.

Furthermore, you will see how I have been led to conclude that

---

[1] Over the years this disorder has been variously called Hyperactivity-Impulsivity, Minimal Brain Dysfunction, Attention Deficit Disorder (ADD) with or without Hyperactivity (H), and most recently Attention-Deficit Hyperactivity Disorder (ADHD) and even Undifferentiated-Attention-Deficit Disorder (U-ADD). All these terms are considered by most clinicians and researchers to represent one and the same syndrome. And the lacronym used most frequently is ADD.

the vast majority of concentration disorders—*even the mild and transient symptoms that are common to us all*—are often physiologically or chemically determined by a permanent or temporary malfunction within the inner-ear system and its interconnections with alerting and attention/activity modulating centers of the brain.[2] You will also learn that ADD is much more than just a concentration and distractibility disorder. It is a problem that encompasses a wide variety of symptoms affecting activity levels, impulsivity, mood, memory and learning, balance and coordination, just to name a few.

Finally, and most important, you will learn that if you are among the estimated 90 percent or more of all patients whose ADD-based problems stem from this common inner-ear disorder, the kind of *medical* help and understanding you have prayed for is finally here. And you will learn that there are a variety of nonpharmacological therapies available for *all* with concentration-related symptoms. In other words, all symptoms can now be clearly explained. And all patients can now be properly diagnosed and effectively treated.

---

[2]When I say the inner-ear system, I am really referring to the cerebellar-vestibular system (CVS), a complex network comprised of the vestibular system (the inner ear) and the cerebellum. The CVS is discussed in detail in Chapter Eleven. Note that the inner ear is not to be confused with the middle ear, the small air-filled space between the eardrum and inner ear where our sense of hearing originates. In addition, the alerting system of the brain and its modulating structures will also be reviewed in the same chapter.

Chapter II

Is There a Physiological Basis for Your Concentration Problems?: A Self-Test

Are your concentration problems the result of a *physiological* problem? The following simple test will give you your first clue.

The symptoms and behavior patterns in the test may appear to be totally unrelated to what you normally think of as a concentration dysfunction. But all of the symptoms noted actually stem from the very same physiological problem that is responsible for most concentration problems: *a malfunction within the inner ear and important interrelated systems of the brain.*

Therefore, if your concentration problems are due to an inner-ear malfunction, one or more of these seemingly unrelated symptoms and behavior patterns may also be present.

CONCENTRATION AND DISTRACTIBILITY

1. Do you have difficulty concentrating and find yourself distracted by the slightest noise or thought?
2. Do people accuse you of being spacy or scatterbrained?
3. Do you tire easily or get "foggy" quickly when you read, write, or study?
4. Do you have difficulty reading a book from cover to cover, or find "dry" reading a torture?
5. Can you listen to music and study at the same time?
6. Do you tend to ignore, or have difficulty following, written instructions?

HYPERACTIVITY, OVERACTIVITY, AND IMPULSIVITY

7. Were you hyperactive or overactive as a child?
8. Were or are you restless, fidgety, driven to rapidly shift from task to task, idea to idea, job to job, person to person?
9. Do you have a low frustration tolerance?
10. Are you prone to temper outbursts?
11. Do you tend to act before you think? Are you impulsive?

SPECIFIC ACADEMIC DIFFICULTIES

Reading

12. Did or do you have trouble remembering the shapes and sounds of letter and word configurations?
13. When reading, do your eyes lose their place as they scan letters, words, and sentences?
14. Do you often find that you remember little or nothing of what you have read?
15. Do you sometimes have to reread sentences or paragraphs in order to understand them?
16. Do you ever use your finger to guide your eyes from letter to letter or from word to word?
17. Do you dread having to read aloud in front of others?
18. Do you sometimes have to read aloud to yourself in order to remember and comprehend what you've read?

Writing

19. Is your handwriting sloppy?
20. Do you prefer printing as opposed to script (cursive writing?
21. During the process of writing, do you often omit letters and words or displace them to more distant parts of the written passage? Does your writing drift up or down on blank paper?
22. Do you often reverse letters and words when you write?

23. As a child, did you ever engage in "mirror-writing" (i.e., writing in reverse)?
24. Do people often tell you that they can't read your writing?

Spelling

25. Do you often forget the letter sequences of words?
26. As a child, did you forget words shortly after a spelling exam? Or even before an exam?
27. Do you often reverse letters and syllables?
28. Do you spell orally better than when writing?
29. Do you rely heavily on a dictionary, "spelling calculator," or other person to help you spell at school or at work?

Mathematics

30. Did or do you often forget addition, subtraction, multiplication, or division facts?
31. Do you rely on finger counting or mental counting?
32. Do you tend to reverse or scramble numbers when reading or writing?
33. Do you have trouble writing numbers in columns and then adding or subtracting them?
34. Do you reverse directions when performing arithmetical functions (i.e., adding columns from left to right rather than the reverse)?
35. Do you occasionally reverse or confuse $+$, $-$, $\times$, and $\div$ with one another?
36. Do you have difficulty counting change or making change?

Grammar

37. Did you (or do you now) have difficulty understanding and/or using simple grammatical forms?
38. Do people ever accuse you of using "bad" verbal grammar?
39. When you write, do you tend to "ramble on"?

40. Does your writing or speech have a "run on" quality to it?
41. Did you (or do you now) have difficulty understanding rules of punctuation?

Speech

42. As a child, were you a late talker?
43. When speaking, did or do you tend to start and stop or use "um" as a bridge between words?
44. Do you stutter, slur your words, or frequently stammer?
45. Do you hate having to speak in public?
46. Do you avoid activities that require speaking (i.e., meetings, social gatherings, etc.)?
47. Are you prone to slips of the tongue, saying words out of sequence, or reversing directions such as up and down or left and right?

GENERAL ACADEMIC DIFFICULTIES

48. Do you make dumb mistakes all of the time, even though you feel that you're smart?
49. Were you viewed as an underachiever, an overachiever, a late bloomer, or an academic puzzlement?
50. Did you hate or avoid school and/or school-related activities?
51. Do you suspect you are, or were you ever diagnosed as, dyslexic or learning disabled?

MEMORY

52. Do you have difficulty remembering names, faces, dates, spelling, grammar, lists, directions, or sequences?
53. Do you find yourself endlessly making lists of things you need to do because you don't trust your memory?
54. Are you absentminded, forgetful, or prone to experiencing mental blanks or blocks?

55. Do you make the same mistakes over and over again, almost as though you had no recollection of the last time you made the mistake?

56. Do you have difficulty remembering simple addition, subtraction, and multiplication facts, and/or do you count on your fingers?

VISION AND HEARING

57. Do you have poor depth perception or limited peripheral vision (i.e., tunnel vision)?

58. Do you tilt your head when you read, have to lie down, lose your place easily, or use your index finger to help you?

59. Do you scramble words and sentences when you read, or tend to confuse letters (such as *b* and *d*), numbers (such as 6 and 9, 14 and 41, etc.) or words (such as *saw* and *was*)?

60. Do you experience any of the following while reading: headaches, nausea, dizziness, blurred vision, double vision, or word and sentence movement?

61. Do things not "sink in" the first time you hear them, forcing you to ask people to repeat what they've just said (and making them accuse you of not listening)?

BALANCE AND COORDINATION

62. When you were young, did you have difficulty with balance and coordination tasks such as skipping, hopping, jumping rope, roller-skating, gymnastics, tumbling, or riding a bike?

63. Is your handwriting messy, poorly angulated, infantile, or difficult to read?

64. Are you clumsy, klutzy, or accident-prone—always bumping into things, or tripping or falling?

65. When you were young, did you have difficulty mastering fine-coordination tasks such as tying your shoes, using utensils, buttoning buttons, and zippering zippers?

66. As a child, were you prone to bedwetting or soiling?

67. Did you, or do you currently, have any of the following speech difficulties: stuttering, slurring, stammering, slips of the tongue, saying words in reverse, or rambling?

SENSE OF DIRECTION

68. Do you have difficulty distinguishing left from right? East and west? North and south?
69. Do you easily get disoriented, lost, or confused?
70. Do you need directions every time you go somewhere, even if you've been there many times before?

SENSE OF TIME

71. Do you have difficulty judging elapsed time or making time projections?
72. Did you have problems learning to tell time?
73. Are you always late or always early?

MOTION SENSITIVITY

74. Were you prone to dizziness or motion sickness as a child? (Are you still?)
75. Do you dislike or avoid buses, trains, boats, amusement-park rides, and other motion-related activities?

OBSESSIONS AND COMPULSIONS

76. Do irresistible, repetitive thoughts and actions (obsessions and compulsions) drive you crazy and render you unable to relax?
77. When you leave your house, do you often find yourself going back repeatedly to make sure you locked the door, turned off the gas, etc.?

78. Do you find yourself driven to check and recheck, touch and retouch, think and rethink?

RELATED MENTAL SYMPTOMS

79. Do you have headaches, migraines, stomachaches, nausea, or other psychosomatic symptoms that have sent you from doctor to doctor to no avail?
80. Were you an anxious, nervous child?
81. Are you prone to mood swings?
82. Do you have hypochondriacal worries, or are you prone to worrying about nothing?
83. Do you suffer from sleep disturbances such as insomnia, nightmares, or sleepwalking? Or are you overtired—sleepy—for no apparent reason?
84. Do you procrastinate and have difficulty making decisions?
85. Are you self-conscious about your intelligence, speech, or appearance?
86. Do you often feel inferior, stupid, ugly, or clumsy?

The significance of each of these questions and many others will be discussed in detail in the Chapters to follow.

Chapter III

Trapped in a Nightmare

When patients with Attention Deficit Disorder come to my office for the first time, they are usually worried, distraught, frustrated, and confused. They cannot understand why they're not able to bear down on a subject and stay with it, or why they suffer from seemingly endless distractions and procrastinations that prevent them from dealing with the job at hand.

In many cases, patients have spent huge amounts of time and energy searching for answers in the offices of psychologists, psychiatrists, neurologists, general practitioners, allergists, food therapists, acupuncturists, or chiropractors. While some with ADD have been helped by these health care professionals, the majority continue to suffer in silence and to wonder why they cannot be "cured." In time, many become convinced that their difficulties are caused by a character flaw, or a "bad nature." Some individuals even believe they are being punished for something that they did wrong at an early age!

In the pages that follow, you will learn that 90 percent or more of all people who seek help for impaired concentration and related symptoms of ADD suffer from a *physiological* problem within their inner ear. This theory isn't something you'll read about in magazines, pop-psychology books, or even in the vast and sometimes perplexing scientific literature. Nor is it something that your doctor will necessarily know of or understand. In fact, it is something I discovered almost accidentally—and only after twenty-five years of psychiatric and neurological practice.

Yet once I recognized this physiological basis, it was immediately obvious that clinical researchers, and the medical community at large, had overlooked the most important piece of the ADD puzzle. Today, having treated more than twenty thousand patients, and having analyzed the appearance and disappearance of a vast array of ADD symptoms, I can share this crucial missing piece with you.

In most books written about medical problems, the reader is told about the cause-and-effect relationships that determine symptoms, not shown. But this isn't how I learned about the physiological basis of ADD, and I don't think it's how you should learn. My theories and my treatment approach developed after I examined, talked with, and listened to thousands of patients. I feel you should have the opportunity to come to the same understanding. After all, it is the real-life experiences of people who have ADD, not the opinions of experts, that ultimately define this disorder.

In this chapter, and in many of the chapters that follow, you will find a wide variety of case histories, ranging from typical to extreme, that will greatly enrich your perspective on this elusive problem known as Attention Deficit Disorder.

All of the patients whose stories appear in this chapter suffer from what I call Type III ADD: their condition stems from a malfunction within the inner-ear system that secondarily affects other interconnecting brain structures via impaired circuits or chemical transmitters. As you will see from these stories, there is no typical Type III patient. A malfunctioning inner-ear system may be present at birth or develop later as a result of accident, disease, or stress-related events. It can create a wide variety and combination of symptoms. Therefore, your own experiences may be extremely similar to those of some patients and totally dissimilar to those of others. Yet there is something to be learned from every story.

Listen carefully to these Type III ADD individuals. Their experiences will help you to better understand your own struggle with concentration. Furthermore, their stories will give you new and valuable insight into how to help yourself and others who suffer. Indeed, *acute and reversible forms* of this disturbance can simply and readily explain the concentration symptoms that affect us all at one time or another during our lives. With this kind of understanding and insight, you will be well on your way to achieving your own personal level of total concentration.

Alan B.

Because of the superficial *mirage* created by gifted and compensatory functioning, it can be very difficult if not impossible to spot individuals—especially adults—with ADD. Yet they may be suffering and hurting severely on the inside.

If you spend a little time in the tiny beach community of Marina Del Rey in California, sooner or later you'll catch a glimpse of Alan B. You'll see the fifty-five-year-old building contractor scurrying in and out of one of the apartment houses he manages, or you'll find him explaining complicated building plans to a group of subcontractors. In the evenings, you might find him on a neighbor's rooftop, putting the final touches on a new satellite dish he's just installed. Watching this man go about his daily business, you would be impressed by his apparent breadth of knowledge and be struck by his ability to handle, seemingly without effort, an incredible variety of details. You also would probably conclude that Alan B., a relatively successful businessman, has no difficulty concentrating. During our first meeting in my office, Alan revealed details quite to the contrary:

"For the past thirty years, I've spent my life in a fog. There's a fuzziness that surrounds me wherever I go. I space in and out. I have trouble concentrating on the simplest tasks. I get confused when I'm at the grocery store—trying to read the labels makes me dizzy. And I get distracted by all the visual configurations of people moving. Even their voices affect me. Often I see things as a blur. And then my mind gets even fuzzier—and sometimes goes blank. If I'm in the car, I have trouble staying focused on road signs and I often get lost. If I'm ordering lumber or materials, I get confused even if I have a list in front of me—I may see the word *socket*, but when I say it, it comes out *sprocket*. Things that are easy for other people are hard for me. Dialing the phone can be traumatic—I forget the numbers, or dial them in the wrong sequence. Recently I purchased a programmable phone, and that helps a lot.

"Even when I'm at home I can't escape this abnormal thing that lingers inside me. If I go into the kitchen to get a glass of milk, by the time I get there, I've forgotten what I came to get. Just looking inside the refrigerator overwhelms me. If my wife asks me to put something in the oven, I'll either forget to put it in, or forget to take it out before it burns. Sure, I have some days that are better than others. . . . But for me, even a good day is bad.

"Over the years, I've tried to figure out what's wrong with me. I've been to food therapists, allergists, you name it. They all claimed they could cure me. I even spent eighteen months in therapy with a psychiatrist trying to get a handle on it. He told me that I had concentration problems because of 'unsettled business' with my father, who died twenty-three years ago. He compared me to a pressure cooker, holding a lid on my inner feelings. And he said that when these feelings start to surface, the energy and concentration powers needed to hold them in check become enormous and thus leave me feeling numb or depersonalized—unable to focus and properly feel and think. In my opinion, his diagnosis is bunk. It doesn't explain the fogginess, the spaciness, or the fact that I get confused when I stare into the refrigerator!

"His diagnosis also doesn't explain why, despite all my problems, I'm pretty successful in my business. There are a couple of reasons for that which have nothing to do with my father, mother, or anyone else—except genetics, maybe. First, I was born with golden hands. I've always been able to master mechanical things. I have a clear vision of seeing something finished before it's done—I can look at an empty lot and visualize a new building and see every board and nail in place. Second, I have a lot of tenacity to me. I can force myself to do things. It's sheer willpower, or stubbornness, that has allowed me to get where I am today.

"Also, I've always had an excess of energy. Physically, I'm tireless and have always been that way. Until lately, that is. I'm starting to get depressed and tired. For the first time in my life, I feel myself giving in. Giving up. And it's scary. I guess my nuclear fusion processes are burning out. And I no longer seem to have the concentration, energy, and effort needed to prevent my forgetting or bungling things. Perhaps this all also has something to do with my age. Maybe my ability to compensate is just losing ground."

Clearly, Alan is a man of intelligence and sensitivity whose concentration problems have demoralized him. Alan suffers from Type III ADD.

Larry

Larry is a twenty-six-year-old electronic engineer who recently sought treatment for concentration-related symptoms. In his own words:

"My job is getting harder and harder to do well. I'm continually required to focus on, learn, and solve at least two new design projects every time I finish one 'old' one. And it's getting tougher and tougher to do. I just don't have the concentration and learning powers to meet the expectations—which increase continually with prior successes. Until I read *Smart But Feeling Dumb*, I never knew what was really wrong with me. You see, I've always been called either an underachiever or an overachiever—depending on what they thought my basic potential was. But now I understand my symptoms, and that has kept me going. But I'd like help.

"Throughout my whole life, I've felt as if I were trying to see through a fog. Unless I was concentrating at maximum levels, words I was reading would get blurry and dance around, or even reverse and blur out. My eyes would continually lose their place and I'd need a finger or marker to keep focus. Conversations I was listening to would pass me by. And it would take me extra time to process what I heard. In fact, words I heard and even said would scramble, reverse, and blank out just like words I read and even words and sentences I wrote. To compensate, I had to develop extraordinary concentration and organizing skills. But it wasn't easy. And now these skills are either insufficient or are failing me.

"I remember as a kid being called lazy, spoiled, inattentive. My friends even called me 'air head' as a nickname. At that time, I truly was spacy and disorganized, forever being distracted by any slight sound—even a pin dropping—or movement. It was hard to see, hear, and perform things in sequence. Apparently I didn't have the concentration energies to see, hear, do, and think things out to completion. It was like I was stuck on one simple step at a time. I was also stuck in time, in the moment. There was no way to anticipate and plan! There was no future—and I couldn't recall the past too well. Only the present existed. I guess I didn't have the concentration and energy and optimism needed to look ahead. And the worst of it was that I didn't realize all this until I was better.

"Now that I'm an electronic engineer and write programs, it's relatively easy for me to understand what was—and is—wrong. But I couldn't before. Your simple explanations make the most sense to me.

"I remember forcing myself to concentrate and think—and trying to filter out all sorts of stupid background noises—but I couldn't. That is, I couldn't until around fifteen or sixteen.

"I was always very klutzy and clumsy, forever falling and breaking things, including my bones. I avoided group sports like the plague. It was always an embarrassment. Not only was I picked last, I was usually not picked at all by teams unless they were forced to take me. I can't remember all the names I was called by other kids, but they all had to do with stupid idiot and terms like that. Were I not already calling myself those names, I would have been completely devastated on hearing them from others. But it still hurts more when others call you stupid than when you just say it to yourself.

"In any event, I decided to start running. I was feeling lethargic all the time, I think because trying to concentrate, block things out, think, and remember . . . were burning me out. So I ran. And as I ran longer and longer, and faster and faster, a strange thing happened.

"All of a sudden I started to do well in school. My grades went from C's, D's, and even a few F's, to A's and B's. My concentration dramatically improved and my distractibility lessened. It was like a miracle. And like all miracles, you accept them without asking too many questions—for fear they will disappear as rapidly as they came.

"From that point on, I was able to complete high school and do fairly well in college and even graduate school. It wasn't until I read your explanation in *Smart But Feeling Dumb* that this miracle of mine suddenly made sense."

He then picked up my book, showed me his highlighted portion, and asked, "Didn't you say that athletes often show enhanced concentration and academic functioning when *in training*? As an engineer, this makes perfect sense if your theory is correct. By fine-tuning the inner-ear system, you may then enable enhancement of related concentration and academic functioning. That's exactly what happened to me. That explains my miracle! But I need another one now if I'm to continue with my job."

Marty

Marty is currently a fifty-five-year-old physician and researcher who was chief-of-service at a major university medical center. Although he recently sought treatment for depression and severe sluggishness and a subnormal mental and physical drive, his history revealed him to have been hyperactive as a child and overactive thereafter. Indeed, he attributed his scientific and medical successes to being able to eventually channel his enormous energy reserve into academics. "However, I wasn't always able to sublimate my energies and concentration this way. When I was younger, I was always in school-related troubles. And I found it impossible to concentrate in class: I was either daydreaming about sports or looking out the window while fidgeting in my seat. In fact, I still remember the teacher trying to embarrass me by asking me a question while I was watching the snow falling in a semitrance. I think I devastated her by answering the question correctly. Then I finished her off completely by telling her that 'I think best when I look abstract!' Although I was being a wise guy at the time, what I told her was really true. It was easier to listen when I wasn't forced to concentrate. Yet my writing was illegible—completely so—unless I concentrated on it severely and drew it like an artist does calligraphy. And my spelling was not too hot, either. Interestingly, I still find it hard to spell simple words correctly, whereas I never have trouble spelling medical terms. I guess that's because I must have outgrown my spelling problems by the time I got into college and certainly by medical school. My writing improved only when my 'life depended on it'—to pass an exam. Thank God for true-and-false tests and oral exams.

"In school, *trouble* and *teasing* were my first and second names. Not at home! My mother was strict and would have killed me. So I let it all out whenever and wherever I had the chance. And most of the time that was in school, except when I was out playing. I was also very stubborn. And when I was frustrated, my temper would flare. Later on, however, I seemed to become determined and forceful instead. Come to think of it, I still have trouble sticking to one thing for any sustained time period. I always have multiple projects and am always reading many journals and books, all at the same time. I just keep moving from one to another and back again until I'm finished. What I lack in patience I make up for with a very good memory. That way I scan things rapidly and seem to learn easily. If I had to read and reread things in even a normal time span, I don't know that I could ever have made it. In fact, I seemed to read, concentrate, and remember more easily when I feared failing in medical school. That fear seemed to stimulate my adrenalin. It was like taking a shot of Dexedrine. And I just sailed right through everything without fatigue, boredom, or even daydreaming.

"My wife repeatedly tells me that I have no listening patience. That I listen to people for only a few seconds and then my eyes and mind are off somewhere else. She is a psychologist. I guess her observations are correct. Come to think of it, there is no way I could have ever been a psychologist and listened to anyone for even a forty-five minute hour. It would have killed me—and them, too! In my specialty, I examine many patients in a day, but I'm always moving around and see each one for only a few minutes, consultations aside. But even when I'm examining them, I'm standing and moving and talking. I don't know that I could sit in one place and listen for any length of time. That is, without daydreaming, jumping up and down, falling asleep, or getting stir-crazy.

"In fact, I have the same problem with friends. I know a lot of people and I'm liked. But I'm not outwardly close to anyone. I'm equally distant to all. And I sort of keep track of those I like without really getting into any deep personal conversations. You know,

I've never been able to talk to anyone about anything personally or real serious for more than a few minutes before I got depressed. This is the first time in my life that I had either the need for or the feeling of being able to talk about 'deep stuff' for any length of time. And that applies to my wife and children as well. Don't get me wrong, I care about them and love them very much. But I have the same trouble listening to anyone too long. And speaking to people—it's easier if I'm moving than if I'm standing still.

"I think I sort of get claustrophobic when I'm stuck in a conversation without being free to move on! And I'm the same way, if not worse, with personal telephone calls.

"Interestingly, I never thought of myself as hyper, even though everyone else did! By the way, might my depression now be related to all this in any way?"

ADD-H IN PRESCHOOL CHILDREN

Since the term ADD-H was originally based on hyperactivity and impulsivity, as well as concentration and distractibility symptoms, and as most older children with this diagnosis date their initial symptoms back to early childhood, it seems appropriate to present two cases described in the literature before those from my own practice.

Case 1

In a single case study of a two-year, eight-month-old child by Husain & colleagues, on interview the mother reported that the child was beyond her control. He was "on the go" from early morning till night, refused to sit still or play with games or peers for any more than a few minutes at any one time, was destructive of his toys and furniture, and was shunned by his peers and siblings because of his unpredictable and physically aggressive behavior. He was negative, stubborn, and given to temper tantrums. His sleep was disturbed with initial insomnia and early rising, which often resulted in destructive behavior before the family rose.

Case 2

The description of another preschooler by Cantwell is significantly instructive as well:

> This boy had distinguished himself shortly before his third birthday by being expelled from nursery school. In itself, this was not particularly significant, since the school itself was a very rigid one. What was unusual was the statement to me by his teacher that under no circumstances would they take him back: he was simply too disruptive.
>
> When I interviewed his parents, the history they gave was a disaster. They described a small tyrant who ruled the house: he was up all night running around, had learned to unhook the screen door and had been found walking down Ventura Boulevard in his Pampers, had put himself in the clothes dryer and turned it on, and so on. My next move was to examine the child himself. He appeared abnormal in some minor respects: an articulation problem that made his speech hard to follow . . . yet he played reasonably quietly with the Fisher-Price dollhouse for some forty-five minutes. To his parents and teacher he was a disaster, yet to me he looked pretty good, so I began to wonder what was going on.
>
> [After Dr. Cantwell examined the child] the boy then walked outside the consultation room, where there is a group of secretarial desks. One woman was away from her desk, and he climbed up on her chair and started pounding the typewriter. When she returned and asked him to get down, he jumped down, kicked her in the shins, and yelled—because of his articulation problem—"Duck you, bitch!" He then lay down and began kicking and screaming; it took his mother another forty-five minutes to calm him sufficiently to take him home.

ADD-H IN A CHILD BEGINNING SCHOOL

Kathy

Kathy is a bright, charming, coquettish, and charismatic five-year-old whirlwind who rises and shines at 4:00 A.M. She remains in perpetual mental and physical motion from dawn to dusk, except when absorbed in art work. Indeed, Kathy's activity level was first experienced while she was in the womb, when she first began moving and kicking her mother, just as she now does in her sleep.

When coloring, she is calm, fully alert, and completely tuned in to the task at hand, impervious to any and all distractions. She appears to function magnificently on the basis of rapid and accurate intuitive assessment—sizing up and manipulating people, her siblings included, and situations at lightning speeds.

She excels in both details and global perceptions when not engaged in an "energy frenzy" or relatively harmless mischief. Aggressive spurts appear to reflect energy and frustration impulse-discharges rather than sustained acting-out due to unconscious conflicts. Once when approached she spontaneously verbalized: "I'm sorry, I'm sorry." When asked why she was sorry, Kathy just shook her head, smiled in bewilderment, and claimed she didn't know. She was obviously apologizing for something she had done, planned to do, or knew she'd do in the future.

Were it not for a loving and limit-setting home environment, Kathy would no doubt have been completely out of control, and even chronically aggressive. Often she apologized spontaneously to her mother: "I just can't be good. I'm sorry. I can't control myself." But she tried her best to behave, if for no other reason than to please her parents. When forced to nap in school, she became anxious and even depressed, almost school-phobic. When placed on a modified Feingold Diet by her mother, Kathy's activity level decreased, her mood stabilized, and her overall concentration improved, especially at school. But all too often, she comes home and begins acting like a tornado. It's as if she suddenly fatigues and there is a sudden relaxation of all efforts at controlling her boundless energy.

While standing and "dancing" on a bathroom fixture during one of her "fits," she was warned by her sitter, "Kathy, you're getting completely out of control." She answered rapidly, "What difference does it make if I'm a little or completely out of control?" In a sense, Kathy was right. She was either in or out of control. And maintaining any semblance of control was very, very difficult.

ADD-H AND ADD IN OLDER CHILDREN

Joey

Joey is a six-year old who was brought to me by his father for "extreme restlessness and distractibility." He seemed foggy and preoccupied and found it difficult to maintain eye contact. In fact, he appeared unable to concentrate when looking and thinking or speaking at the same time. School discipline and restraints bothered him no end. Indeed, the only times he was quiet were when he periodically came home spent or burned-out. When he was controlled at school, he was wild at home. And no two days were the same, although the overall pattern was similar. Sometimes he would bounce around from hyper- to underactive in the same day. Most of the time, these variations would occur at intervals of several days.

Joey was short and stocky—strong, but clumsy. As a result, he found it difficult to run off his energy without tripping or falling. Speech functioning was delayed and evidence of articulation problems were still apparent. In fact, he was too impatient and lacked the persistence to complete sentences and thoughts. Were it not for an intelligent glint in his eyes and facial expression, one might have thought Joey's IQ to be below average, especially as he also evidenced severe learning disabilities in school affecting reading, writing, spelling, math, memory, grammar, and sense of direction and time.

Although Joey's mother was greatly concerned about his impaired overall functioning, his father seemed quite confident—even overconfident. "I used to be just like him, perhaps worse. And now I'm practicing urology. The only thing different about me was that I was never fearful. Joey is fearful of heights—he was always that way, since he was an infant. Bouncing him up and down terrified him. And he would even get motion-sick, too! Stairs terrify him, especially going down. Sometimes he just slides his way from step to step on his backside. And see-through steps are the worst for him. The same is true with escalators. He panics going down them. And his nights have been terrible since infancy. He has had night terrors since birth. And sometimes I think he is afraid of strangers and has day terrors as well.

"Stubborn! That's Joey. He gets his mind on something he wants or doesn't want, and that's it. There is no dissuading him. He is the same way with practicing things. If he is interested in basketball, he'll dribble or shoot baskets forever. And you can't stop him, except by force. Sometimes he is like that with conversations. He'll get stuck on one theme and there's no way to sidetrack him. I think that is also why he had temper tantrums as a baby. It's like there is no way for him to do things in moderation. Either he won't or can't try at all, or he won't or can't stop what he's doing.

"His overeating and overplaying are similar. When he's into eating, especially sweets, there's no stopping him. He'll even cheat, remaining completely undaunted by punishment. That's strange, especially when you think about how fearful he is about most other things. Getting him to wind down at night is equally impossible. Sometimes I think he would just play right into dawn if we let him. But once he falls asleep, he's dead to the world unless awakened by his night terrors. When he was younger, we'd sometimes find him sleeping on the floor under the kitchen table at odd hours. It's just as if he would run himself into a sudden exhaustion and drop 'deadlike' in his tracks wherever he happened to be."

Laurel

Laurel's mother describes her daughter's ADD-H symptoms as follows: "Laurel, now age seven, has always been a very active, restless, and fidgety child. And she never liked nor needed much sleep, even as a newborn and infant. Naps were out of the question. Many nights we succeeded in lulling her to sleep only by rocking her in a swing. However, if we then tried to place her in a crib, she would invariably awaken and we'd be back to square one. Strange! But it seemed she needed motion to relax sufficiently enough to sleep. As she grew slightly older, it didn't matter how early we put her to bed, or how many stories we read to her.

She wouldn't or couldn't fall asleep until nine or ten at night. At times, she even rocked herself to sleep, but it was always very, very late. It's like she tried to fall asleep and couldn't. It's not like she wouldn't, as many tried to tell us.

"No matter how late she fell asleep, Laurel was up and ready to run by seven o'clock on weekdays. So it was never a case of staying up late and sleeping in late. This pattern has continued until the present day. Only recently has she begun to sleep in a little later on weekends. And that's only until around eight.

"She's never still. Even when she's asleep, some part of her body is always moving. I've questioned her pediatrician about this. All he said was, 'She is just a restless sleeper.' However, watching her sleeping in motion, it seems impossible for her to be getting any rest.

"Laurel has boundless energy. As a result, she has to be involved in numerous events throughout the day. Even after a major activity which leaves her peers worn out, she wants to know (and is ready for) 'What's next?' A good word to describe her is 'scattered.' She goes from one thing to the next at lightning speeds. And Laurel can't stick with anything long enough to complete it. As a result, many things she does remain incomplete, disorganized, and messy. Either she is forced to race through everything, leaving her no time to finish, and/or she gets too distracted and forgets what she was just doing or thinking a moment before.

"Laurel began to show signs of unpredictable behavior as an infant. Rapidly changing mood swings emerged which included tantrums and severe acting-out behaviors. She's always been a very demanding child and requires constant attention. Were it not for our continuous supervision, Laurel and things around her— including her siblings—would rapidly deteriorate into bedlam and chaos.

"When I explained Laurel's mood swings to Dr. K., a clinical psychologist, she recommended a referral to a pediatric neurologist. Interestingly, she noted none of the mood swings that I had reported but did observe a definite restlessness about her that suggested a mild hyperactivity. The neurologist felt she probably had ADD, but not severely enough to warrant medication. However, Laurel needed something to calm her down—to help her concentrate! Besides, she was a lot calmer in his presence than in mine or even the teacher's. In fact, when I think about all his comments now logically, Laurel's functioning was minimal and her disorder was severe. In addition, the neurologist also noted a delay in her fine-motor coordination. But he didn't feel it was medically significant at this time, either. It may not have been significant to him, but it certainly affected the way Laurel read and wrote. For example, whenever she tried to read, she kept losing her place and needed a finger or a marker. And her writing was completely atrocious—unrecognizable. It's as if she had no control over the pencil or the angles and directions her writing was supposed to go. She was also accident-prone. Not only because she was active and impulsive, but because she was really, really, klutzy. When I think back over her development, it appears very easy to understand that her poor coordination corresponded with difficulties that she had with buttoning and zippering and even attempting to hold a pencil in a normal way, rather than the awkward grasp she still maintains. In any event, the neurologist suggested a sleep EEG. This turned out to be an awake EEG because the fifty milligrams of Benadryl given her did not put her to sleep. Her EEG results were normal. However, the medication calmed her down significantly and she was more alert and less distracted than ever before.

"Shortly thereafter, we took Laurel to an optometrist for vision therapy. He also noted a definite eye/hand fine-motor coordination problem as well as difficulty distinguishing right from left.

"Since Laurel started school, I have noticed definite and increasing problems with reading, writing, spelling, and organizational skills. These problems led me to read up on learning disabilities. And when I discussed all these many problems with Laurel's school psychologist, she agreed with me that Laurel was dyslexic, but did not feel the case was severe enough to be overly concerned. But I am! When I finally realized and understood the nature of all of Laurel's symptoms as well as her response to Benadryl, I decided to consult with you!

"In the meantime, we even had her fitted with colored lenses. She claimed to see the letters and words more clearly, and some decrease in reversals and word movement occurred. But most of her other symptoms persisted."

John

John was first examined by me when he was eight years old, for severe hyperactive-impulsive behavior together with sustained aggressive acting-out. His attention span was described as "nonexistent" by both his teachers and parents. Distractibility was pervasive and intense, triggered by minor background visual, acoustic, and even olfactory or smell stimuli. He had difficulty sustaining both tactile (touch) and emotional contacts, appearing more comfortable at arm's length, momentary lapses aside. Indeed, he seemed academically as well as socially dyslexic, never seeming to learn from mistakes and discipline. Indeed, he appeared fearless, impervious to punishment and even injury. His demands were insatiable; he was driven from one toy or event to another without any apparent relief or sustained satisfaction. He appeared to function on a moment-to-moment basis without a sense of sequence, perspective, purpose, or future. As a result, his sense of time seemed flat, and lacked the depth of those with only two-dimensional vision. Stimulant medication, diets, and psychotherapy were only of minimal help.

With increasing age and strength, his acting-out became more serious and his aggression more violent. Truancy, lying, and inevitably stealing and drug abuse became dominant personality characteristics. Weight lifting, strength, and bullying were used to compensate for inner feelings of stupidity and hopelessness . . . and escalating frustrations.

Many years after initial contacts, I was informed that John had been repeatedly arrested for assault and robbery, and eventually for murder at age nineteen. From the time I last saw him at fourteen, and once he became addicted to alcohol and drugs, all ensuing attempts at various therapies by a wide range of therapists proved to be of little help.

Chapter IV

Attention Deficit Disorder: Diagnosis "By the Numbers"

Attention Deficit Disorder is commonly recognized as a physiologically based syndrome characterized by distractibility, hyperactivity, and impulsivity, as well as problems with concentration, learning and memory, mood, and sleep. Despite the growing attention this elusive disorder has received since it was first recognized several decades ago, alertness, arousal, ADD had remained a scientific enigma, defying precise attempts at medical understanding, diagnosis, and prediction. For the most part, researchers and clinicians have been unable to comprehend and accurately define the physiological basis and mechanisms responsible for its wide range of fluctuating educational, medical, mental and behavioral symptoms.

This does not mean that clinicians and researchers haven't attempted to describe criteria for diagnosing ADD. On the contrary, the medical community has over the years developed a somewhat straightforward list of symptoms attempting to help us identify patients with this disorder. The list can be found in the third revised edition of a huge tome called the *Diagnostic and Statistical Manual of Mental Disorders* (DSM-III-R).

When I first began examining patients who were said to have ADD, I viewed the DSM-III-R, and its predecessor, DSM-III, as helpful and necessary tools for diagnosis. After all, my colleagues used it with apparent success; why shouldn't I? Being something of a newcomer to the world of ADD, I was also comforted by the fact that the criteria were extremely specific. Not only had the creators of DSM-III-R described fourteen behaviors to watch for, they also indicated that *eight* of them had to be present for *six months* in order for a diagnosis to be accurate. They also stated that the onset of behaviors should occur *before the age of seven.* With these guidelines before me, I believed there would be little room for diagnostic error. By taking a look at the criteria listed below, you'll understand what I mean.

Criteria for Diagnosing Attention Deficit-Hyperactivity Disorder from the DSM-III-R:

Note: Consider a criterion met only if the behavior is considerably more frequent than that of most people of the same mental age.

A. A disturbance of at least six months during which at least eight of the following are present:

   (1) often fidgets with hands or feet or squirms in seat (in adolescents, may be limited to subjective feelings of restlessness)
   (2) has difficulty remaining seated when required to do so
   (3) is easily distracted by extraneous stimuli
   (4) has difficulty awaiting turn in games or group situations
   (5) often blurts out answers to questions before they have been completed
   (6) has difficulty following through on instructions from others (not due to oppositional behavior or failure of comprehension), e.g., fails to finish chores
   (7) has difficulty sustaining attention in tasks or play activities
   (8) often shifts from one uncompleted activity to another
   (9) has difficulty playing quietly
   (10) often talks excessively
   (11) often interrupts or intrudes on others, e.g., butts into other children's games
   (12) often does not seem to listen to what is being said to him or her
   (13) often loses things necessary for tasks or activities at

school or at home (e.g., toys, pencils, books, assignments)

(14) often engages in physically dangerous activities without considering possible consequences (not for the purpose of thrill-seeking), e.g., runs into street without looking

Note: The above items are listed in descending order of discriminating power based on data from a national field trial of the DSM-III-R criteria for Disruptive Behavior Disorders.

B. Onset before the age of seven.

C. Does not meet the criteria for a Pervasive Developmental Disorder.

Criteria for severity of Attention-Deficit Hyperactivity Disorder:

Mild: Few, if any, symptoms in excess of those required to make the diagnosis and only minimal or no impairment in school and social functioning.

Moderate: Symptoms of functional impairment intermediate between "mild" and "severe."

Severe: Many symptoms in excess of those required to make the diagnosis **and** significant and pervasive impairment in functioning at home and school and with peers.*

Like many other physicians, I used the DSM-III-R as a reference for tracking patients' symptoms. After examining, testing, and talking with a patient, I'd jot down the symptoms I'd observed. When I interviewed the child's parents, teachers, peers, or siblings, I'd note what they'd said about the youngster's behavior at home, school, and play. Then, I'd review the diagnostic criteria

*Reprinted with permission from the *Diagnostic and Statistical Manual of Mental Disorders. Third Edition, Revised.* Copyright 1987 American Psychiatric Association.

in the DSM-III-R to see how the patient's symptoms matched the official list of behaviors. Sometimes I was able to find eight or more of the criteria. Occasionally, I even met patients who'd exhibited the "correct" number of symptoms for a period of six months or more. But more often than not, I found exceptions to the "rules" listed in the highly regarded diagnostic manual.

First, I discovered that patients' behavior often deviated from the stated criteria. This was true for each and every one of the fourteen behaviors listed. I observed that:

1 Not all ADD patients fidgeted or squirmed. Some were able to keep their bodies at rest by dint of sheer willpower; others seemed hypoactive and even non-responsive;

2 Not all ADD patients had difficulty remaining seated when required to: some could control themselves all day in the classroom setting but would become whirling dervishes when they got home;

3 Not all ADD patients were easily distracted by extraneous stimuli: some patients could concentrate only when there was a radio playing nearby; others became distracted only under certain conditions—if fluorescent lights were shining overhead or if noises like sirens disturbed them;

4 Not all ADD patients had difficulty waiting their turn in games or group situations: some would either tune out their surroundings and appear disinterested or would fixate on someone else's behavior and act like an observer or outsider to the game or activity;

5 Not all ADD patients interrupted or intruded on others, or blurted out answers before questions had been completed: some were not impulsive at all and were highly skilled at monitoring themselves so that they never interrupted or asked a question; others became withdrawn and tuned out their surroundings to the extent that they were not even aware that a question had been asked;

6 Not all ADD patients had difficulty following through on instructions from others: some patients had no difficulty with *verbal* instructions, only with visual or written material; the reverse was also true;

7 Not all ADD patients had difficulty sustaining attention to tasks and play activities: some patients had great attention spans as long as certain *specific* distractions did not occur—i.e., some were distracted only by noise but not by nearby physical activity; others were distracted only by movements that caught their eye, not by sounds;

8 Not all ADD patients shifted from one uncompleted task to another: some exhibited symptoms of perseveration—they seemed to get "stuck" on one task, repeating or perseverating it again and again;

9 Not all ADD patients had difficulty playing quietly: on the contrary, many patients were so adept at tuning *everything* out, it was as if they were in a dreamlike state; others could become so preoccupied with play, they would perseverate, or glue in, playing quietly with the same toy over and over again;

10 Not all ADD patients talked excessively: some never uttered a word because they had difficulty concentrating while speaking in sequence, or had problems lining up the words in order; others seemed to experience cycles of overactive speech—they could be excessively chatty one day, silent the next;

11; Not all ADD patients interrupted or intruded on others: many were shy, some were withdrawn and preoccupied within themselves, while still others were able to control their impulsiveness with peers and strangers—but not at home;

12 Not all ADD patients had difficulty listening to what was being said: some could listen attentively to narratives about sports, for example, while others could remain adequately focused on verbalized stories or fables; although many patients appeared *not* to be listening to what was being said, some were able to correctly answer questions related to the verbal comments made to them—apparently they *had* listened;

13 Not all ADD patients were extremely messy or careless, or lost things necessary for tasks: some patients spent a great deal of time organizing their desks, or dressing themselves; some perseverated on organizational tasks to the extent that they seemed incapable of doing anything else; and some had exquisite memories for details;

14 Not all ADD patients engaged in physically dangerous activ-

ities without considering possible consequences: many were underactive and behaved flaccidly; others engaged in cyclic behavior—one day they would be overactive and behave impulsively, the next they'd be underactive and withdrawn.

Second, I began to see even more variations in my patients' symptoms. Some of them experienced difficulties with reading, writing, spelling, or math. Others were plagued by memory problems, poor coordination, and difficulties related to time or directions such as right and left, north and south, east and west. Some of them had seemingly irrational fears of objects or situations: they might be terrified of lightning or snakes, for example, or be extremely fearful of elevators or heights. Others exhibited behaviors that could be more readily observed on a daily basis: head tilting, blinking, stuttering and slurring of words, and postural reading preferences such as lying down or tilted. Many patients frequently complained of so-called psychosomatic symptoms: headaches, dizziness, nausea, stomachaches, depression, panic attacks, and sleep disturbances—just to name a few! I was observing these and other symptoms in the *majority* of my patients; yet no such signs were accounted for in DSM-III-R. Were my observations inaccurate? Or were the "rules" incorrect? Or incomplete?

Third, I discovered that the DSM "rule" about eight or more symptoms for six months or more did not seem to apply to the majority of these individuals. Some youngsters had only five symptoms; others had only two or three or four. Did that mean they *didn't* have ADD? Furthermore, no matter how many signs could be counted, not all kids exhibited consistently *severe* symptoms: Johnny might be fidgety before a test, but calm down while doing routine class assignments; Jill might talk excessively to her best friend, but hardly speak at all to the child seated behind her. In addition, some kids had experienced problems for only four months prior to their referral to me; still others showed symptoms for an even shorter period of time.

What about the edict regarding onset before the age of seven? This rule troubled me for two reasons: not only did it suggest that attention deficits must start at an early age, but it also implied (as did most of the scientific literature) that this disorder could not be *acquired* by older children, adolescents, and adults! This was clearly not the case in my practice. In fact, more than one-third of the patients I examined were adults. And many had first experienced symptoms in their twenties, thirties, and beyond!

Over time, I became disenchanted with the DSM criteria. Although DSM is widely used in clinical settings, I found that it was seriously flawed in several respects: (1) it stressed *behaviors* rather than impacts on learning or academic and occupational productivity; (2) it implied that ADD represents a uniform group of patients who must be children or adolescents; (3) it suggested that affected individuals had identical or nearly identical therapeutic needs; (4) it failed to recognize that there is considerable variety in the degree and nature of patients' symptoms, and that in some cases—such as those involving perseveration—an equal but opposite behavior might occur; and (5) it failed to account for many patients—children, adolescents, and adults—whose cases differed widely in terms of onset, cause, progression, prognosis, and even drug-responsiveness.

There is always a need in medicine or in any scientific field to try to organize observational data in a step-by-step fashion. Indeed, an organizational or classification system often leads to greater understanding of a process, phenomenon, or disease. But it is my belief that such systems, in order to be effective—i.e., to serve clinicians and researchers *and the patients they are studying*—must not rely on "magic" numbers. As you have seen in this chapter, the widely used DSM-III-R classification system for ADD does just that: it outlines fourteen behaviors, eight of which—present for six months or more—must have occurred before the age of seven.

By tallying up symptoms and their duration and by calculating age of onset, many clinicians are ignoring the *quality* of ADD—a quality that has never before been clearly recognized and appropriately described—and its diffuse and varied symptomatic fallout. Of course, the reason for this failure is tragically simple: patients with ADD cannot answer questions they have never been asked! They do not specifically and spontaneously relate and describe their many symptoms and feelings to researchers or doctors who are only interested in matching behaviors to a prescribed list of numerical criteria.

Numbers most certainly have their place in science and research. They are most effective in biological research, especially where the subject tested cannot verbally respond, as in the case of apes, dogs, and unconscious patients, and in chemical assays. But as scientists, we should not rely so heavily on numbers when attempting to understand the symptoms experienced by human beings who are desperately attempting to verbalize and clarify the nature of those symptoms.

Instead, we should ask patients what is wrong with them or how they feel. We should let *them* tell us! Then we should record the details in the same meticulous manner that we would record quantitative data. When a pattern of symptoms emerges, we should ask more specific questions in order to further pin down and define this pattern. When we do all this, what will happen? Much of Attention Deficit Disorder will materialize before our eyes!

You are about to embark on a path toward understanding ADD[1]. Along the way, you will meet scores of my patients—some with mild, some with moderate, and some with severe forms of the disorder. But first, I want to introduce you to an extraordinary woman whose search for the truth about ADD parallels, to some extent, my own quest to understand this sometimes baffling disorder. As you read her story, you will begin to see, as I did, that the symptoms of ADD cannot be fashioned into a tidy package containing fourteen behaviors. Listen carefully to her story—in it you will find new insights, and perhaps a better understanding of yourself or a loved one.

[1]In an attempt to capture the basic essence of ADD in children, Dr. Paul H. Wender, an outstanding clinical researcher, lists and describes the following important characteristics:

(1) attention difficulties and distractibility
(2) impulsivity
(3) hyperactivity

(4) attention-demanding behavior of an *insatiable* quality

(5) school difficulties related to dyslexia, learning disabilities (LD), or the recently named specific development disorder (SDD)

(6) impairment in balance and coordination, including fine and gross motor in coordination, often resulting in handwriting and eye tracking difficulties

(7) resistant and domineering social behavior, which has *three* distinct characteristics:

- ☐ a resistance to obey social demands: "do's," "don'ts," "should's" and shouldn'ts"
- ☐ increased independence, i.e., those with ADD often tolerate separation anxiety exceptionally well when very young
- ☐ domineering behavior with other children

(8) emotional difficulties of physical origin affecting mood, reactivity to pain, overreacting to excitement—including excessive irritability, frustration and anger, "unsatisfiability," low self-esteem.

(9) immaturity—the emotions and behavior of children with ADD are often normal, but applicable to children several years younger.

Wender also described the changes of these many symptoms over time and attempted to highlight the *residual* or *leftover* symptoms characterizing ADD adults, termed ADD, RT(residual type). In fact, only during the last ten years have ADD-adults been recognized for study. Previously, it was erroneously thought that ADD-H as well as its favorable response to stimulant medications disappear by puberty.

CHAPTER V

Why Can't Josh Concentrate? A Search for the Truth

When Evelyn D. brought her eight-year-old son to my office for an evaluation several months ago, she was bitter, confused, and exasperated. So severe were Josh's concentration problems, she explained, that she had begun to worry that he might be mentally retarded. "But it just *can't* be that," she said, angrily shaking her head. "I know he's a bright boy—I know he has the ability to do well in school! But no matter what I do to try to get him to concentrate on his schoolwork, he just can't . . . or won't. Lots of times he refuses to try—he just gets mad and throws a temper tantrum. Sometimes I think it's because he's just lazy and stubborn, but even punishment—spanking, isolation, withholding treats—have no effect! He's flunking everything now, and I'm worried that he'll never be able to catch up. Even his teachers have given up—and I am about to."

Quickly, she grabbed from her briefcase a rather thick stack of papers. She thumbed through the sheets until she found a letter that Josh's third-grade teacher had written. She thrust it at me, then stood up and began pacing back and forth. "Before I say anything I want you to look at this," she commanded. I opened the letter, which was addressed to a school psychologist:

"I have been watching Josh with concern since the beginning of the 1987 school year. That concern has only increased in the past two months. The problem started out with Josh not doing his work, but has grown into much more. It is very hard to explain Josh's behavior. The only way to understand is to observe on a daily basis. I have tried everything to get Josh to do his work, but *nothing* works. He will do it at home, but not at school where there are many distractions. I believe that it goes much deeper. There seems to be something missing somewhere—an imbalance in the mind. His attitude, relationships, and schoolwork are suffering greatly.

"Some of the symptoms that I see in Josh include the following. He seems fidgety, restless, irritable. He's easily frustrated and very impulsive—he seems to overload easily and will fly off the handle at the slightest provocation, or for no apparent reason at all. Even if he's given a task that's simple, he burns out after a few seconds. He's unable to participate in group sports and can't seem to socialize with more than one child at a time; he gets lost and confused when two or more things are going on around him.

"If I'm talking to him and there's noise in the background, he's a goner. He seems to tune me out . . . and tune the noise in. He responds to every little noise—even a pin dropping or a bird flying by. In fact, he's the first one in class to hear that it's raining, and sometimes I even think he can hear the sun's rays hitting the window or the sound of clouds rolling by. It's as if his filter is "off," or leaky; he can't tune me in, yet he can't tune the other things out.

"Maybe that's why loud noises drive him crazy. I've seen him hold his ears with his hands and hide beneath his desk when an ambulance or fire truck goes by with the siren blaring. He also seems terrified of thunder and lightning.

"Josh's workbook and appearance are disheveled and disorganized; they seem to symbolize his inability to concentrate long enough on any task to either sequence it or complete it. Maybe that's why he's such a procrastinator—he doesn't have the concentration power to begin a task, let alone complete it, in a neat, organized way.

"Although he is often a whirlwind of unfocused activity, at times he seems so tuned into things that he 'gets stuck' in or on them. For example, if he's writing something, he may continue to write the same sentence over and over again until he's off the page and onto the desk. Or if he's playing with a ball in the school yard, he'll keep bouncing it again and again in a compulsive sort of way. He doesn't seem to be enjoying it . . . it's more like he's mesmerized by it. At these moments, he seems to have tuned everything else out and is exclusively preoccupied with one repetitive task which he cannot disconnect from.

"I'm completely baffled by Josh's behavior. In a word, he seems 'spacy.' I hate to use that term, but it fits. He doesn't seem to realize that when the others are working, he is supposed to be working, also. His mind is very active but it is somewhere other than school. He cannot keep his attention on any one thing. He forgets what he is supposed to be doing. He always has a look of frustration on his face."

As I folded the letter and returned it to her, Mrs. D. stood up and began pacing again. "I've got lots more to show you, but first, I want to tell you a few things," she said. "There's much more you should know."

Mrs. D. sat quietly for a moment, collecting her thoughts, then added the following details to her story:

"When I gave that letter to my husband Bob to read, I figured he'd be just as upset as I am. Not so! Fact is, he actually laughed, and told me not to worry, because he says he had the exact same symptoms when he was a kid! Then he said, 'And look at me—I'm successful in spite of it.' Doctor, I don't have the heart to tell my husband that he *still* has problems! He still can't concentrate on things too long, even relationships. When I try to talk to him about something, he's off somewhere in two seconds; he can't stay with a conversation. Now, I can tolerate that in Josh, because he's a kid, but my husband is forty-eight years old! It makes me really angry! When I complain to him about it, he either ignores me or he'll get mad and say he just can't hear things right! We fight about this all the time!

"Bob's problems have affected our social life, too. He hates going to parties—says they're just too noisy, too many things going on at once. And if I do manage to drag him to some social gathering, he talks so loud it's embarrassing! It's as if he has to shout in order to hear himself think!

"To tell you the truth, Doctor, if my husband didn't have his own business, I swear he'd be out of a job. Any boss would fire him because he can't focus on any one project for more than a couple minutes. He has to do ten things at once. He also has trouble concentrating when he's in the car; he can get lost just going around the block! If he didn't have a secretary to drive him to his appointments, he'd never get anywhere.

"I know I'm ranting and raving. I apologize for that. But it's just that our whole family seems to be affected by some mysterious illness, or whatever it is! Take my other son, Bob Jr., for example. He's fourteen now, and in high school. He was never really interested in school, but always did exceptionally well—it was like he could intuitively grasp things. Until now, that is. Now he's totally uninterested in his schoolwork, bringing home *D*'s and *F*'s instead of *A*'s and *B*'s.

"He can't seem to remember anything! If I drill him on his spelling words, he knows them that night, but forgets them when he has to take the test. If he has to read a chapter in a book for class, he can get through it but can't tell you anything about what he read. He can't even remember to give me his dirty clothes for laundering—they just sit in a pile in his room.

"All of his homework is sloppy, especially writing assignments. He'll start a sentence, then cross it out, then try again, but there are so many spelling errors, it's hard to figure out just exactly what it is he's trying to say! And if you ask him to read something aloud, he stammers and stutters and sometimes slurs his words—it's like each word is a giant hurdle that he just can't get over!

"Something else about him baffles me. He can spend hours playing Nintendo; he can really concentrate on that game! But if anybody interrupts him while he's playing—look out! He gets extremely irritated and upset. He also knows every major league ball player's stats by heart and could tell you, in excruciating detail, everything you ever wanted to know about a player or a team. But if he has to do anything related to school, he can't stick with it or remember it. His teachers say it's adolescence, or puberty, or that he's just gotten interested in girls. Some of them have even blamed me for not disciplining him enough!

"None of those things make sense to me. If he's so interested in girls, then why doesn't he pay more attention to his appearance? He's unkempt; he won't take a shower unless I remind him. It's as if he just doesn't care about himself . . . or anything else! Of course, when I try to discuss this with his father, I get the same old line—'Don't worry, Bob Jr. is doing better than I was at his age! Give him time. He'll snap out of it.'

"Maybe he will, maybe he won't. I even took Bob Jr. to a psychiatrist—he's been in therapy now for six months. He says he feels better, but he still can't seem to concentrate in class or at home. So far, the shrink hasn't given us any answers, but he suspects Bob Jr. has emotional problems. Like my husband, the psychiatrist just keeps telling me that 'these things take time.'

"Maybe the psychiatrist and my husband are right. Maybe both Bob Jr. and Josh will eventually snap out of it. But since my husband still has *his* problems, isn't there a good chance the boys will continue to as well? Isn't it just possible that—"

Mrs. D. stopped abruptly in mid-sentence. She folded her arms across her chest defensively, as if to protect herself from the terrible answer she thought she would hear. Then, with a look of fury in her eyes, she said abruptly, "While I have been waiting for the members of my family to 'snap out of it,' I've done a considerable amount of research on the subject of concentration. But instead of getting answers to my questions, I've just gotten more confused! Let me show you what I mean."

After sorting through her papers, Mrs. D. produced a number of articles that dealt with concentration, attention, and distractibility. As she pointed to each one, she gave a running commentary:

"This one is a real joke. It says, 'If you're overcome by anxiety and fear before a test or a big game, concentration will go right out the window. The solution? Laugh. Watching a funny video or cracking jokes with friends can break the tension and make it easier to concentrate!' Here's a fascinating one: It links concentration problems to diet . . . says that if you avoid food dyes, artificial flavors, and forms of aspirin, your problems will disappear! Oh, here's another—this one says that caffeine is the culprit! You know what, though? A little caffeine from soda pop will drive Josh up the wall, but if my husband doesn't have his five cups of coffee in the morning, he can hardly function at all! And here's an article I found that talked about a group of hyperactive kids who were given caffeine. Guess what? They calmed down!"

Next, she produced from her briefcase a thin, worn book, by

Melvin Powers entitled *A Practical Guide to Better Concentration* (Wilshire Books Co., Hollywood). "Listen to what these Californians have to say," she said, turning to the introduction.

"'Undoubtedly, you have reached a point where you feel that your lack of concentration is a handicap and your inability to attain it is a constant frustration. There is no need to continue this pattern however. The ability to increase your powers of concentration is inherent. *Desire and motivation* . . . will bring out this latent asset.'"

Mrs. D. paused for a moment, heaved a sigh, and continued:

"'Developing the ability to concentrate and learn is a matter of harnessing the latent characteristics that everyone possesses. After all, poor students do become good students, and those who are successful in certain areas of achievement become proficient in areas where it was thought they had no aptitude. These changes are possible because the individual changes his feelings about himself and translates them into purposeful action. Our theme is that the initial impetus for improving your concentration must come from a changed attitude and increased self-esteem. Actually, *a complete reconstruction of one's psyche is essential.* This necessitates a substitution of good habit patterns for the ones that have been handicapping you, a belief that you can overcome your mental shortcomings and a willingness to test yourself by facing your problem.'"

She slammed shut the book. "According to the authors of that book, then, my sons and my husband are either stupid, lazy, or they have a bad attitude."

Next, Mrs. D. pulled from the stack an article that had appeared in *The New York Times Magazine* in November of 1987. She pointed to the headline, "Out of a Darkness."

"I really thought I was onto something when I found this one," she said. "In some ways, the writer seemed to be describing my husband. Listen to this. Describing his problem, the writer says, ' . . . the world rushes in unimpeded. At lunch, a nearby conversation threatens your ability to listen to the person across the table, however interesting; in the quiet of a library, the noise of someone adjusting his chair can disrupt a train of thought. Disorganized, unwanted information pours in ceaselessly. It is a very egalitarian kind of disability: the trash collector in the alley demands as much attention as the boss on the phone.'

"Doesn't that sound like my husband . . . and like Josh? And how about this: The author says, 'Distractibility is one related problem; others are impulsiveness, trouble with organizing and planning, difficulty in completing tasks, large mood swings, immaturity, low tolerance of stress.' Sound familiar?

"The man who wrote the article goes on to say that his problems are caused by 'a group of symptoms usually associated with childhood . . . a disorder known to psychiatrists as Attention Deficit Disorder.' He goes on to say, 'According to the American Psychiatric Association, ADD is a syndrome that begins before the age of seven and has fourteen symptoms—inability to complete tasks, distractibility, hot temper, etc.'; any eight can constitute a positive diagnosis.' He also says that ADD is probably caused by something faulty in the brain.

"After I read that, I figured that my husband and Josh have ADD, and that maybe even Bob Jr. does, too. But then I got to thinking—the article said a person with ADD had to have *eight* symptoms! Josh has maybe seven of them, and my husband probably has five. Bob Jr. doesn't have near that many. If they don't have the right number of symptoms, does that mean they *don't* have ADD?

"Something else occurred to me. Sure, my kids and my husband seem to have concentration problems, but theirs branch out in so many directions! Take Josh for example. He seems to have a hearing problem, too; it's like he hears too much! But we've had his ears tested, and have found nothing wrong. And what about his compulsive behavior—the writing and rewriting and the continuous bouncing of a ball? What does that have to do with concentration?

"I thought some more about my husband, too. Why does he hate socializing? Is it because he can't concentrate on a conversation—or does he have a psychological problem? Why does he have such trouble driving the car? And what about Bob Jr.—what accounts for his speech problem, his sloppiness, and his memory problems?"

Mrs. D. heaved a sigh. "You can see why I'm confused and worried," she said. "Do they all have something wrong with their brains? Do my husband and my sons have ADD? Or do they have something else? A diagnosis of ADD just doesn't seem to explain their other problems.

"I'm also concerned about medication. The man who wrote that article took a drug called Ritalin—he said it changed his life and that it had helped others with ADD. But I've heard it can make people act crazy, and I'm worried that if my kids took it, they would become addicted to it. That may be beside the point, though. Even if the drug could solve the concentration problems, wouldn't we still be left with the other difficulties?

"So where do we go for help? Should we be seeing you for ADD—if, in fact, that's what they have—and then try to find a psychologist for the other problems? Should we consult a speech therapist for Bob Jr.'s stuttering. Is he dyslexic?

"Please tell me, Doctor. What's causing all our troubles? And how can we solve them?"

If you're like most people, you probably found Mrs. D.'s account of her family astonishing. And you probably found the number and variety of the family's symptoms overwhelming. So did I when I first began examining patients who were said to have ADD or ADD-H. By painstakingly collecting and analyzing the symptoms of thousands of ADD patients over the past twenty-five years and by studying their responses to treatment, I have been led to the insight that a vast number of problems—dyslexia or learning disabilities, even phobias and mood and behavior disorders—are part and parcel of Attention Deficit Disorder. In fact, I have come to realize that anyone with ADD will have one or more of the following symptoms:

- □ Impaired concentration, distractibility, hyperactivity, overactivity or impulsivity
- □ Difficulties with balance and coordination functions, i.e., walking, running, skipping, hopping; children have difficulty tying shoelaces and buttoning buttons
- □ Memory instability for letters, words, or numbers

- ☐ A tendency to skip over or scramble letters, words, and sentences
- ☐ A poor, slow, fatiguing reading ability prone to compensatory head tilting, near-far focusing, and finger pointing
- ☐ Reversal of letters such as *b* and *d*, words such as *saw* and *was*, and numbers such as *6* and *9* or *16* and *61*
- ☐ Messy, poorly angulated, or drifting handwriting prone to errors in size, spacing, and letter-sequencing
- ☐ Memory instability for spelling, grammar, math, names, dates, and lists, or for sequences such as the alphabet, days of the week, months of the year, and directions
- ☐ Speech disorders such as slurring, stuttering, minor articulation errors, poor word recall, and auditory-input and motor-output speech lags
- ☐ Right/left and related directional uncertainty
- ☐ Delay in learning to tell time
- ☐ Fears of the dark, heights, getting lost, going to school
- ☐ Fear or the avoidance of various balance-, coordination-, sports-, and motion-related activities
- ☐ Mood disturbances
- ☐ Obsessions and compulsions

Remember Josh? He had at least five of the above symptoms. Remember Bob Jr.? He had four symptoms. Remember their father? He had at least two. Each of these individuals suffers from Attention Deficit Disorder.

If you are still a bit confused by the many faces of Attention Deficit Disorder, don't despair. By introducing you to Mrs. D. and her story, I wanted you to see all the disparate parts of the puzzle right up front—the way many patients and clinicians do when they encounter ADD for the first time. In the next chapter, we will begin to put the pieces back together again.

CHAPTER VI

Paths to a New Discovery

Two roads diverged in a wood, and I—
I took the one less traveled by,
And that has made all the difference.
                                        —Robert Frost

Although the shortest distance between two points is a straight line, it has been my experience—in the study of medicine and in nearly every other endeavor of my life—that the straight line, while perhaps the quickest and easiest route, is rarely possible to take when heading for an unknown destination. Indeed, my interest in and beliefs about Attention Deficit Disorder and related problems crystallized from a series of circuitous and indirect paths, where straight lines formed loops and parallels intersected.

As you will see throughout this book, those paths have led me to five basic and novel conclusions: (1) that the diagnostic symptoms of ADD are far greater in number—and thus, far more complex in their shapes and guises—than anyone has yet dared to recognize or admit; (2) that over 90 percent of ADD subjects referred for diagnosis and treatment have typical dyslexic or learning disabled (LD) symptoms; (3) that over 90 percent of these referred patients also have balance, coordination, and rhythmic neurological signs (stuttering, hopping, skipping, etc.) suggesting an inner-ear dysfunction; (4) that the vast majority of symptoms associated with ADD, with or without hyperactivity (H), are consistent with this physiological or inner-ear problem; and (5) that most symptoms, for the vast number of individuals with this disorder, can be treated and corrected medically.

These are clear in retrospect, but all the above-mentioned

straight lines were seen and drawn only accidentally. And were it not for my prior research with dyslexia, I would never have stumbled onto and solved the many and perplexing riddles characterizing ADD.

During my years with the Bureau of Special Reading Services of the New York City Board of Education, where I examined children who had dyslexia or were learning disabled (LD), I observed many patients who suffered from concentration difficulties, distractibility, and related problems. As I watched them read from right to left or scramble letters in their writing assignments, for instance, it was easy to understand why such children might have trouble listening to a teacher or starting a simple assignment. They were so busy concentrating on and attempting to compensate for their academic difficulties with reading, writing, spelling, and math that they couldn't possibly absorb the words of the speaker as well. And it was easy to see why they burned out and became inattentive. As for those who were easily distracted, who wouldn't prefer watching a passing fire truck to reading a sentence that, to a dyslexic, looks as if it had been written in Serbo-Croatian? And were not these frustrated children preoccupied with inner distractions, feeling stupid or anxious?

At the time, it appeared obvious that the impaired concentration and distractibility of these children were *secondary* to their dyslexic or LD problems. Indeed, when these very same hyperactive, impulsive, inattentive, and distracted dyslexic children were examined out of a classroom and in a one-on-one situation, they invariably appeared calm, cool, collected, and attentive. This further convinced me that their deficient concentration and their distractibility—even their hyperactivity and impulsivity—were psychologically based. Otherwise, these symptoms wouldn't have disappeared so rapidly in a different situation. Little did I know how much remained to be learned!

In those days, many clinicians and researchers—myself included—believed that the reading and academic disturbances of dyslexic or LD children were primarily of psychological origin. As I listened carefully to my patients talk about themselves, they often used descriptives such as "dumb," "ugly," "hopeless." Weren't these psychological symptoms? And what about the fact that many of my dyslexic patients were also prone to emotional and behavioral "acting out" or aggressive disorders, as well as to phobias, obsessions, compulsions, mood disturbances, and even psychosomatic symptoms such as bed-wetting, headaches, dizziness, nausea, vomiting, and abdominal pain? Didn't these symptoms also fall within the psychiatric and psychological realms? And as stated earlier, did not emotional conflicts serve both as distractions and mental energy drains? Does not anxiety make children jumpy—as well as impulsive, moody, irritable, and aggressive?

Since the learning difficulties of dyslexics or LD youngsters were said to be of psychological origin, it seemed logical to assume that their concentration difficulties were psychologically based, too—via a vicious cycle. That was how clinicians explained the inexplicable—by drawing a short, straight line from the disability to the psyche. When in doubt, blame it on the intangible! This tendency served a dual purpose: neurologists were relieved of the responsibility of delving further into the brain; and psychiatrists had a ready-and-waiting way to explain all these poorly understood phenomena. There was only one rub! They were all wrong! Had we been more open-minded, we might have asked at least two crucial questions: Might an overlooked, hidden, physiological disorder be responsible for all these symptoms? And might not psychological factors secondarily intensify this physiologically-based disorder and/or its symptoms?

Over time, it became increasingly difficult for me to accept all the psychoanalytical theories that linked reading and writing disorders to such emotional causes as sibling rivalry, competitive difficulties, fear of success, parental abuses and/or pampering, sexual and/or aggressive fantasies, Oedipal conflicts, classroom abuse, etc. As I listened carefully to each person, it made little sense that a young boy's infatuation with his mother, or a young girl's battle with her sister, could trigger the specific mechanisms found shaping the many unique symptoms and qualities characterizing dyslexia or LD. I also began to question the assumption that all these patients' concentration problems also stemmed from psychological causes.

Despite all my initial efforts to link reading-disabled symptoms with psychological theories, I simply could not make them meld into a cohesive, rational whole. As a result, I began to wonder: Was I somehow inadequate because I could not apply the theories championed by respected analysts to the reading disorders I examined? Or was it possible that my teachers and countless researchers were mistakenly developing theories that had little or nothing to do with clinical reality? Could it be that the key to unlocking the mysteries of dyslexia or LD—and the attendant concentration problems—might be found somewhere *other* than within the psyche? Perhaps in our brains' physiology and chemistry?

I had to find the answer. Not only were my many patients and their families frustrated, so was I! And there's nothing like frustration to stimulate answers and solutions. Suspecting that I might discover answers in some aspect I'd overlooked, I vowed to listen more carefully to my patients and to delve more deeply into the available research. Eventually, my efforts were rewarded beyond my wildest expectations, although the path to the truth was fraught with continuous trials, errors, and retrials.

As I continued to observe dyslexic or LD patients in greater numbers and with increasing intensity, I began to notice that most of them experienced symptoms either *identical* or similar to what was commonly called Attention Deficit Disorder—a malady assumed to be of unknown physiological origin. Initially, this observation surprised me, since many tended to view and define these two disorders as if they were separate and even mutually exclusive: Only those patients with *severe* reading and writing problems could be diagnosed as dyslexic, while only those patients with *severe* hyperactivity/impulsivity/distractibility/concentration problems were considered to have ADD.

As I continued to examine more and more *dyslexic and ADD* patients, the artificial boundaries traditionally established between these separately named and defined disorders seemed to disappear! My ADD patients certainly had concentration problems, but a majority also exhibited dyslexic or LD symptoms. And while my dyslexic or LD patients invariably experienced a host of reading and writing problems, they almost invariably had impaired concentration and distractibility, overactivity, hyperactivity, and impulsivity symptoms as well. Indeed, the symptoms overlapped to such an incredible extent that it seemed to me that there must be a common denominator.

As I examined more and more patients, I was thrown yet another curve. To my dismay, I stumbled upon hyperactive or overactive individuals without concentration problems. And the reverse. Indeed, I even found distractibility present with intact concentration powers, and the reverse. In other words, all these ADD symptoms were found to occur either alone or in various combinations. And their intensity ranged all the way from mild to moderate to severe—and even overcompensated.

Not only did I find radical variances among patients with ADD-related concentration, distractibility, hyperactivity, and impulsivity symptoms, I also uncovered striking variations in the associated dyslexic symptoms, and even in moods. While some youngsters had considerable trouble with many skills—reading, writing, spelling, math, grammar, and speech—others seemed deficient in only one or two areas. Within these groups, concentration/distractibility/hyperactivity/impulsivity levels also varied widely. I also found that while some patients reported fears or phobias and depression, still others never complained of any anxiety symptoms or mood changes whatsoever! In fact, some were pathologically fearless, and their mood remained stable despite tremendous frustration and failures.

Needless to say, there were no straight lines that fit the symptoms characterizing all subjects. And even loops were difficult to attach from one symptom to another. Eventually, I came to recognize that curved or broken lines—the exceptions—often highlight the hidden or unifying concepts or rules, if only we are patient or interested enough to wait and objective enough to listen to what our patients desperately attempt to tell us.

At this point in my research, it became increasingly impossible to fit my patients into neat diagnostic categories. Some exhibited "classic" symptoms of dyslexia, but they also had symptoms—of varying intensity—closely associated with ADD. Others, who had been referred to me as having "pure" ADD, showed varying degrees of dyslexia or learning-related problems. Indeed, my patient-universe was comprised of individuals whose symptoms rarely fit any of the then perceived rules. There were always exceptions. But as I listened to more and more patients, I made a startling observation: While not all of my patients' symptoms were alike in severity or quantity, almost *all* of their symptoms and underlying mechanisms were similar in *quality*—they all had some common, basic, characteristics. They had a common feel, a feel that could only be grasped by an interested physician after years and years of studying and listening to thousands and thousands of cases.

That observation soon led to another. Since nearly 90 percent of my dyslexic or LD patients had problems related to concentration, distractibility, hyperactivity, and impulsivity, and as 90 percent of my ADD patients had symptoms related to dyslexia or LD, it was clear to me that all were suffering from the same underlying disorder—regardless of the diagnostic terms used.

But how could these findings be? After all, textbooks—and the researchers who wrote them—often stated unequivocally that if subjects had severe reading problems, they were *dyslexic*. When the problems were less severe, they were *LD*. If their writing problems were most apparent, they were called *dysgraphic*. If they complained of great difficulty with math, they were said to have *dyscalculia*. If they were clumsy, they were *dyspraxic*. If they forgot words and names while speaking, they were *dysnomic* or *dysphasic*.

When there were other aberrations, an entirely different set of terms was applied: If their activity level was way beyond normal, they were called *hyperactive*. When impulsivity, as well, was present, they were considered *hyperactive-impulsive*. If their concentration was significantly impaired, they were considered to have "pure" Attention Deficit Disorder, or ADD—now called Undifferentiated-Attention Deficit Disorder, or U-ADD. And if the latter were also hyperactive, they had ADD-H and now ADHD, or Attention Deficit Hyperactivity Disorder.

With respect to ADD, ADD-H, or ADHD, clinicians and researchers believed (and many still do) that only those patients who exhibited a certain number of severe behavioral symptoms could be said to have this disorder. Interestingly, the same quantitative factor was mistakenly used to define dyslexics: to be dyslexic, your reading scores had to be two or more years below your peers or potential. If not, you were called learning disabled. In other words, the same pseudoscientific mistakes were made in attempts to define both disorders: both were defined quantitatively rather than qualitatively; and both were artificially fragmented and described by various names, depending on the leading or "pure" symptom catching the clinician's often biased eye.

Although I was observing both dyslexic and ADD-like symptoms in roughly 90 percent of all my patients, each leading symptom was given a different name as if each was, in reality, a different disorder. Yet, to my mind, all these so-called separate disorders—really symptoms of a single disorder—overlapped in the majority of patients. Accordingly, I wondered: Could one and the same patient possibly have so many different yet seemingly related disorders? Or was I dealing with one disorder with many different symptoms and names? If, as I suspected, the latter was true, it meant that most of my patients had a problem that stemmed from a common, but hidden source—a source with varying dysfunctioning and compensatory mechanisms that shaped both the typical and the so-called atypical, exceptional symptoms that characterized the overall group. But what was it? And where was it?

In an effort to find answers, I began to look more closely at ADD patients who had been referred to me. In some of them, the hyperactive symptoms were so ingrained it was not surprising to hear parents say that their hyper children had been "born that way." Some mothers even claimed that fetuses, while in their wombs, "climbed all over the place." Such subjective accounts fascinated me because they hinted at a genetic, constitutional, and therefore physical etiology. Moreover, outstanding clinical researchers had shown several decades ago that hyperactive children with and without attention and distractibility symptoms responded remarkably to stimulants—medications that one might ordinarily think would make them more excitable, more active. Instead, paradoxically, it appeared as if stimulants calmed these children down. Since these very same stimulants also helped the concentration and distractibility symptoms that these hyperactive and overactive children almost invariably displayed, it seemed logical to assume that the root of all these symptoms was *physiological or chemical*. But where in the brain could I find it? The answer lay in a renewed study of my dyslexic patients and in a renewed search of the scientific literature. After all, these very same stimulants also improved the concentration, distractibility, activity, and impulsivity symptoms in my dyslexic patients!

Once again, evidence suggested that both these differently named disorders—dyslexia and ADD—were reflections of an underlying common denominator. Since most of my experience had been with dyslexics, I decided to focus my research effort on this group. As you will recall, I had not been able to accept the psychological theories about this disorder that were then in vogue. In time, however, I became intrigued by the prevailing neurological theory, and endeavored to learn as much about it as I could. What I discovered was that dyslexia and its related symptoms were considered to stem from a disturbance within the cerebral cortex—the thinking, speaking, IQ-endowed brain. Researchers then and now assumed that this disorder was due to a structural and/or neurophysiological defect within the dominant half of the brain—the side responsible for the ability to recognize written symbols and see objects, the side responsible for and determining meaningful speech functioning and handedness.

Initially, this theory made sense. However, listening to and studying countless dyslexic patients told me otherwise! A good many of my dyslexics were extremely bright, even gifted, and eventually did well by compensatory processes. So how could it be that there was something structurally or seriously wrong with their thinking brains? In addition, neurological examinations revealed no signs suggestive of such a dysfunction. If the facts did not fit the theory, then once again the theory appeared wrong or incomplete. Thus, I was not surprised when I learned that my findings were consistent with those of most other researchers.

Although there were myriad drawbacks to the cortical theories of dyslexia (they are discussed in my other books), I shall not go into the details here. Suffice it to say that I eventually concluded that *both* the traditional neurological and psychiatric theories contained more fiction and fantasy than fact. As a result, I was forced to look elsewhere for the elusive cause of dyslexia.

During the early 1970s, I reevaluated and analyzed all available scientific data concerning the neurological findings in dyslexia. I searched for any hidden clues. But only when I very carefully reviewed my own data—which I had gathered during the late 1960s—did I stumble upon the missing link I had been searching for all along. After reexamining one thousand consecutive dyslexic cases for evidence of a cortical dysfunction, I accidentally noted that over 50 percent showed distinct evidence of impaired balance and coordination. (Only 1 percent of the cases exhibited evidence suggesting a possible cortical dysfunction.) To my surprise, the vast majority of patients reported similar histories, involving delayed ability to sit, crawl, walk, and/or talk; difficulties skipping, hopping or running, and/or participating in sports; problems learning to ride a bike or walk a balance beam; tripping, falling, accident-proneness; and fine-motor incoordination in areas such as tying shoelaces, buttoning, zippering, holding and using a pencil for writing, using crayons, drawing within guidelines, awkward use of a knife and fork. Also common were difficulties fixating and tracking letters and words when reading; dyscoordinated and dysrhythmic speech functioning, such as slurring, articulation impairments, stuttering, or stammering; and difficulty with gross balance, coordination, and rhythmic functioning related to sports, etc.

And what did these clues mean? That the majority of my dyslexic patients, who also exhibited these balance, coordination, and rhythmic difficulties, probably had an *inner-ear*-related problem! These findings were confirmed in repeated studies, one of the latest consisting of the examination of four thousand learning disabled children, adolescents, and adults.

Interestingly, Paul Wender and other leading researchers had also come to recognize that up to 50 percent of their hyperactive or ADD cases had similar balance and coordination symptoms, and that up to 50 percent of these very same cases had dyslexic or LD symptoms! I was beginning to see straight lines.

As I searched for a means to treat dyslexia, several facts became apparent to me: (1) most dyslexics evidenced eye tracking coordination difficulties when reading—they'd lose their place, and their eyes seemed to jump wildly about the page, lost in space and time; (2) this impairment appeared similar to those experienced by normal individuals when reading in a car traversing a bumpy road, or while in a boat tossed by waves or after spinning; (3) dyslexia could thus be viewed as a form of dizziness or motion sickness and might therefore be treated with, and respond favorably to, the antimotion-sickness medications.

Although I initially expected only the reading symptoms to improve with medication, to my surprise I found that a whole series of sensory-motor and related symptoms had improved, including visual, hearing, and touch sequencing functions! Most important, with medication, dyslexic symptoms—and their concentration problems—*improved or disappeared roughly 75 to 80 percent of the time.*

Armed with this information, I retested my ADD patients neurologically and attempted to evaluate their responses to the antimotion-sickness medications. By now you can guess what must have happened. They, too, had shown the very same balance, coordination, and dysrhythmic problems as the dyslexic patients. And with medication, their concentration, distractibility, hyperactivity, and impulsivity symptoms—as well as their dyslexic-related problems—all began to disappear as well! ADD patients who were hyperactive calmed down. Those with distractibility and concentration problems were now able to focus on and complete difficult tasks. And those with learning problems showed remarkable improvements! Indeed, the favorable responses to medications—antimotion-sickness, antihistimines, and stimulant drugs alike—served as a dissecting tool by highlighting the symptoms and mechanisms characterizing ADD and dyslexia, a single disorder that had two distinct names.

Having now examined and medically treated more than twenty thousand children and adults with both dyslexic and ADD symptomatology, I have concluded that both these disorders have an underlying common denominator, and that this neurophysiological or chemical malfunction lies primarily within the inner-ear system for the vast majority of referred patients. As noted earlier, this conclusion is perfectly consistent with the findings of other researchers who have found these very same disorders to significantly overlap with one another. However, their findings did not lead them to take the last and most difficult step: to finally recognize that prior definitions might be significantly incomplete and even wrong, and that a new conceptualization of these overlapping disorders was vital if patients were to be properly diagnosed and treated!

Eventually, my research efforts led me to recognize *four* primary and *one* secondary types of concentration disorders (CD). And this insight led me to develop a new classification of ADD based on mechanisms of origin rather than on superficial descriptions of the symptomatic fall-out. According to this new classification:

☐ *Type I CD* is due to realistic emotional trauma
☐ *Type II CD* is due to unconscious neurotic conflicts
☐ *Type III CD, or ADD*, is due to a primary neurophysiological and/or neurotransmitter dysfunction of the cerebellar-vestibular system (CVS), or inner ear, as well as interconnected circuits of the alerting and concentration modulating centers
☐ *Type IV CD, or ADD*, is due to a primary non-CVS neurophysiological and/or neurotransmitter dysfunction of the reticular activating and concentration modulating systems of the brain, perhaps with secondary or associated involvement of higher centers as well as the inner ear. This disorder may account for those with extremely severe and pervasive symptoms and tends to have a poorer prognosis than Type III ADD.
☐ *Type V^2 CD* is due to the secondary effects of "energy drain" resulting from a variety of conditions such as anemia, metabolic, or chemical disturbances.

As a result of this new classification, all patients and all symptoms can now be clearly defined in terms of their specific and overlapping origins. And all symptoms can be more specifically and thus effectively treated. Furthermore, the transient and temporary concentration-related symptoms that periodically affect us all can now be readily explained by these very same mechanisms. In other words, there now appears to be a simple way of understanding all concentration-related symptoms—the mild, the severe, and even the transient and reversible Freudianlike slips of functioning that periodically affect us all.

Within the pages of *Total Concentration*, you have met and will continue to meet those who suffer from Type III ADD. However, you've still to meet individuals who have Types I, II, IV, and V^2 concentration disorders. Since any one patient may have any number of overlapping types of concentration disorders, and as many of the resulting symptoms appear somewhat similar both in quality and intensity, it is imperative that you listen carefully to all these patients.

By presenting a significant number of additional case histories in the chapters that follow, I hope that you will eventually find it possible to recognize which symptoms are caused by which of the Types I through V^2, how these many and varied symptoms are interconnected, and how they affect one another and overlap. Although the task may not be easy, it will not be as difficult for you as it was for me. Ultimately, you will be rewarded for your time, effort, and thought: You will, I hope, attain your own personal level of *Total Concentration!*

Chapter VII

A Model for Concentration

In our daily lives, we are constantly bombarded by more information than we can possibly comprehend, absorb, or process. Not only that, we're faced with far more activities than we can ever hope to pursue in a day, a week, or even months. As a result, we're forced to select information and activities out of the chaos that surrounds us—often on a moment-to-moment basis.

For people like Josh, the youngster you met in Chapter V, the process of selection is an insurmountable obstacle. "He seems to overload easily," his teacher wrote, "and will fly off the handle at the slightest provocation, or for no apparent reason at all. Even if he's given a task that's simple, he burns out after a few seconds. He's unable to participate in group sports and can't seem to socialize with more than one child at a time; he gets lost and confused when two or more things are going on around him."

Why does Josh burn out? Why do *you*? To answer those questions, we must begin by examining two of the functions that are crucial to concentration: selective *attention* and selective *intention*.

SELECTIVE ATTENTION

Although many researchers have attempted to define the process of selective attention, I prefer to describe it as the dual ability to focus on what's important and to simultaneously filter out what's not. According to Melvin Levine and other researchers, there are eight steps involved in the process, many of which are analogous to the act of tuning in and watching a television set:

1. Turning on
2. Tuning in
3. Initial focusing
4. Tuning out irrelevant details
5. Fine-tune focusing
6. Feedback (continuing to watch, or changing the channel)
7. Responding
8. Turning off

People who do not have a concentration dysfunction say the process feels automatic—they're not even aware that they're moving through the steps. To understand how selective attention operates, let's take a look at the following example:

Mary is sitting in her office, working on an assignment the boss has just given her. Toiling away at it, she hardly notices that her co-worker has entered the room. However, at the moment she hears him say, "We've got to talk now," Mary *turns on*; she's alert to the fact that her colleague wants something. Within seconds, Mary's phone begins to ring and her secretary buzzes on the intercom: she now *tunes in* to all the stimuli around her. Faced with a variety of choices—should she answer her phone, or the intercom, or ignore both and give her co-worker her complete attention?—Mary will instantaneously begin the process of *initial focusing*; she'll think about what's the most important thing to respond to, weighing the pros and cons of each choice. At this point, she'll begin to *tune out irrelevant details*; she may ignore the jangling phone and her secretary's voice, or she may choose to keep her colleague waiting. Assuming Mary decides to listen to what he has to say, she begins *fine-tune focusing*. With her eyes, ears, and all the intuition she can muster, she tries to assess what he's trying to say. Then, after hearing him out, Mary begins the process of *feedback*: she quickly analyzes what's been said and determines whether or not it is really useful to her. (She'll also be deciding whether to continue listening to her co-worker, or to turn him off—i.e., do something else, like daydreaming.) If Mary decides that his comments are worthwhile, she will start *responding* to what he's said: she'll either write down his comments, vow to memorize them, or decide that she must act on them in some way. Eventually, after realizing she has gleaned everything she needed from this conversation, Mary will decide to *turn off*. She'll either change the subject because there's no point in belaboring the current one, or she'll return to her work.

For Mary, these eight basic steps of selective attention occur with lightning-fast speed. And because they occur properly—i.e., the steps are not sabotaged by a dysfunction—she isn't even aware that she has followed them. What she is aware of, however, is what the steps enable her to do: to produce a business memo or a letter to a friend, for example, or develop a friendship or other social exchange—even to play a sport or draw a picture. When the process of selective attention is intact, we can produce an infinite number of short-term or long-term "creations"—some of them tangible, some intangible, but all uniquely ours.

When, however, selective attention becomes impaired—as in ADD—there is often a spontaneous decomposition or falling-apart of this total "invisible" process into its component parts. Patients are then forced to compensate, consciously and deliberately, by attempting to relearn the missing steps. For those who luck out, this relearned process once again becomes smooth, effortless, automatic. When ADD subjects respond favorably to medical treatment, the impaired and thus obvious subfunctions or "steps" suddenly disappear, and the previously awkward and obviously decomposed process is rapidly transformed into a reflex, viable but invisible recomposed whole.

What can we learn from these observations? Namely, that there are two parallel but interrelated mechanisms responsible for modulating and implementing the process called selective attention—and *total concentration*. The reflexive, automatic determining mechanism is inner-ear-based and is also responsible for regulating all sensory-motor-related academic processes. And the conscious and deliberate, or intentional, mechanism is determined by higher order cerebral or thinking functions.

Under normal circumstances, these two neurophysiological determinants of selective attention are completely interconnected and interwoven via feedback circuits, and thus act as one indivisible whole. In the presence of ADD (Type III and/or IV), the functional unity of these two determining mechanisms becomes unglued and thus clinically apparent. Compensatory processes acting on and enhancing either the inner-ear and/or cerebral mechanisms facilitate a reunification of this whole process.

The same insights also apply to the related process of selective intention. Overall, this rather "simple" but general overview has enormous implications for understanding and diagnosing this disorder and, most important, for effectively treating it via a wide range of medical and nonmedical modalities.

SELECTIVE INTENTION

Even before we begin to create something, we have to do a certain amount of planning. This activity, called *selective intention,* helps us to anticipate the outcome of our actions and to select the best ways to accomplish a task. There are ten basic steps:

1. Setting the goal or objective
2. Reviewing possible methods
3. Predicting possible outcomes
4. Choosing the best route
5. Suppressing negative actions
6. Persisting
7. Monitoring
8. Fine-tuning
9. Issuing a stop order
10. Reviewing the outcome

How do the steps of selective intention operate in the lives of people who do not have a concentration dysfunction like ADD? Consider the following story of an advertising executive who accomplished what he calls "the toughest task of my life"— passing the Graduate Record Exam so that he could qualify for graduate school and eventually become a full-fledged professor.

For twenty years, Gene S., now fifty-four, was president of a large advertising agency in Chicago. After realizing that he was "sick and tired of all the backbiting and hustling," he sold out his interest in the agency, became a visiting lecturer in the graduate business school of a nearby university, and simultaneously began work on his Ph.D., a move that would eventually help him reach his goal: to become a full-time professor. "I was working seventeen to eighteen hours a day then," he recalled during our phone conversation. "It was a grueling schedule, but I was determined to reach my goal in four years or less! I felt that nothing could stop me . . . until I reached the point when, like all PH.D. candidates, I had to take the Graduate Record Exam.

"The GRE was very troublesome to me because the questions are evenly divided between quantitative and qualitative information. I knew the qualitative stuff wouldn't be a problem, because I'd always excelled at it. But anytime in my life that I've had to deal with quantitative information, it's as if I suddenly become brain-damaged—I simply cannot concentrate on it. Even as a kid, I recognized that this was my major problem. The teacher would be at the blackboard, teaching the multiplication tables, and my mind would just wander. I'd discover myself in a strange fantasy or reverie and get furious with myself. I'd try to focus, but to no avail.

"The quantitative part of the GRE involved algebra, trigonometry . . . all the things that had been my nemesis all my life. Somewhere in childhood I think I'd gotten the message that quantitative data was "the enemy," or that I was just dumb when it came to numbers and mathematical concepts. I was completely inhibited from being a performer in that area and avoided it whenever I could. I remembered zero of the stuff they'd taught me in high school, and I'd failed—and had to repeat—virtually every math class I'd ever taken. So you can imagine my dilemma: I wanted desperately to get my Ph.D., but feared that the GRE would totally block my chances.

"I knew I had to force myself to try to overcome this problem at least minimally in order to pass the test. So I employed a tutor to work with me for an intensive period of two months prior to the exam. We worked together several times per week. It was holy hell for me, a nightmare revisiting all these things that I thought I had safely put in my past. The tutor would tell me things and I'd sort of get it, then I'd come back two days later and have totally forgotten what I'd learned. Even when he gave me hints to try to refresh my memory, I'd just go blank.

"I was so super-stressed during this period I felt I was mentally ill! I felt such a sense of resistance, of trying to run away from it. I'd sweat profusely and my heart would pound in my chest; my whole body reverberated with fear. I also felt a rage inside—a rage at my inability to overcome this psychic block! I've never been tolerant of my limitations and flaws, but this was somehow the most insufferable insult! But the more I fought it the more it became a problem. I was wrestling with it as if it were alive!

"About three weeks before the exam, both the tutor and I were becoming exasperated. It appeared that none of this stuff would ever sink in; it seemed clear that the GRE would conquer me. One day, before we started in, the tutor pulled out a bottle of vodka from his briefcase and said, 'Gene, let's have a drink before we begin.' He poured three fingers into my coffee and I started sipping away, and suddenly I was beginning to perform!

"That became our ritual. As soon as I'd come in, we'd drink. I never got sloshed, but just got the edge off this tremendous anxiety that was destroying my ability to concentrate. When I could relax myself sufficiently, I started to assimilate the information. It seemed terrible to have to court alcohol to solve the problem, but I was prepared to do whatever I had to do.

"In the days that followed, I began to feel more in control of the data I was studying. In fact, I felt I had reached the point where I could work the problems—and remember them—without having to imbibe. We stopped our vodka ritual and, lo and behold, I remained calm enough to grasp concepts and recall facts. With each passing day my mind felt stronger and stronger; I began to believe that I actually had a chance of passing!

"The night before the exam, I crammed until three in the morning. Over and over again, I'd repeat the basic theorems and formulae. But all the while I kept thinking about walking into the classroom and remembering absolutely nothing. Just the thought of it made me hysterical.

"On the morning of the exam, something peculiar happened. As I walked through the snow, I felt a sense of calm coming over me. Not that I knew everything, but I was so tired and emotionally spent at that point that I felt a sense of fatalism about it. I believed that I'd given it my very best shot and that within the limitations of my mind there was nothing more I could do. And I was now prepared to accept the consequences. I walked in, didn't get crazed or hysterical, and functioned at my maximum level. I think I broke through the incredible tension by forgiving myself my limitations. I simply relaxed and was able to perform. I didn't excel on the exam. But between the superior performance on the qualitative and the acceptable performance on the quantitative, I passed on the first go-around, which I'm told is unusual. I believe my motivation was so powerful, as was my determination not to put myself through this hell again, I just somehow drove myself to overcome this tremendous concentration problem. But three weeks later, when I picked up my workbook, I drew a complete blank. I couldn't remember one theorem."

During the months that Gene was struggling to pass the GRE, he was not conscious of having moved through the steps of selective intention. Nor was he aware that each separate step naturally requires simultaneous operation of many of the steps of selection attention discussed earlier. Yet when we reviewed his motives and behavior during that important episode in his life, each part of the process became evident:

1. Because he was dissatisfied with his job in the world of advertising and was intrigued by academia, he *set a goal* for himself: to leave his present job and pursue a career that would satisfy his intellectual cravings.

2. *Reviewing the possible methods* for achieving the goal was easy: Gene knew he would have to attend graduate school, but first, he'd have to pass the Graduate Record Exam—a grueling test that required an adequate performance in math, his weakest area.

3. Although he considered quantitative data his "nemesis," Gene was extremely motivated to pass the test. While *predicting the possible outcomes* of his goal, his fears were offset by his desire to achieve; in his heart and soul, he not only wanted to succeed, he knew he must succeed. With enough hard work, he believed the goal was within his reach.

4. While *choosing the best route* to take, Gene knew he'd have

to study long and hard. For him, the "best" route involved employing the services of a math tutor.

5. During his tutoring sessions, Gene was forced to *suppress negative actions* that had plagued him all his life: a poor memory for math, a feeling of being "brain damaged," and high anxiety. According to Gene, the "three fingers of vodka" helped suppress those negatives—the alcohol relaxed him enough so that he could concentrate.

6. Now able to focus on the task at hand, Gene *persisted* at it by reviewing equations and other mathematical rules; he was able to keep at it long enough to feel competent.

7. Of course, Gene experienced moments of great frustration during his tutoring sessions. And he often worried that, despite all the work, he might not pass the test. Yet when he *monitored* his progress, he was confident that he was making headway—he was beginning to assimilate the information needed to pass the test.

8. As Gene's confidence increased, he no longer felt the need for the vodka ritual. By eliminating alcohol from the study sessions, he took a step toward *fine-tuning* his actions.

9. On the morning of the exam, Gene felt calm and relaxed, knowing that he had given the work his "best shot." He was ready to take the exam, prepared to "accept the consequences." On an emotional and intellectual level, Gene had *issued a stop order*: he knew "there was nothing more I could do." Happily, he *had* done enough; he passed the exam on the first go-around.

10. *Reviewing the outcome* of the exam was a pleasant experience for Gene. He had overcome the odds against him and discovered that the agony he'd experienced along the way had been worth it.

As you read about Gene's experience and traced the steps of the process of selective intention, you may have noticed that from time to time he experienced some of the symptoms associated with a concentration dysfunction—forgetfulness, excessive stress or burn-out, agitation, irritability, and mood swings. Did you wonder why *he* was able to overcome them—and why in many situations *you* or your child can't? Were you also curious as to why he had difficulties with math? In the next chapter, we'll fit more pieces of the puzzle together by examining the behavior of people who have Attention Deficit Disorder—individuals whose processes of selective attention and selective intention have somehow gone awry.

CHAPTER VIII

A New Way of Looking at ADD

As we saw in the previous chapter, the processes of selective attention and selective intention are fundamental to the ability to concentrate on a task, however complicated or simple it might be. When everything is working right, we slip through the steps with ease, completely unaware that we're doing anything of consequence. Unfortunately, these functions become obvious only when they fail. And they fail in those with Attention Deficit Disorder, resulting in underachievement and self-defeating behavior unless conscious and deliberate compensatory efforts are made and/or compensatory reflex mechanisms kick in.[1]

As you'll recall, selective attention is the ability to focus on what's important and to filter out what's not. The process involves steps similar to those used when we operate a television set: when we are confronted with a task or activity, we turn on and tune in, then begin initial focusing. Almost unconsciously, we tune out irrelevant details and attend to what's important. After deciding whether the information we've selected is useful to us, we respond to it until we feel it's time to turn off.

To understand what happens when the process of selective attention becomes disabled, I'd like you to consider the following

---

[1] In accordance with these observations and my research, two parallel but interrelated neurophysiological determinants were shown to contribute to the processes of selective attention and intention: a conscious and deliberate function or mechanism of cerebral or thinking origin and a reflex vector of inner-ear origin. Any dysfunction of these vectors may result in a corresponding breakdown of these processes into their component parts. And compensatory or therapeutic enhancement of these respective vectors is required to effect a recombination of these subfunctions or parts into a functional whole—total concentration.

case history, based on an interview with one of my patients with ADD.

Jacqueline D.

When she was in high school, Jacqueline D. had high hopes for her future. "My friends were all headed to white-collar jobs," she says, "and I always expected I'd become a teacher. When I was feeling really good about myself, I thought I might even become a doctor or an astronaut, but things didn't turn out that way. I'm qualified to do nothing except clerical work, which is what I've done ever since.

"I think I managed in the earlier grade levels because the volume of work wasn't too large. Back then I was able to compensate for the problems I have since become aware of. But once I started my first semester in college, all of a sudden there was just too much to read and remember. I found it very difficult to concentrate. After reading or writing a sentence or a paragraph, I'd get very tired and have to stop and rest. I'd feel sick if I had to continue without a break.

"For tests, I would have to memorize entire texts, word by word. It took forever, but it was the only way I could remember something. I couldn't just read something two or three times and get it—sometimes I felt compelled to go over a sentence fifty or sixty times. I spent all of my time studying, even though I only took four courses. I dropped out before the end of the first semester. It was really demoralizing.

"I find difficult any activity where I have to keep my eyes focused on something. Watching or playing tennis is impossible. Instead of focusing on where the ball is going, I may find myself concentrating on what the players are wearing, or what people in the crowd are doing. I have problems adding columns of numbers unless the columns are clearly divided by a line. If there's no line, every time I add the columns I get a different answer. I cannot ride a bicycle and talk to someone at the same time—if I do, I feel wobbly and cannot control the bike.

"My concentration problems have really hindered me in my

work. I can only perform one task at a time. For example, if my boss calls me into her office and tells me to do three tasks, I have to repeat them over and over again to myself on the way back to my desk, and then I have to write them down right away or I will forget. If, on the way back to my desk, I get distracted by something—like an interesting painting on the wall—I'll focus on that and forget what my boss told me to do.

"At all times, I carry a huge diary and constantly make notes in it about what I have to do and when, including things that other people don't even think twice about doing, such as ironing clothes, getting dressed, etc. If I don't write down that I have an appointment, I know I'll miss it. If I go grocery shopping and have to get just three things, if I don't write them down, I'll forget.

"At home and work, and on every job I've ever had, there always seems to be this big backlog of work to do which I can never seem to keep on top of. I used to think it was the job and that the place was understaffed, but after a few jobs where the situation was the same, I realized that it's me and not the job.

"Typically, ten minutes before a work day ends, I'll discover that there are still urgent tasks to do, and I invariably end up staying very late to complete them. I barely get by at work—if I do, it's only because I check and recheck things so many times to make sure I haven't made major errors that would have major consequences. My boss thinks I'm a better than average worker, but it's just because I overcompensate and try so hard. It's exhausting!

"If I have to think about anything that's more complex than what I'm going to have for dinner, I have to sit down and just try to concentrate on that. Sometimes I can concentrate with the radio or television on and find the sounds somehow comforting. But more often than not, I have to have total silence and be doing absolutely nothing in order to think about something.

"I also have trouble working in groups—it seems like everyone is talking too fast for me to comprehend them. In these instances, I give up on listening to what's being said and will focus on something else, such as what people are wearing. If I'm in a crowd, I get overwhelmed and feel anxious, dizzy, and light-headed. The thought of having to speak in front of a group terrifies me—I avoid such encounters at all costs.

"I am disturbed by the fact that I have trouble grasping concepts that a child could understand. For example, while traveling abroad, I couldn't comprehend the traffic lights—I was never sure which flash sequence meant it was okay to walk across the street. Making change is a nightmare: if someone gives me a ten-dollar bill for something that costs $4.80, I can do it. But if they give me a ten and a nickel because they want a quarter back instead of twenty cents, I can't figure that out; they have to tell me.

"I've always felt stupid. Yet I know there is a smart person inside of me. I know that a lot of the things I think could only come from someone who has a reasonably intelligent mind. Yet almost everything I do or try to do seems to contradict this assumption. I'm at a point in my life where I feel like giving up hope for good. I wonder if I will ever lead a normal life."

Jacqueline's symptoms are important for many reasons. Adults with ADD are seldom reported in the scientific literature and thus there currently exists no way to reliably understand and diagnose them. And yet in my experience, over 90 percent of children with ADD will show some residual signs in adulthood (this compares with a one-third figure reported by DSM-III-R). And some with ADD will *first* experience or recognize symptoms as adolescents or adults, when overloading suddenly destabilizes the prior equilibrium established between dysfunctioning and compensatory mechanisms, or when ADD is newly acquired.

Although the DSM-III-R diagnostic criteria apply only to children (and as I've already stated, only one-third of them), it seems worthwhile to compare Jacqueline's *residual* symptoms with those highlighted in DSM-III-R:

1. She certainly appears to have trouble following through on instructions from others.
2. She doesn't seem to listen to what's being said to her.
3. She's sometimes easily distracted by extraneous stimuli, such as a radio playing or people talking.

It appears, then, that Jacqueline has at least three symptoms of ADD, according to the criteria used for diagnosing children. But, in fact, she has many more symptoms related to this very same disorder. And *all*—including difficulties with memory and sequencing tasks—must be clearly recognized both for diagnostic and therapeutic purposes.

Based on my research, I believe it is imperative that clinicians, researchers, and patients *broaden* their view of ADD. We must go beyond simplistic lists of symptomatic behaviors and recognize the panorama of traits that characterize this disorder. And we must attempt to analyze these symptoms so as to recognize their underlying mechanisms. How do we do it? First, we must dissect the function of selective attention into its component parts and view the wide range of negative patterns that can occur. By doing so, we can account for many of the subtleties in symptomatic behavior and academic performance that are often overlooked. Then we must attempt to separate symptoms resulting from impaired functions from those resulting from compensatory attempts to get around these impairments. Later on, we can evaluate these symptoms to determine their *mechanisms of origin*. The ensuing insights will inevitably suggest ways to compensate for the specific functions and mechanisms found deficient.

A dysfunction in selective attention is characterized by "improper tuning": wandering focus, distractibility, and reduced response to feedback. As you review these obstacles to concentration, highlighted below, think about yourself. Do you have similar "tuning" difficulties? Remember that some with ADD will experience many of the symptoms, while others exhibit just a few. In either case, problems may vary in intensity from mild to moderate to severe—and even become completely compensated for. Let's take a closer look.[2]

---

[2]As noted, many and varied symptoms characterize ADD. These result from hidden dysfunctioning or from compensatory mechanisms. As a result, symptomatic characteristics vary from one extreme to another, depending on which vector is dominant: when the two opposing vectors neutralize each others, no symptom is apparent. It becomes hidden, masked, or subclinical. When two or more impaired mechanisms overlap, then multiple combinations and variations of symptoms occur.

THE DETAIL DILEMMA: Overloading and "Burn-out":

Because some with ADD have trouble concentrating on and processing relevant particulars, they tend to prefer the "big picture." Like Jacqueline, they may understand concepts of math, but can't seem to properly focus on the columns and remember facts. When the number of details increases—as they did when Jackie entered college—these patients simply cannot concentrate, remember, and process or cope with all of them. They become overloaded! And "burn-out," or depletion of already limited concentration and processing reserves occurs. As you might expect, the dilemma with details can occur when a person is faced with written or verbal information.

A WIDE-ANGLE VIEW

By recalling Jacqueline's difficulty with watching or playing tennis, you'll understand what I mean by a wide-angle view. She has trouble focusing on what's important—i.e., the ball—and instead concentrates on peripheral details. Her train of thought can be easily interrupted by irrelevant information: if she sees a painting on the wall on her way back to her office, she focuses on that instead of her boss's instructions. People with ADD constantly notice and learn from things around them, but they're usually off-target: they have a tendency not to learn the right thing in the right place at the right time. It's as if their "background filter" is leaking. And thus irrelevant details and perceptions that should have been filtered-out instead bombard their consciousness or "attention spheres."

When driving, Jason W. becomes confused about where he's going and how to get there. "Even if I've looked at a map and have a sense of my destination, I get distracted by flashing lights, signs, and buildings. I lose my sense of direction rather quickly, and wind up getting lost most of the time." As noted, this wide-angle view often results from a failure to filter out background, peripheral, or irrelevant details. And this problem, in turn, may even intensify other problems, for example, a poor sense of, or memory for, direction. The analysis of countless cases with ADD suggests that there are several reasons for this wide-angle phenomenon and that any of them may be responsible for this symptom in any given individual. Many with this disorder have fine-motor eye-tracking problems—the same problem that makes it difficult for them to read letters and words in sequence without losing their place or reversing the order. This visual fixation and sequential tracking problem creates a compensatory tendency to rapidly scan and grasp the whole—a wide-angle view. This tendency is reinforced by the difficulties ADD patients experience in selectively picking out foreground or important details for perception and concentration while simultaneously filtering out unimportant background events. The result is sensory scrambling—unless secondary factors, such as rapid wide-angle scanning, are learned or developed to compensate.

THE FATIGUE FACTOR

To be attentive, one must be reasonably alert. But such alertness can be compromised by a variety of fatigue factors. Some people with ADD have trouble getting to sleep at night; others experience periods of restlessness at night, resulting in tiredness during the day. For some people, like Jacqueline, concentrating on reading or writing fatigues them—they feel "sick" and have to stop and rest. Indeed, many such patients must exert excessive degrees of concentration effort to compensate for impaired sensory-motor and related academic functions. The compensatory energy drain further destabilizes and depletes their attention and intensifies their symptoms.

It is interesting to note that some patients who seem fatigued during the day will "get a second wind" in the evening and be quite attentive and alert. Unfortunately, however, these late-night spurts of energy often contribute to overtiredness the next morning. Needless to say, reversals and/or poor modulation of arousal and sleep cycles is typical of many with ADD.

OVERFOCUSING AND UNDERFOCUSING

Although you might suspect that people with ADD concentrate too briefly on information because of inadequate "energy reserves," the reverse is also true. Some patients tend to overfocus on material, getting "stuck" on it to the point of perseveration. This can often result in compulsions or obsessions. Individuals may reread sentences over and over again like Jackie did, or perseverate in other ways: writing repetitively, or constantly fiddling with objects, thinking the same thought again and again. They have difficulty turning off.

Some individuals who overfocus become anxious and fretful about seemingly unimportant details. Joan S., an elementary-school teacher, told me that when she left for work every morning, she would "run back to the apartment several times to make sure I've turned off the lights, or the iron or toaster. If I don't recheck things, I'll feel upset all day long." During subsequent interviews, I also learned that Joan overfocused while at home and at school. She would spend hours rearranging her closets, for example. And at work, she found herself constantly organizing her desk. If unable to do these tasks, Joan said she felt "lost." Obviously, she had impaired memory functioning. To compensate, she had to pay excessive attention to details, checking and rechecking them for errors to the point where her behavior might be called obsessive-compulsive.

Under- and *overfocusing* may also result from improper fine-tuning or modulation of concentration: too little or too much. Also, conscious efforts at enhancing tracking and focusing often compensate for underlying impairment in these very same reflex mechanisms. As noted, Joan's repetitive checking and rechecking—or overfocusing—served to minimize anticipated errors and disorganization—and the inner feelings of stupidity and fears of losing control.

ONE-TRACK FOCUSING

Imagine that you are listening to someone giving a speech. What do you notice most? The speaker's clothing? Her tone of voice?

The way she uses hand gestures for emphasis? The facts she's using to illustrate her point? People with ADD have difficulty simultaneously processing all the stimuli bombarding them; they are not "reflexively" adept at selectively attending to and perceiving all the parts that make a whole. Instead, they focus and concentrate on one element that may appear to be insignificant. Recall Jackie's problem in groups: because multiple conversations confuse her, she concentrates on group members' clothing. One-track focusing is similar to what I call single-targeting. Patients with ADD often have difficulty with sensory-motor and related thinking functions unless they focus all their concentration efforts on each step of a sequence or whole—one at a time. They attempt to compensate in this manner for a failure to naturally and reflexively scan, concentrate on, and process the total automatically.

Furthermore, many with ADD experience tunnel vision. Often, they find it easier and more helpful to concentrate on and perform one task well than to mess up the total that they can't see, perceive, and act on. In other words, one-track focusing may result from either an impairment in selective attention and intention or from specific attempts to compensate for this problem by deliberately narrowing the field of vision and action.

You may also recall that Jackie couldn't ride a bike and talk to someone at the same time. About that problem she said, "There's just too much going on all at once. I've got to watch where I'm going, hold on to the handlebars, and push the pedals. At the same time, I'm hearing a conversation or being asked questions and watching my friend out of the corner of my eye. It's hard to keep track of all the details and to keep my balance, too." As you can readily see, overloading in subjects with ADD scatters concentration—which in turn destabilizes inner-ear-based balance and coordination functioning. Stated another way, intense and focalized concentration serves to stabilize and enhance inner-ear-based functioning.

Over the years, my research has clearly shown that most people with ADD suffer from a disintegration or coming-apart of a total process into its single parts. And to compensate, they often must consciously make efforts to reintegrate the whole—one single sensory, motor, or thinking step at a time. For those who luck out, reintegration processes become relearned on an automatic basis. And thus they appear to function normally and effortlessly once again.

INCONSISTENT FOCUSING

Many parents say to me, "I'm stunned by the fact that my child can sometimes concentrate for hours on a video game or television show or book. Yet later, he'll tune out completely when confronted with another task." This inconsistency frustrates many parents—they're convinced their youngster can *will* himself to concentrate, because they've seen him do it many times. The fact is, children and adults with ADD have extreme difficulty controlling their attention spans; more often than not, their ability to concentrate fully seems to hinge upon whim or chance. More specifically, the concentration and related mechanisms in patients with ADD are improperly and thus inconsistently fine-tuned. And just as a TV picture may come and go, depending on a host of variables, so do the attention and related symptoms of vulnerable patients.

In fact, this inconsistency is characteristic of ADD. Most clinicians recognize that the symptoms constituting ADD are *situation-specific*: apparent at one point in time and gone at another.

Jackie once told me that a friend had described her as being "shifty-eyed." During interviews with her, it became apparent why such an accusation was made: Jackie's eyes would dart about the room, often focusing on irrelevant details such as my tie or the model of the brain that sits upon my desk. When examined, she evidenced a neurological sign of inner-ear dysfunction called nystagmus—spontaneous and reflex rapid to and fro eye movements. Needless to say, this problem certainly explained the inconsistent focusing of both her eyes and her attention. My research has found that many subjects with ADD have mild and subtle forms of this disturbance, often absent to the naked eye and thus requiring special testing to uncover.

However, when I asked Jackie why she looked at everything

the way she did, she rationalized, "Everything seems so interesting. It's difficult for me *not* to look at all this stuff." Many individuals experience reading or dyslexic difficulties because their ability to visually fixate and sequentially track important foreground events is impaired, as is Jackie's. When reading, for example, they may insert words that are not a part of the text, or when writing they may omit or reverse letters and words. "I've always been a poor speller," says Jackie. "Even if I know the word is 'dog', I'll spell it 'g-o-d'."

Inconsistent focusing may be caused by mechanisms similar to those previously discussed. In other words, similar mechanisms may result in functions that appear different because compensatory factors have shaped the final outcome, and symptoms that appear similar may result from different mechanisms. For example, not everyone with high blood sugar has diabetes, and not everyone with high temperature has an infection.

ACUTE LISTENING

If you recall Josh, the subject of Chapter Five, you will understand the acute listening problem. His teacher said it was as if his "filter was off": he tuned in to irrelevant sounds, such as raindrops and even pin drops. And he often complained of excessive noise levels—he'd cover his ears when he heard sirens or thunder. Josh's father experienced some of the same symptoms: at parties, which he thought were too noisy, he spoke loudly, as if trying to hear himself think. I consider this problem to be the result of a "leaking filter"—too much input getting in. As a result, the sensory input—whatever its nature—appears louder, more intense.

AUDITORY DISTRACTIBILITY

Persons who experience auditory distractibility problems may find that social gatherings trigger anxiety. Explained Jane L., a registered nurse, "If I'm in a restaurant where there are lots of people talking, I have trouble hearing what my friends are saying. All the sounds blur together. I get embarrassed and feel stupid in these situations, and avoid them whenever possible. My friends tease me about it; they say I have a restaurant phobia." In other words, some people experience difficulties in filtering out background or unimportant noise so as to better focus on, listen to, and comprehend important foreground events. As a result, foreground and background become scrambled—and anxieties, avoidance, and even social phobias result.

BODY FOCUSING AND "PSYCHOSOMATIC" SYMPTOMS

It is not unusual for people with ADD to be distracted by their bodies. In other words, they experience difficulties in properly filtering out various *inner*, or somatic, sensations. And they thus experience the symptoms characterizing their disorder as especially intense. These symptoms often include headaches, dizziness, nausea, and myriad other "psychosomatic" problems. As a result, these individuals are usually referred to as hypochondriacs. However, an opposite response is sometimes noted in these very same ADD patients. Sometimes their filters shut out *too much*. They then can complain of nothing. And what might we call them: brave, stoic? Regardless of the moralistic names we superficially give them, these individuals have in common a defective filter. Needless to say, this filtering defect is often sensory-specific and may thus apply to any (and all) sensory stimuli.

When faced with reading a "dry" report, Albert F., a forty-eight-year-old salesman, experiences great bodily discomfort. During an interview he told me, "Before I even start reading, I get nervous. My palms sweat and my heart races. Once I begin, I feel light-headed. Sometimes the words seem to jump around on the page, and I'll get dizzy. Eventually, I can't focus on the reading; I can only focus on me."

How do you analyze this sequence of symptoms? Pending confirmation, I would assume that the task of reading a "dry report" triggers anxiety and psychosomatic symptoms only in someone with impaired concentration and/or reading abilities. And anxiety, boring content, and the ensuing distractibility further destabilize the inner ear—which is responsible for these symptoms in the first place. Were there not a preexisting dysfunction, why would this patient become so anxious? And why would the trigger be a "dry" or boring one? And why would the psychosomatic symptoms triggered suggest involvement of the inner ear?

THE "SPACINESS" FACTOR

Spaced-out. Spacy. Space cadet. We've all heard the terms used to describe individuals who daydream or who simply "tune out" during meetings or conversations. They feel mentally asleep. Not there or with it. They feel unreal,—even depersonalized or estranged from themselves. In fact, the presence of this "spaciness" factor and its related symptoms—including other difficulties with arousal and sleep—in ADD patients has suggested that the mechanisms of the brain that modulate alertness and concentration are impaired in ADD. Some researchers have even thought that these subjects suffer from free-flight distractibility. However, it appears to me that their filtering mechanisms are "leaky." Too many thoughts and ideas penetrate too quickly to be adaptively processed. Accordingly, these subjects are flooded and overwhelmed—and become exhausted. Some begin to feel "unreal" or depersonalized—not there. Then they become frightened that they've lost their minds. And the resulting anxiety then intensifies these already existing feelings. Jeffrey S., a university student, complained: "I had been up all night studying. Around midnight, while working through an equation, my mind started to race. I'd have a flood of ideas, but they were coming so fast I couldn't keep track of them. I felt like I was going to jump out of my skin. I couldn't see straight, then I'd experience tunnel vision. All of this happened within a six-hour period."

Some people with ADD act as if they are driven by a "racing motor"—they cannot stop or slow the flow and speed of information nor inhibit the background thoughts. This "flooding" often triggers or is associated with anxiety and panic, which further destabilizes concentration and related inner-ear functioning. To compensate and thus attempt to minimize overloading, tunnel vision may occur.

INSATIABLE CRAVING AND IMPULSIVITY

A while ago, the mother of one of my patients told me a story that clearly illustrates the problem of insatiability. Referring to her twelve-year-old, she said, "He's got to have everything—*right now*. With Scott, it's always 'I want, I want, I want.' Yet he never seems satisfied with anything. As soon as he gets the thing he so badly wanted, he thinks of something he wants even more." Such youngsters—and many adults—seem restless, cannot tolerate boredom, and seem to have a voracious appetite for excitement. Many with ADD have difficulty tuning in on and being satisfied by any one thing or activity; some try to create situations—even dangerous ones—that supply them with the intensity, activity, and excitement they dearly crave.

"Margaret gets bored very quickly," the mother of this fourteen-year-old told me. "Perhaps it's because she has a poor sense of time. A minute seems like an hour to her, and she'll get aggravated if she has to slow her pace. Within a half an hour, she may try to read a book, play her tape cassette, watch part of a television show, call a friend, and ask me to help her bake cookies. She seems to want to keep moving all the time. When she can't, she'll throw a fit. If she doesn't get instant gratification, she gets extremely frustrated and will do things like pick fights with her brother."

In retrospect, impulsive behavior seems to be the result of poorly filtered or "slowed-up" discharges—so that sufficient time is unavailable for thought and adaptive checks and balances.

DETACHED SELF-MONITORING

Unlike Jackie, who checked, double-checked, and triple-checked her work, some individuals resist any sort of self-monitoring.

They seem unable to review what they've done or to reread assignments to catch mistakes. "Sam, my ten-year-old," wrote a mother, "does all his schoolwork at breakneck speed. He refuses to slow down, even if I point out that he's made a mistake." Sometimes, in social situations, such individuals appear to ignore negative feedback from their peers: "When Daryl's friend tells him to go away and stop bugging him," explained his mother, "it's like he doesn't even hear him. He tunes out the negative feedback and just keeps going back for more!" Obviously, this symptom may also be viewed as mental impulsivity, or a failure to neutralize, check, or slow down responses sufficiently to accomplish "normal" or adaptive behavior.

By examining some of the negative patterns of selective attention, we have begun to get a clearer and more accurate picture of ADD. But we cannot stop here; we must continue to add to our canvas by taking a look at the many problems that affect the spontaneous and reflexive planning that is required before and during a task. This activity is not easily accomplished by individuals who have ADD.

If you recall Gene, the advertising executive who went on to become a university professor, you'll remember that despite a math block, he was able to pass a difficult exam that was necessary for entrance to graduate school. To briefly recap his story, he succeeded because he had clear goals, selected the best means of achieving his objective, and suppressed negative actions that might have defeated his purpose. He also persisted at all the tasks necessary to achieve his goal, monitored and fine-tuned his performance at various stages, and finally stopped his grueling study schedule because he knew he'd done all that he could. Exhausted but calm, he passed the exam and eventually moved on to the next phase of his graduate work.

Gene moved easily through the steps of selective intention because he was able to exert both conscious and reflexive control over his behavior. In particular, he was able to *select* certain behaviors and *inhibit* others. To use a military analogy, we might think of these actions as "advance" or "retreat" orders: when confronted with the enemy—his math block—he advanced toward positive solutions and retreated from negative ones.

On the academic or professional battlefield, we are all required to make selections from a wide variety of behaviors. We can choose either positive behaviors or negative ones in order to carry out our missions and reach our goals. Do we make mistakes? Of course. But people with ADD tend to make more mistakes in these two areas. To understand why, let's take a look at some of the traits of disabled intention. They will further enhance our understanding of ADD.

Although *intention* appears to have a consciously willed and purposeful function, it is crucial to understand that there is also a hidden reflexive basis to this activity as well. In normal subjects, all goes well and both conscious and reflexive mechanisms function as one. In ADD, problems arise and these two mechanisms separate. The reflexive mechanism becomes impaired as a result of inner-ear dysfunctioning and interferes with efficient overall performance—despite all our conscious efforts.

INAPPROPRIATE SPEAKING

Instead of choosing words carefully—i.e., thinking about and then selecting statements and responses that will help achieve a goal—people with ADD tend to impulsively say things that get them into trouble. Jack B., a patient of mine who is an editor at a large publishing concern in New York, told me that during story-planning meetings he was often "called on the carpet" by his boss for blurting out seemingly nonsensical statements. "Several times," he explained, "I've lost complete control of myself, calling other people's ideas 'stupid' and sometimes even verbally attacking a colleague. I tend to say the first thing that comes to my mind; I have difficulty censoring remarks that are spiteful or hurtful. I sometimes stutter and stammer in these situations and may use bad grammar. I just ramble on without thinking." Like many people with ADD, Jack has trouble planning or really controlling and inhibiting impulsive and background thoughts.

IMPULSIVE ACTIVITY

Allen provides us with a good and clear illustration of the impulsive behavior people with ADD sometimes exhibit. His fourth-grade teacher wrote, "If there's a fight on the playground, Allen has usually started it. It's not as if he plans to get into trouble, he simply responds to situations impulsively. He has a short fuse, you might say. You'd think he'd have learned from these episodes by now. At my request, he spends most recesses sitting in the classroom—but it's almost as if he can't control his impulses. He rarely looks before he leaps."

IMPULSIVE PERFORMANCE

It's a familiar scene in high school. The teacher passes out a multiple-choice exam and instructs students not to open the exam booklet until told to. Students who have ADD, like sixteen-year-old Carrie, ignore such remarks and plunge right in. "I always want to get started right away," explains Carrie, "because I want to get it over with." Performing without planning or "thinking" contributes to Carrie's poor grade average. So does her poor memory, a problem encountered by many with ADD. "When I do listen to instructions, I've got to start quickly, or else I'll forget what they are." Impulsivity may be confused with and even intensified by behavior that appears similar but is differently motivated. Thus, some race through tasks as a way to minimize the torment that they associate with schoolwork. Explains Carrie, "I know I'm going to fail anyway. So why should I spend a lot of time on my work?" Others with impaired or slowed reading, writing, and recall race through academic tasks in order to complete them.

INCONSISTENT PERFORMANCE

Do you recall Josh's older brother, Bob Jr.? According to his mother, he'd always done well in school—until he reached fourteen. Then, his work became slovenly, his memory for math deteriorated, and he did poorly in most classes. This inconsistency of performance, seen in many individuals with ADD, is a source of frustration for all concerned: parents accuse children of "not really trying—we've seen you perform well before"; bosses demote employees who are "not consistently performing at a high level." Such sporadic behavior often leads to name-calling as well: people with ADD are frequently accused of being lazy, undisciplined, even schizophrenic. How unfortunate this is, because many with ADD do not really know how to "turn on" to certain activities, particularly those that are not compelling. Hence, Bob Jr. was turned off to math and English, whereas he was extremely tuned in to Nintendo and baseball statistics. This inconsistency in performance is as situation-specific and function-specific as that already described for selective attention functioning. And for the very same reasons. Also, a host of secondary destabilizing factors may play a hidden but important role, e.g. diet, fatigue, stress, anxiety, motivation, and interest—even dyslexic difficulties with math and English.

INAPPROPRIATE BODY MOVEMENTS

Like many with ADD, Jim T., a middle-management executive at an insurance company, has difficulty reflexively selecting proper body movement. "Because I feel I have to be supercareful when writing reports, I get anxious quite a lot. The only relief I get from the anxiety is to flex different muscles in my body. It almost seems involuntary. I have memories of doing this when I was a child: I can remember tensing the muscles in my calf or forearm, and doing it over and over again. When writing, I will purse my lips or roll my tongue around between my teeth. My mother says I did that when I was younger, and that I also kept moving the fingers of my left hand in a way that mimicked what my right hand was doing while I was writing. She said it looked like I was writing with one hand and conducting an orchestra with the other." While "tics" and other unusual movements are common in preschool children and fade out of the behavioral repertoire at an early age, these behaviors in their extreme—called Tourette's Syndrome—

occur rather infrequently. However, when present this phenomenon is important to diagnose, especially since these symptoms often intensify when using the stimulant medication found so helpful for the typical and related ADD-based symptoms.

EXCESS ACTIVITY

Joann C. could be described as a "whirling dervish": she's constantly active and productive; because of her high energy level, she's often referred to as an overachiever. She reaches goals, performs well, and is the envy of her peers. What distinguishes Joann from some people who have ADD? Her energy is funneled into productive activity. For the sake of contrast, consider Joann's sister Beth. Her mother describes her this way: "Beth has plenty of energy, but it translates into fidgeting. If she's reading a book, her feet are tapping a mile a minute, she's fiddling with her hair, and she's either whistling or humming her favorite song. I wish she could harness all that energy and put it into learning." Curiously, some individuals with ADD say that they can concentrate better when their attention is slightly diverted by extraneous motor activities. "When I listen to someone giving a report," says Jim, the insurance executive, "I will often doodle or take notes. It helps me focus on what's being said."

NONPERSISTENCE

Karl W., an eighteen-year-old high school dropout who is now working as a clerk, reflects on his problems with impersistence: "Whenever I think of high school, I see half-finished reports, assignments that were started but never completed. In shop class, we once had to make a step stool, which meant sawing the wood, sanding it, putting the pieces together, and painting the finished product. The other guys found it really easy and fun to do—they were like busy little dwarves in Santa's workshop. I'm pretty klutzy, though; working with my hands is hard for me. So I burned out right away. Every time I got to class, I'd start sawing away, but I kept on doing it wrong. My teacher kept criticizing me because I was doing sloppy work, but I couldn't help it. As a result, I just couldn't stay interested in the project."

Paradoxically, individuals with ADD may also overpersist, focusing on a detail or task much longer than is necessary. Explained Karl, "When we painted model airplanes, I got 'hung up' on making mine look realistic. I was the last kid to finish, and got a lower grade because it wasn't done on time." So-called over-persistence may also be due to a failure in checking or stopping an act-perseveration; or it may be due to the compensatory need to mask severe feelings of inferiority by getting things perfect and beyond criticism.

NONRESPONSIVENESS

In the paragraph above, you may have noticed that when his teacher commented on his sloppy work, Karl took no heed of the criticism. He didn't try to improve; in fact, he proceeded on a course of self-destructive behavior that led to failure. The reason? Karl said he "didn't care," but the truth is, like others with ADD, Karl was unable to exercise any quality control. He had no internal sense of his own progress, and he didn't respond to external cues from his teacher. Many persons with ADD seem to be oblivious to any form of feedback, and they tend not to respond to either punishment or reward. According to Karl's mother, "Even after he was warned that he would fail shop class, he didn't straighten up. When I threatened to ground him for two weeks, he just shrugged his shoulders and told me to mind my own business." One might also view this impairment as a failure in selective fil-tering. In other words, realistic warning signals are blocked out or inhibited, whereas impulsive and aggressive drives go improp-erly checked!

As you read the case histories in this chapter, you probably noticed that many of the traits of ADD are associated with con-centration, distractibility, impulsivity, hyperactivity, and reduced response to feedback. Although such behaviors are an important part of our expanding picture of ADD, they do not represent the disorder in its entirety. What remains?

In the next chapter, we will complete our picture of ADD by taking a look at a number of symptoms that one might not normally associate with a concentration dysfunction. In fact, many of those symptoms have already been alluded to here. Do you recall that Jackie had problems with math, reading, writing, and spelling? Do you recall that some patients described difficulties related to memory, direction, and time, and that others had trouble with balance, coordination, and speech? Do you recollect that still others had symptoms often associated with compulsions, obsessions, and phobias? These, too, are symptoms associated with ADD.

Chapter IX

Completing the Picture of ADD

In the last six chapters, you've met scores of my patients who have ADD. As you read of their experiences, you no doubt realized that their difficulties with concentration cannot be boxed into the brief list of fourteen behaviors contained in the DSM-III-R manual. By now, you must surely know that ADD—its mechanisms, its symptoms, and its compensatory style—is far from a simple disorder.

Just how complex is ADD? In this chapter, we'll add to our knowledge by exploring yet another level of symptoms: the myriad behaviors and academic difficulties that have been ignored by clinicians and researchers.

As I have stated many times throughout this book, years of painstaking clinical and theoretical effort have taught me that patients, not experts, truly define ADD. In other words, it is the patients and the *quality* of their revealed symptoms that are diagnostically correct. If those symptoms do not fit established and ingrained theories, then the theories are either wrong or incomplete and must be changed.

Thanks to the honesty and sensitivity of many of my patients, we discovered in previous chapters that persons with ADD have problems with concentration and distractibility that are far more subtle and complex than previously realized. We've also learned that they exhibit levels of hyperactivity, overactivity, and impulsivity that are far more varied than a simple list can reveal. Most important, we have observed that *any one* or *any combination* of these symptoms can justify a diagnosis of ADD.

Now I would like to take your understanding of ADD a step further. As you read the case histories that follow, you will arrive at the obvious conclusion that anyone who has this disorder may experience difficulties in *any one* or *any combination* of the following additional areas—difficulties typical of dyslexia or LD:

Reading
Writing
Spelling
Mathematics
Memory
Direction
Time
Speech
Grammar
Balance and coordination
Phobias and related mental and behavioral disorders

Although many of these dyslexic problem areas are described by ADD patients, many clinical researchers have not fully recognized that they are also part and parcel of ADD. At this point, it may be helpful to consider an analogy. What happens when a common virus affects five members of a family? Do all members exhibit the same symptoms with uniform intensity? Obviously not. Most frequently, each member will evidence some symptoms of the virus, but the *leading* symptom may be different for each, and the symptom's intensity may vary from one extreme to another. In fact, one member of such a family may even feel "almost" well, his illness thus escaping clinical detection altogether. The same is true for many a person with ADD. To help you to understand this concept, I'd like you to "eavesdrop" on a conversation that took place in my office not long ago. As you listen to Mrs. W.'s story of her son, you will begin to see how I first arrived at my conclusion about the above problem areas. You will also witness the damage than can occur due to misdiagnosis.

Jeremy W.

"If only I'd known then what I know today," laments Jeremy W.'s mother. "There were signs of a problem back when Jeremy was in first grade, but we just didn't know what to look for. We got absolutely no help from his school or his teachers; I often think that if we had, maybe most of my son's traumas could have been avoided.

"Originally, I thought Jeremy was sort of a Jekyll and Hyde child. At home, he was like a little Ford tractor—he went ninety miles an hour, and his mouth never hushed. And he found it difficult to concentrate on anything for more than a few seconds without getting distracted by the slightest movement, sound—anything. He also jumped into things without thinking—impulsively. Yet once he got to school, teachers said they couldn't get him to respond or participate. In fact, his teacher told me that if she tried to hug him to reward him for something, he'd pull away from her. She said it was like he couldn't stand being touched.

"At the time, I thought the problem was a conflict between Jeremy and his teacher. On the one hand, she was elderly and set in her ways; on the other, Jeremy definitely marches to the beat of a different drummer, and she was annoyed by that. She didn't want to spend time helping him and commented at P.T.A. meetings that there would be no way for him to go on to second grade with his reading ability. She also said that his concentration abilities were immature. I thought she was exaggerating . . . until I had lunch at the school one day and watched him through the classroom window.

"When it would come his time to read, he would hesitate, like this: "The . . . uh . . . uh . . . ball . . . uh . . . uh . . . hit . . ." It was like he couldn't find the words on the page. But then, to make matters worse, the teacher would snap her fingers and shout, 'Just go on to the next one!' The two of them really had a time of it that year. She did things like shove him into a corner to punish him for daydreaming, or make him stand by himself at the back of the room if he couldn't answer her questions fast enough. Things got so bad between them that very often he'd refuse to go to school and he'd scream and cry something fierce! Then I'd have to take him myself, and when we'd get there, she'd say that he was a big boy now and that she didn't want me personally escorting him to the classroom!

"As I look back on all this, I think we did get some clues to Jeremy's problem, but maybe we weren't smart enough to understand what they meant. He was always terribly uncoordinated and clumsy . . . had a hard time learning to tie his shoes. He had a rotten sense of time. If you told him he could do something in an hour, he'd keep coming at you every ten minutes asking 'Now? Is it an hour now?' He never baby-talked and we never went through the transition of trying to teach him correct language. It's like he picked up his verbal skills right away. But if you'd try to get him to write something, forget it. Everything was illegible—a mess! In fact, at one parent-teacher conference, his elderly teacher told me she was really puzzled by something. She said Jeremy could say his letters frontward and backward—*literally*—but that he couldn't tell you whether Z was at the beginning of the alphabet or at the end. Unfortunately, none of us, including the teacher, knew what this meant.

"By the time he reached second grade, he refused to read altogether. He didn't even try. He just couldn't seem to focus on anything; he became even squirmier, and very sensitive to criticism. Even if you tried to encourage him, he'd fly into a rage. Most of his grades were D's and F's; if he came home with a C, we were thrilled! In desperation, we went through three pediatricians, two optometrists, an allergy clinic, a child psychologist, a learning center, private tutoring, and summer school—all to no avail. For a time, he did great with the tutor, but once he'd get back into class, he'd just bomb and forget whatever he and the tutor had gone over the day before!

"We just felt like giving up hope. Things at school got worse. When he got into third grade, his teacher put him through a psychological evaluation, but it said there was nothing wrong. The teacher told us he was just immature and to give him time—he'd pull out of it, she told us. But we didn't feel we had time. We needed help *now*.

"We had him IQed to death. And the results almost made us feel worse. His verbal score was 122, performance was 112, and his full-scale IQ was rated at 123. Psychologists told us he had the mental age of a ten-year-old with the performance age of a five-year-old. Yet they said nothing was wrong. They said he just didn't want to sit down and do the work. And that was their final analysis.

"Then we got a small break. After the school had determined that nothing was wrong with Jeremy, I got a call from a special-education teacher who had worked with him. What she basically said was this: 'Please do not repeat my name. You came up with this in a dream, because it could cost me my job.' She said, 'Do not accept the school's evaluation, please. There is something there, I know there's something there, I can see it when I work with him. I can't put my finger on it, but I know it's there.' She also told me, 'My heart bleeds for Jeremy. I can see how hard he's trying and how he's failing, but when I talk to him, he's talking about things way above his level. He's fascinated with dinosaurs and volcanoes and could carry on a conversation with adults. Yet he can't read a kindergarten primer. There's more than meets the eye here . . . so please don't take the school's evaluation.'

"Had it not been for that remarkable teacher, we might never have had the strength to continue our search. We might never have discovered that Jeremy has a form of Attention Deficit Disorder. Still, I'm bitter—I feel I have the right to be. An incompetent school system put my child through mortal hell and it's going to take him a long time to pull out from it. Our school system is not educating its teachers the way it should . . . it's not exposing them to what needs to be done."

What symptoms did you notice in the story about Jeremy? He was hyperactive, inattentive, and easily distracted at home, yet was nonresponsive at school. He was an inconsistent performer. He seemed to have trouble with *coordination*, had a poor sense of *time*, and had problems with *writing*. He sometimes exhibited overactivity—i.e., his energy was often channeled into fidgeting or squirming. He also stuttered and stammered—examples of a *speech* problem. Most obvious, however, were Jeremy's immense difficulties with *reading*.

During several sessions with Jeremy and his mother, it became apparent that this youngster had problems with *memory* as well. Mrs. W. told me:

"After spending $25,000 on all kinds of treatment, including a so-called 'progressive' learning center that guaranteed—but failed—to bring him up one grade level, Jeremy was just barely holding on by the skin of his teeth; things weren't improving for him one iota. And just when I thought things couldn't get worse, they did. Jeremy experienced what I would call severe memory lapses. They scared me half to death!

"The first time it happened, we were driving to a private tutor who was forty-five miles away. To try to make these outings as much fun as possible, we always stopped off somewhere for lunch. On this particular day, I asked Jeremy where he wanted to eat, and he said such and such a hamburger joint. I told him that we'd been there before, so I named a different place and he thought that was fine. As we started up the highway, all of a sudden he threw himself in the backseat and screamed, 'Momma! You passed it! You passed the hamburger place!' And I said, 'Honey, we just decided that we were going up the road to someplace new. . . .' Right then, you could see that surprised look on his face, and he just slumped down in the seat and said 'Oh . . .'

"That was pretty bad, I thought, but things got worse that weekend. His daddy and I redecorated his bedroom. We painted the walls, put in new curtains, new sheets, new bedspreads—we did everything just the way Jeremy wanted it to be. We both worked on it all day Saturday and Sunday. Jeremy was so excited, he just kept running in and out of the bedroom and telling us how neat he thought it looked.

"Then on Monday, something strange happened. About a half hour before his daddy got home, Jeremy kept running to the window, watching and waiting to see the car pull up, and then he'd run back to his room and look at it. Then back again to the window to watch for the car. It was like he had a secret or something, a surprise for his daddy. Well, when my husband finally got home, Jeremy grabbed him by the hand and pulled him toward the bedroom door. Then he flung the door open and said 'Ta-dah!' and threw his arms out. My husband kept saying 'What? What is it, honey? What should I be looking at?' Jeremy looked real frustrated and said, 'My room! Look at my room!' His daddy said, 'Yeah, I know it looks great. Your momma and I did a good job on it.' Then Jeremy scrunched up his face. 'No, Momma did it by herself,' he said. 'You were at work.'

"My husband and I were just stunned. We walked back down

the hall together, and I watched this big tough man with these big old tears just running down his face! That was when we really hit rock bottom—we just fell off the cliff real fast! And there stood poor Jeremy. We didn't blame him or anything, but it was like we'd slapped him in the face. He just slinked away to watch television."

On the basis of his concentration, distractibility, impulsivity, and memory problems alone, I would have diagnosed Jeremy as having ADD. But since he also experienced some hyperactivity, I determined that he had ADD-H, or Attention Deficit Disorder with Hyperactivity. With proper treatment, he improved dramatically—as you'll find in Chapter Fourteen.

What about some of the other typical dyslexic symptoms I listed? What about his coordination symptoms—including those affecting his eye tracking, writing, and speech? Let's meet a few more patients.

Jerry H.

Jerry H., a Ph.D. research scientist at a well-known chemical company, did not display any of the symptoms of ADD until after he turned forty. The triggering event: a bad car accident in which he sustained severe injuries to head and body. During our first meeting, he recalled:

"Soon after getting out of my body cast, and before I started the months of intensive physical therapy, I could tell that there was something wrong with my eyes," Jerry explains. "Any time I looked off center, such as looking down through my bifocals to read, I would see double. As it turned out, besides breaking about half of the bones in my old six-foot-two body, I had also damaged the nerves that control my eye muscles. It took six rounds of eye surgery to get them back to near normal.

"Even after I got my eyes fixed, I didn't enjoy reading anymore. It was simply an irritating struggle for me, and it didn't matter what I was reading. I had just as hard a time concentrating on the newspaper or a magazine as I did with books, because whenever I came to the end of a line, I had trouble finding the beginning of the next line. Plus, I wouldn't always remember what I had just read, so nothing made much sense unless I carefully read and reread. To compensate for these mental-mechanical problems, I held a three-by-five card under the line I was reading and moved it down the paper. This was particularly irritating to me, because I used to enjoy reading a book while watching TV and could read so fast that I would usually finish a novel in a few nights. In fact, if it was a book like *The Godfather,* I could read it in one evening.

"Before the accident, my oldest son used to be amazed at my powers of concentration and how fast I could read! He was always asking me to read something that he had either written or found. It was like a game to us: I would 'glance' at the document and tell him what it said or if there were any mistakes on the paper. And ninety-nine percent of the time, I'd be right! Thus, before the accident I would essentially read whole lines (if not paragraphs) at a time and remember the content. After the accident, I'd try to comprehend what I'd read, but couldn't remember a thing. And while reading, I'd become distracted as hell by any sound or movement within miles.

"After the accident, my balance was terrible. In fact, I first learned how to walk again in the high-school swimming pool, and I was very proud to graduate from a wheelchair to crutches and finally up to a cane. Despite my physical progress, however, I still couldn't read, write, or speak well, and my memory was terrible—I couldn't remember names or faces! Even several sessions with a speech therapist, months after I came home from the hospital, didn't help the way I talked. I knew what I wanted to say, but the words just wouldn't come out correctly. I spoke slowly, hesitantly, and erratically.

"For years after I went back to work full-time, I always felt off balance, and I would trip over any little thing that was in my path. I was so bad that I always had to walk slowly or hold on to a piece of furniture or a wall, if I could reach one, as I walked through a room. I wouldn't even try to walk down the block alone! If I did, I had to have my cane or hold on to my wife's shoulder. I became quite fearful of any place where I was likely to fall.

"I also suffered from spatial confusion. I'd get easily lost—but only if I was driving the car. For some reason, if someone asked me for directions, I could give them with ease—with a map, I could conceptualize directions with no trouble.

"My writing was terrible—I often couldn't remember what I wanted to say at the end of a sentence, let alone at the end of a paragraph—and my speech was hesitant, jerky and broken with lots of 'Ahs' or 'What I mean is . . .' None of my doctors recognized that these problems had anything to do with Attention Deficit Disorder and dyslexia."

Again, we see typical dyslexic *reading, writing, and speech* problems in this patient who has ADD. We also find a *memory* dysfunction. What else do we find? Jerry also had difficulties with *balance and coordination and direction.* Again, all these symptoms characterize dyslexics. Does Jerry have both ADD and dyslexia? Or are both disorders due to one and the same common denominator—an inner-ear dysfunction? And since this disorder was *acquired* after head trauma requiring neurosurgery, one would have to consider his acquired ADD disorder due to Type II, III, and IV mechanisms.

Debbie L.

When Debbie L., now twenty-four, moved from California to the Midwest, she developed an inner-ear infection. "I don't know whether it was the cold climate or what," she explains, "but I experienced attacks of nausea and loss of equilibrium. Very often I just feel 'off balance.'"

Since then, life for Debbie has been, as she puts it, "like living in a fog—and it's getting thicker all the time. I just can't concentrate on anything anymore. And I'm forever distracted and preoccupied. It's funny. As a child, my reading and spelling skills were always above average. But as I've gotten older, I find that I am drawing more and more 'blanks,' either in spelling, finding the appropriate word I need to express a thought, or—most disconcerting—remembering the names of people I have been introduced to or whom I'm speaking with on the phone. My memory is really shaky—long term or short term. My numerical skills are a disaster: I confuse computational signs and have particular trouble with multiplication. I can do twos, threes and fours pretty easily, but at five and above, I get confused.

"Simple words or names of people I *know* will fly right out the window. Simple computations suddenly become totally mysterious. Spelling of common words—words that I may be writing several times a day—become unknown.

"My vocabulary is becoming ridiculously limited. Words that mysteriously disappear from my recall must be replaced with miserably inadequate substitutes. If I'm writing a letter or something, I can pause to consult a thesaurus, but very often there's not enough time to do that. If I'm in a conversation when these word 'blocks' occur, I get embarrassed, pause while searching for the right words, then make excuses for not completing the thought while I furiously try to grasp the elusive word that seems to be right on the tip of my tongue. Usually by then, though, I've rambled off the subject.

"I've lost my ability to focus on one thought or concept at a time. My mind jumps around from one subject to another, and I lose the ability to completely comprehend a concept or a thoroughly answered question.

"I've also become hyperactive for extended periods of time. This results in insomnia, and sometimes I won't calm down enough to sleep for twenty-four to forty-eight hours. After I 'burn out,' a period of distraction and lethargy follows. During this period I'm usually extremely cranky or unbelievably happy. My mood level swings on a roller-coaster ride of extremes, while my temper and levels of depression have achieved record lows."

For Debbie, poor *reading, spelling, math and speech* skills are sources of frustration. So is a dysfunctional *memory.* All these symptoms are typically those of dyslexics. She also suffers from impaired concentration, distractibility, overactivity, mood swings, insomnia, fatigue, etc.—symptoms typical of ADD or ADD-H. Since all her symptoms *first* started after an ear infection, it appeared likely that an inner-ear impairment was responsible for her acquired ADD and dyslexic symptoms.

Sally K.

After housewife Sally K. visited me, her husband Peter wanted to give me the clearest picture possible of his wife's condition. He felt that the bizarre nature of her symptoms needed to be explained in greater detail. He paid me a visit and recalled:

"Sally has at different times been diagnosed as hypoglycemic, or as having premenstrual syndrome, in attempts to define her problem. Although she's had many symptoms throughout her life, I believe they became much more severe after the birth of our first child. She immediately became severely depressed. It was called postpartum blues, but it did not ever go away. She would not come out of her room for weeks and did not want to see anyone. This was a very definite change in her personality, not gradual, but sudden and intense.

"Sally's always had trouble reading and refuses to read aloud, except bedtime stories. Now, even that is so traumatic that she often makes excuses for why she cannot read that evening, which leads to arguments with the children.

"She's always been a 'dizzy dame,'—distracted, preoccupied, and foggy. Even hyper and disorganized.

"She has no sense of time. She uses a timer for nearly everything. She can't remember to wind a watch. She confuses past and present events and memories. She can tell the time with her wristwatch, but cannot figure out what time it will be in ten minutes. She does not remember to check cooking food and will often let it burn. She does not remember to check timed events like clothes in the dryer—sometimes they will sit for days.

"She has no sense of direction. She will get lost on the expressway, not knowing where she is but uncertain as to whether to turn around. Once she wound up more than fifty miles away without knowing how she got there or how to get back. She cannot read a map and confuses directions on street signs. She must have directions written out, and once she has learned the way to a place, she will not deviate and go there by any other route. When she drives she has a mask of intense concentration on her face: Squinting eyes. Looking straight ahead like into a tunnel. She will hardly ever drive at night.

"When she is nervous, she will get dizzy, nauseous, say the room is spinning, and have to hold on to something or someone. This often happens in crowds or when she has to deal with certain people who make her nervous. When she's with someone who intimidates her, she will withdraw to the point of meekness. But sometimes she will explode with anger. When she blows, she uses expressions like 'he don't' or 'she ain't.' Her use of bad grammar particularly surprises me; she attended a good university and has a degree."

Difficulties with concentration, distractibility, activity, and organization are suggestive of ADD.

No sense of *time*. Poor sense of *direction*. *Reading and memory* difficulties. *Grammar* problems. These were just a few of Sally's symptoms. Are they not dyslexic symptoms? During subsequent interviews with her, I learned that she also suffered from panic attacks and phobic behavior. As her husband explained it:

"Sally has been treated by two different psychologists for a total of eleven years and is presently being treated by a psychologist with counseling twice a week. She has suffered from severe depression and anxiety, wide mood swings, and panic attacks. A few years ago, the depression got bad enough that she entertained suicidal thoughts and lost all emotional control. She entered a psychiatric hospital for around four weeks for treatment. She has never actually attempted suicide, but she felt that she would if not helped. She has been given several different medications, including Valium, without much improvement. Presently she takes Triavil, which does seem to help, but it still does not completely relieve her symptoms. She feels totally dependent on the medication and her therapist, and feels overwhelmed by everyday events. She is afraid of doing without the medication she is now taking.

"She constantly makes lists of things to do. She will spend three to five hours sitting and making lists of things that will require only one or two hours, total, of actual activity to complete. She worries continually about what is wrong with her and has bought hundreds of self-help books of every description.

"Sally's mood swings, depressions, angry outbursts, confusion, short-temperedness, headaches, fears, etc., have all placed a great strain on her and our family. You make it sound as if they are all related to each other, with the inner ear as the underlying cause. We hope you are right. We want to have reasonable expectations. We hope that your treatment will relieve her of her symptoms."

The information Sally's husband shared did not surprise me. In the course of interviewing thousands of individuals with ADD or ADD-H, I have observed that patients periodically complain of phobias, panic disorders, compulsions, and obsessions that are *identical* to those that I treat in my psychiatric practice. Moreover, ADD patients often describe themselves as stupid, dumb, and ugly—the very same labels that my phobic (and dyslexic) patients unfortunately attach to themselves. Most important, I have found that many ADD patients with phobic symptoms also have an inner-ear dysfunction. When they are medically treated for this physiological problem, 80 percent spontaneously report significant improvements in their phobias and self-esteem, as well as in their more typical ADD symptoms.

Of course, not all phobic behavior is caused by an inner-ear malfunction. Some phobias are realistic—they develop after traumatic exposure to danger. Still others are considered neurotic in nature—they develop "all in the mind" through a series of subconscious or unconscious Freudian processes. Yet my clinical evidence suggests that realistic and neurotic phobias *together* may account for less than 10 percent of all phobics referred for treatment. The other 90 percent can be traced to an underlying malfunction within the inner-ear system!

At present, the phobic component of ADD is not well understood by most clinicians and educators. Perhaps that is because they've not listened closely enough to those who suffer from it. Perhaps they've focused only on the phobic triggers—not on the more important underlying mechanisms that create and shape the phobic behavior that may accompany ADD or ADD-H. Perhaps they've been misled because many subjects with ADD appear fearless. As you read the final case history in this chapter, I hope you'll begin to draw some of your own conclusions.

Stephen B.

In this summary of his phobias and concentration problems, Stephen B., a bank teller, provides an excellent illustration of the multidimensional nature of ADD:

Fears and phobias: "I'm terrified of heights and will do almost anything to avoid being in high places. In fact, I have quit jobs that required me to use elevators or escalators. I believe I'm also claustrophobic. I can feel walls closing in on me. I can't stand it if someone is standing too close to me—it disorients me. The very sight of a needle will send me into a panic. I've fainted many times at the doctor's office. I'm also deathly afraid of public speaking, because I'm so afraid I'll make a mistake and appear dumb."

Obsessions and compulsions: "I'll sometimes be plagued with obsessive thoughts and actions. Thinking itself is probably my biggest obsession. I have a hard time paying attention to seeing, hearing, and feeling the world around me without constantly drifting off into my own thoughts. It's sort of like my mind gets stuck in a loop—I'll keep thinking the same thought over and over. I'm also a perfectionist and am never satisfied with anything unless it's just right. For example, it can take me all day to wash and wax my car; I'll keep seeing little flaws, or particles of dust that I feel I must remove. I sometimes feel that if I don't do things perfectly, something bad will happen to me."

Concentration and distractibility: "I feel I can only concentrate on things I'm interested in. Otherwise I'll tire easily, become distracted, or get spacy. I'm easily distracted by music, television, my own thoughts, and other conversations. When I'm with others, I periodically lose the drift of the conversation. My mind returns to the conversation, but I must piece it together. This kind of thing happens when I'm watching TV, too. Thus, any kind of reading, TV watching, or concentrating is very difficult and exhausting."

Listening: "I'm slow to understand, especially in lecture-type situations. I feel I don't have enough time to focus in on and comprehend an idea before the next one is presented. In college, I'd take copious notes so that I could go back and try to understand what was presented. People sometimes think I'm not listening—

because while they're speaking I'm still trying to understand what they said previously."

Memory: "I have difficulty remembering things from my past. In college, I definitely had to overstudy to compensate for my poor memory. Everything I'm going to do must be put on a long list or I'll forget it and be totally disorganized."

Reading: "I tire quickly when reading and am easily distracted unless I'm extremely interested in the material. I never read fiction, only educational material. For some reason, I don't have the patience for fiction. I'm a very slow reader and must use a mental finger to keep my place, silently speaking each word in my mind. I have several dyslexic symptoms, too—jerky eye movements, omission and insertion of letters and words, retargeting words and phrases, and tracking problems. I'll get stuck on words or sentences, and the meaning won't come. I'll have to look up and rest a few seconds and then go back. I definitely use single targeting and read word by word, with much blinking and squinting."

Handwriting: "My handwriting is so poor that I have to print everything. In order for it to be presentable, I have to type it."

Self-consciousness: "I am overly conscious of myself around other people. I feel inferior, stupid, ugly, clumsy, and ashamed of myself."

Motion sickness: "I have to drive if I'm riding in a car or I'll feel queasy. Amusement-park rides are definitely out."

Balance: "Generally, I feel off balance, and uncentered. Oftentimes mildly dizzy. Also, I have occasional feelings of being disoriented, light-headed, or floating."

Wandering focus: "It is very difficult for me to make any extended eye contact during conversations. It usually makes me feel disoriented, off balance, distracted, and self-conscious."

Time: "A strange sensation I experienced occasionally as a child was the speeding up of time. It felt like everything around me was happening so fast that I had no time to grasp anything. I would have a sort of swirling feeling in my brain."

One-track focusing: "I have a hard time and get very anxious when I have a lot of things to do at the same time. I always like to do only one thing at a time."

Physical condition: "I have been diagnosed as having allergic rhinitus and a deviated nasal septum. I have a very dry nose, constant stuffiness, bad headaches, and lack of energy. I also have a very poor sense of smell. My ears always feel stuffed up. There's a crackling sound as though I have water in them. There is a definite correlation between how well I feel mentally and physically and how stuffed up my ears feel. I have a very difficult time understanding people when there is any background noise. In fact, sometimes I feel nervous and my ears feel tense from too much noise. At these times, I need to have some real quiet place to be."

As you might have guessed, all of the patients who've "spoken" to you in this chapter suffer from Type III ADD. Yet they all have dyslexic symptoms as well. Many have balance and coordination problems. And a few had fears or phobias and related anxiety symptoms, e.g. obsessions and compulsions. Are all these symptoms derived from a common denominator? Or do these many patients have entirely unrelated, multiple disorders?

In Chapter XI, we'll take a look at how the inner-ear system works, and how a problem in this system can cause the many and various symptoms that constitute ADD.

CHAPTER X

Psychologically Determined Concentration Disorders—Acquired Types I and II

Although the vast majority of clinical data discussed and presented thus far in this book relates to ADD or organic Types III and IV mechanisms of origin, it should be readily clear to the reader:

- □ that overlapping determining mechanisms may coexist in any given subject, and often do; and
- □ that to understand *concentration disorders* in general and ADD specifically, it is crucial to study and understand ADD-like but nonphysiologically-based concentration symptoms and determining mechanisms of a psychological origin.

Once again, I have chosen to clarify these psychologically determined Type I and II mechanisms resulting in concentration disorders by presenting you with clinical vignettes. These cases will suggest how psychologically determined mechanisms result in concentration-related symptoms.

Needless to say;

- □ to really understand and help any given patient, one must fully comprehend all possible interacting and overdetermined mechanisms contributing to symptom formation; and
- □ to really understand ADD, one must truly recognize the psychologically determined mechanisms that result in similar symptoms. How else can we distinguish between the concen-

tration symptoms resulting from physiological or ADD mechanisms (Types III and IV) and those resulting from psychological mechanisms (Types I and II)?

Sally

Six-year-old Sally suddenly became withdrawn and preoccupied, unable to observe and sustain attention in class. She was described by her teachers as moody, easily frustrated, and very sensitive. The slightest trigger provoked either crying or aggressive acting-out. She began to tell stories and to lie. And one of her classmates even accused her of stealing.

Sally appeared tired in the morning and claimed she had had difficulty sleeping the night before. Although previously calm, she suddenly became fidgety and restless in her chair, even during lunchtime.

In an interview with Sally and her parents, it became clear:

□ that Sally's older sister had been recently hospitalized for surgery;
□ that the concerned parents had tried to spare Sally the discomfort they felt by minimizing and even avoiding discussing her sister's hospitalization; and
□ that they were shutting Sally out by not allowing her to verbalize her feelings.

This sudden "rejection" and Sally's concerns that her sister might die or was dying all contributed to her acute symptoms. Several therapeutic family sessions resulted in a complete disappearance of all of her symptoms.

Obviously, Type I Concentration Disorder mechanisms were prominent. However, one couldn't eliminate Type II or neurotic mechanisms as well. It was certainly possible:

□ that "rejection" by her parents triggered anger, and that this anger led Sally to exaggerate the seriousness of her sister's illness; and

☐ that the guilt from this anger resulted in obsessive preoccupation and daydreaming about her sister's illness, and that Sally's aggressiveness, lying, and stealing reflected an acting-out of her unconscious anger toward her parents and sister.

Johnny

Johnny is a seven-year-old who suddenly became inattentive, restless, and inordinately distracted.

On examination, it materialized:

☐ that his parents had been continuously fighting and had just separated; and
☐ that his mother was physically ill and had been recently hospitalized, and that a caretaker was now looking after Johnny.

A few psychotherapeutic sessions with Johnny reversed all his symptoms.

In retrospect, it appears clear that Johnny was suffering from Type I CD, especially as there exists and existed no prior evidence of other determining mechanisms. In other words, a diagnosis was made on the basis of:

☐ positive evidence of Type I CD mechanisms; and
☐ negative evidence of other mechanisms.

Jay

A forty-three-year-old friend of mine named Jay, who happened to be a physician, became normally involved and embroiled in his son's illness. Suddenly, his son developed an acute leukemia with severe complications. Hospitalization was required together with repeated medical and surgical procedures.

During the acute phase of his son's illness, and for a period of years following remission, Jay found it difficult to concentrate and remember, and became forgetful and absent-minded. His mood was unstable and fluctuating; his fuse was short and his drive dampened. Sleep was difficult; he had trouble both falling asleep and rising in the morning.

Although Jay was not obviously depressed, all his mental and emotional energies became focused on his son's illness and medical care. In this area he appeared to function with remarkable clarity. However, in all other areas, including his practice and his social and private life, his concentration-related functions began to fail.

Eventually, Jay's son Rob went into a sustained remission. And slowly, but steadily, Jay returned to his prior functioning.

In retrospect, it appears obvious that all of Jay's concentration-related impairments were due to Type I CD mechanisms. However, as a result of the incredible stress and strain caused by his son's illness, as well as difficulties sleeping, resulting in fatigue, and poor nutrition, one cannot eliminate the possibility of secondary Type V^2 mechanisms.

Karen

Karen, age forty, was involved in a severe auto accident. Fortunately, she was not hurt, just terrified. She became focused on events of the accident, as well as anticipating what could have happened and what might occur in the future when traveling in a car.

For months, to her chagrin, her overall level of superb functioning deteriorated. She found it difficult to concentrate on her family. She became irritable with her children and unable to clearly concentrate on, focus on, and plan for their needs as before. Her home, a model of organization, started to deteriorate, as did her own personal appearance.

Karen was not depressed, just preoccupied with the events leading up to the accident. This is another example of a concentration disorder resulting from Type I CD mechanisms.

Bonnie

Bonnie was my first patient in private psychiatric practice. In fact, her case was eventually written up and published in the *British*

Journal of Psychiatry (1966), entitled "Auditory Hallucinations in a Case of Hysteria."

Bonnie was a twenty-nine-year-old orphan when she first sought psychiatric treatment. At the time of initial examination, she was married and had two children, an eight-year-old boy and a four-year-old girl. Her main complaints at the time were hearing "voices" and a fear of dying. Needless to say, her neurotic disorder created significant difficulties with concentration, distractibility, activity, mood, anxiety, speech coordination, stuttering, and learning.

During a series of psychotherapeutic visits, her many symptoms and their neurotic determinants unfolded:

> "I can't get rid of the voices and fears of dying in my sleep. Please help me," she cried. "The voices are frightening and hound me all day long."

She dated these symptoms back to when she was four years old. They began shortly after she was first taken to visit her dead mother's grave and told about the circumstances of her mother's death. Since that time, she had been completely preoccupied with daydreaming about these voices and her fears of dying, resulting in a variety of psychologically determined ADD-like symptoms:

> "It suddenly hit me yesterday that the voices were really my own thoughts . . . I spoke to the voice and I answered for it . . . It was all my own imagination. I knew this before intellectually, but I hated to part with my mother—the voices."
>
> "It seems that my talking to the voices dates back to when I was very young and was taken to visit my mother's grave. I watched my [adoptive] mother and grandmother talking to the grave as if my mother were alive and could hear . . . This scene frightened me very much."
>
> "I never realized how much I would daydream, even when people are talking to me. I would even talk aloud when alone without realizing it. . . . It's strange, but with all my daydreaming, I never consciously thought of my mother until you first mentioned her. I would usually daydream about my father and myself."

During Bonnie's psychoanalysis, it turned out:

□ that the voices represented a dialogue with her dead mother;

☐ that she missed her mother dearly and re-created her via these auditory fantasies;

☐ that she felt guilty for her mother's death and for the resentment she unconsciously harbored against her for being abandoned.

As a result, the voices were critical and thus satisfied her need to be punished.

Bonnie recalled what was told to her at four and recounted her fantasies as follows:

"My mother caught a cold when sixteen years old and later developed heart trouble, which I assumed to be rheumatic fever. . . . Doctors warned her not to get married . . . and not to have children. . . . She must have loved my father very much to have married him. . . . They were married five years when I was born. My father was later heard saying that he had only five happy years in his life. He must have meant the five years he spent with my mother. . . . My mother was only twenty-four years old when she died. . . . She must have been a brave and wonderful person to sacrifice her life in order to have me."

After Bonnie's "voices" disappeared, a strange and surprising thing happened. Instead of being grateful and happy, she was annoyed and sad and tried her best to bring back the voices in a seemingly conscious and deliberate manner:

A. She became mean and spiteful toward others in a deliberate attempt to sensitize her conscience and force it to react in a threatening and warning way: "It seems every time I get better, I can't take it and I act mean on purpose to antagonize my conscience."

B. She kept suggesting to herself what she should hear and how she should react: "I keep telling myself, 'Bonnie, you're going to die, you're going to die,' over and over, but it doesn't scare me anymore and the voices won't come back. I keep saying, 'What do you say now, little voice?' but it's quiet. Where did it go? It won't answer me anymore!" In another session she again spoke about her conscience telling her what to do, and I asked her if she still heard voices. "I'm not sure.

It seems that I speak to myself and tell myself to do this or that."

C. She concentrated deeply within herself, listening very intently and ignoring all other stimulation, a state resembling auto-hypnosis: "I look around desperately and listen for the little voice, but it won't come back anymore [definitely implying this method worked before]."

In her last session and an ensuing telephone call she explained that she really heard a voice, later recognized it to be a thought, and described the conditions making this confusion possible.

"I sometimes think, 'You're going to die,' when I act mean, but it doesn't scare me and leave me cold."

"Did you ever really hear a voice?" I asked.

"Yes."

The Unconscious Need to Be Ill

When Bonnie's symptoms first disappeared she began to feel increasingly guilty and didn't know why. At the same time she fought desperately to bring back her illness (the fears and voices).

"The voices are definitely gone. . . . It's strange, and I have to laugh at what I do. I keep catching myself saying, 'What do you say now little voice?' and I actually miss it. It's funny how the whole thing is in my mind, and as much as I want to get better I miss it [crying bitterly], because it is my mother. . . . It's amazing how stubborn I am and fight to stay sick." She described the following: "I was resting yesterday when my mind started to race and the thought hit me that my mother was dead. Isn't it funny and stupid? I've known she was dead, but I couldn't stop crying. . . . I knew my holding on to the fears and voices was connected with my mother's death, but I didn't fully realize it until yesterday."

Following therapy, Bonnie graduated college and later graduate school, becoming a social worker. Interestingly, she graduated with honors!

CLINICAL INSIGHTS

☐ Do not these cases highlight rather typical concentration symptoms *and resulting concentration disorders*?

☐ Might not some of these *symptoms and cases be confused with those diagnosed as ADD*?

☐ Might not a series of psychological triggers (illness, separation, divorce, injury) result in impaired concentration, distractibility, moodiness, disorganization, restlessness, difficulties in socializing with peers?

☐ Might not psychologically based triggers not only cause ADD-like concentration and distractibility symptoms in previously normal subjects, but also intensify these very same symptoms in mild and previously unrecognized (because compensated) forms of ADD?

SECONDARY DETERMINANTS OF CONCENTRATION-RELATED SYMPTOMS

Type V^2 CD

Any subject developing diabetes, low thyroid, fever, anemia, low cortisone levels, or fatigue, will inevitably develop a decrease in concentration-related functioning, even in the absence of all pre-existing Type I-IV CD mechanisms.

Needless to say, all these Type V^2 CD triggers may also arise in subjects predisposed to Types I-IV CD and thus intensify their symptoms. These symptoms may be intensified:

☐ via *nonspecific* central nervous system (CNS) mechanisms

☐ via *specific* Types III and IV ADD and related CNS neurotransmitters and/or structures.

Secondary triggers may arise and complicate the symptoms in all patients. Needless to say, the careful analysis of any subject's complaints and *all the determining mechanisms* are absolutely essential for appropriate treatment.

Additional Insights and Considerations

DEPRESSION

Depression's effect on concentration is obvious. It sucks away and withdraws energy from vital functioning areas. In severe cases, even physical functions are affected and life is threatened, not only by suicide, but by inattention to eating and sleeping and by an impaired immune system.

Depression may be directly caused by an inner-ear dysfunction and thus be part and parcel of the ADD disorder—in which case it is a primary symptom in addition to being a secondary destabilizing trigger. Accordingly, it is exceedingly important to carefully evaluate the presence of this symptom and its origin, as well as its overall effect in ADD.

LEARNING DISABILITIES (LD) OR DYSLEXIA VS. COMPENSATORY CONCENTRATION

As previously and repeatedly noted, symptoms affecting reading, writing, spelling, math, and memory appear primarily associated with ADD. These symptoms are vital and trigger severe frustration, requiring exceptional concentration and memory efforts to compensate. The same applies to all sensory-motor and related thinking functions characterizing impaired ADD. They all require extra or compensatory concentration efforts in order for impaired inner-ear-related mechanisms to approach even reasonable levels of functioning.

As a result, the study of depression and LD or dyslexia in ADD is vital for the understanding of *total ADD*—not just an unwittingly biased subsample representing merely a localized tip of the "ADD iceberg."

ANXIETY

Anxiety also plays a vital role in ADD. Needless to say, overreactive anxiety mechanisms significantly destabilize concentration, activity, impulsivity, and memory in ADD. Moreover, anxiety symptoms were also found to be primary symptoms of an inner-ear dysfunction.

Because of the importance of depression, LD or dyslexia, and anxiety in ADD, follow-up chapters will elucidate these issues in much greater detail.

CASE HISTORIES—AND ADDITIONAL EXPERIENCES

Neurotic and realistic anxiety-based factors may be entirely responsible for some concentration problems, and they may contribute to others. But twenty-five years of clinical research have demonstrated to me that the vast majority of concentration problems, including those found in Type I and Type II Anxiety Disorders, can be traced to a hidden and frequently compensated *physiological* problem: a malfunction within the inner-ear system. In other words, Types I and II Anxiety Disorders, mechanisms may either destabilize a prior inner-ear impairment or create a new one.

As you read the following case histories, notice how many of the symptoms are *identical* to those described by patients who have Type III ADD. Is the similarity merely coincidental? You be the judge.

Mike

Mike S., a thirty-six-year-old graphic designer and artist, describes himself as a conservative, down-to-earth person who's at best level-headed, at worst, perhaps too anxious to please other people. Always a good student—he graduated *cum laude* from a major university—this bright young man had never had a concentration problem until he moved from a tiny town in Iowa to New

York City in the hopes of "making it" as a designer for a major magazine. What happened to him during his first six months on the job illustrates, with piercing clarity, how the symptoms of concentration dysfunction can permeate one's personal life, one's career, one's very soul. Indeed, as you'll see, although Mike's concentration problems were "realistically" based (Type I), his behavior, while under stress, was quite similar to the behavior of those who suffer from Type III or physiologically based ADD.

"I fully expected to be successful when I came to the Big Apple," he explained to me during an interview not long ago. "And I had everything going for me: I'd won design and illustration awards for the magazines I'd worked for in Dubuque, I certainly wasn't lacking in the confidence department, and—most important—I really wanted to succeed! I felt I was destined for it. Plus, I was motivated for several reasons: friends were rooting for me; I'd taken out a huge loan to finance the move; and I had convinced myself that I'd find relative fame and fortune in Gotham.

"Despite the fact that I'd envisioned myself living in a wonderful loft in Soho or a small penthouse on Fifth Avenue, I learned quickly that I could only afford a one-room dive in the East Village. It was overrun by roaches, the toilet overflowed at every flush, and the sound of traffic filled my every waking moment. My yuppie neighbors in the building avoided me as if I were a Peeping Tom, and in a few short weeks I realized that I was totally alone in the world—there was no one to talk to, no one to console me when I came home from work. Was it loneliness that triggered my anxiety? I'll never be sure, but I'd say it's a good guess.

"By the time I actually started the job, a few weeks after my arrival in town, I was feeling pretty disenfranchised from everyone and everything. I felt disconnected. All my energy was absorbed by anxiety at first, then depression. So it wasn't surprising that every assignment was too much for me. If I was asked to do the layout on something really simple, like a one-page piece that required only one piece of artwork, I panicked. I'd move the picture around on the page over and over again, but never felt confident that I was putting it where it should go. If, during a layout conference, my boss asked me what I thought about a particular design, my mind would go blank. I'd stutter my answer. Most sentences were prefaced with 'I don't know if this makes sense to you, but . . . '

"The most hideous example of my lack of concentration occurred when I was assigned to do my first 'real' story. I was to do the illustration *and* layout, and my name would appear in the credits. This was really important to me—to have my name emblazoned on a story in a national magazine—and I knew it was the assignment by which I would be judged! Unfortunately, from the moment I began to work on it, my brain became mush, and I spent the next couple of weeks acting like a zombie.

"As I sat at the drafting board, staring at the blank page, all I felt was panic. I'd start a sketch, then erase it. Nothing I drew made any sense to me. I even tried copying ideas from other artists on the staff, but mine all came out looking like a third-grader had done them. I felt like I was a blind person who had been instructed to draw something he'd never even seen! My heart raced, my throat was bone-dry. I'd pace back and forth, wringing my hands; my stomach ached constantly. My head would throb until I felt like it would burst! Several times, I got the dry heaves and would flee from my office to the men's room. Although I never actually vomited, I always felt it could happen at any moment.

"Each day my condition worsened. I'd spend ten or more hours at the office, struggling but getting nowhere. I felt so stupid! It's as if I'd forgotten everything I'd ever learned about art and design. Completely sapped by the end of each day, I'd drag myself home. Once there, I'd chain-smoke. I even tried marijuana in the hopes of anesthetizing myself, of dulling my overactive senses. By midnight, I'd be exhausted yet almost too tired to sleep; when this happened, I'd take twice the recommended dose of over-the-counter sleeping pills. By three A.M., if I was lucky, I'd be asleep.

"When morning came, I'd be groggy and feel sick to my stomach. Then I'd look at the clock and come face to face with brutal reality: in another hour, I'd have to show up at the office and face that drafting board again. And I knew, without a doubt, that I'd spend yet another day staring at a blank page. I dreaded leaving the apartment—it was the only place where I felt safe.

"After six months of this agony, with no relief in sight, I felt convinced I was close to having a nervous breakdown. Believing that no job was worth such a risk to my health, I announced to my boss that I was leaving the company.

"Almost instantly my tension melted away. Within a few days, I felt that I was back to being my old self again. Weeks later, I was out pounding the pavement for freelance assignments; I contacted several magazines, got a number of projects, and performed admirably. Since that time, I've started my own business and make more money than most of my artist friends. I'm happy. I'm at ease with my work. Most of the time, I enjoy what I'm doing. What happened to me back then? Maybe I expected too much of myself . . . of New York. Maybe I was just never cut out to work for a corporate entity. What I do know is this: I hope nobody ever has to go through what I went through. If there's a hell, I lived there for six months of my life."

Although Mike's concentration and performance problems were caused by anxiety, stress, environment, and fatigue, his resulting symptoms are similar to those caused by a physiological problem. Did his feelings of stupidity sound familiar to you? Are they not analogous to those of many Type III ADD patients you read about earlier in this book? And what about his fear—did he not sound phobic as he described not wanting to leave his apartment? His temporary stuttering, too, brings to mind many of my patients. Recently, Mike underwent diagnostic testing in my office. The tests revealed the presence of an underlying inner-ear dysfunction.

- Might intense realistic (Type I) anxiety have led to overloading and destabilized a preexisting but compensated CVS dysfunction?
- Might the relief of this stress have resulted in a rapid recompensation?
- Might the preexisting CVS dysfunction be a coincidental factor?

Tina M.

Forty-two-year-old Tina M., a science writer, generally has superb powers of concentration. "I can sit four to five hours at a stretch," she explains, "and almost not know I have a body. I become totally immersed in what I'm doing and get so focused that my husband can come into the room and say something to me and I won't hear him. On several occasions, he says he's told me he's going out to run errands, and that I've answered him. Yet after I come out of one of these periods of intense concentration, I'll look around and wonder where he went. I literally do not remember him saying he was going out."

At other times, however, her powers of concentration disappear. "It's Fidget City—I get hyperactive, tense, can't stay in one place, have to pace or walk around. Then I get a tenseness in my shoulders, and sometimes have tremendous headaches. Sometimes, I've even experienced panic attacks. They're extremely debilitating and scary. When I'm in the throes of a panic, I feel that I've simply lost control of myself."

I asked Tina to describe her most recent attack:

"I'll tell you about two of them," she replied. "They may interest you because their causes are quite different. One of them happened after I'd been assigned to do a story about gold mining in California. I flew to the coast to tour the mother lode and spent four fantastic days with two geologists. It was the most fun I'd ever had researching a story. When I returned to the office, though, the editors called a meeting. I guess it was intended to be sort of like a 'pep talk.' Two of them gave a presentation wherein they told us, the writers, that we must 'treat every word as a gem.'

"After the meeting, I sat down in the copy room, at my computer, and started writing the story. All I could hear in my head was 'treat every word as a gem. Every word must be a gem.' I sat in that room for hours on end and was literally unable to get past the first sentence. I wrote it and rewrote it and rewrote it until I had a page full of first sentences: 'A team of men came up the hill clear-cutting the mountain . . . Clear-cutting the mountain, a team of men came . . .' and so on until I had written every possible permutation. I became totally obsessed with every word, every punctuation mark, every sentence. I could not stop doing it.

"I felt this incredible sense of anxiety. I felt like I was going to die. There was this feeling that somebody had me around the back of the neck and was squeezing it. Always in my mind was the thought that when they read this, they're going to see that these words are not gems!

"The attack lasted for days. I had trouble sleeping and was totally agitated. I couldn't think about anything else. I had this incredible fear of censure, and I envisioned myself being laughed at or scolded or fired because I just couldn't measure up.

"Eventually, my 'fever' broke. I don't really remember how I got the story done, but I did. As I recall it, somebody came into the copy room and saw that I was foundering and said, 'Look, you can't make it perfect. Just write it.' At some point, I guess I threw up my hands and just did it. But I did it *non compos mentis*. The story got through the editing channels and eventually appeared in the magazine. Nobody ever knew that I'd labored over each and every word."

I wasn't surprised to hear of Tina's insomnia, fear, and agitation; they're all typical symptoms of Types I and II anxiety, which can secondarily trigger concentration and functional impairments. Nor was I shocked to learn of her episodic obsession—it is not unlike the repetitive, seemingly unnecessary actions that patients with phobias often experience.

In relating her second panic attack to me, Tina described an even wider variety of symptoms:

"Shortly after I started working on another story for this same magazine, the magazine was sold to another company. Although I had hoped that the new owners would want to hire me, they didn't. All they wanted was for me to finish the story, which, in principle, they now 'owned.' While all this was going on, my husband had sold a book contract to a publishing house to do a book about the state of Louisiana. Since I was now technically out of a job and we desperately needed money, we knew that we'd be moving to Baton Rouge so my husband could start researching his book. All of that was okay with me, but I still had that damned article hanging over my head!

"Within just a couple of weeks, we had moved to Louisiana. But instead of feeling excited about it, all I remember is feeling a great deal of anxiety and *rancor* about having to do the article.

I kept thinking, 'Why should I finish the story when these people aren't going to hire me and I'm here in Louisiana without a job?' I had no friends, our financial situation was iffy, and I had this nagging feeling that something bad was going to happen. As it turned out, that prediction was pretty accurate.

"The story was due in a couple of days, so the deadline pressure was ever-present. I drank a double expresso to try to concentrate, but it didn't give me the usual 'kick.' So I decided I was going to lie down and take a break. I lay down with a pillow propped behind me so that I could read a novel to relax, but within fifteen or twenty seconds, I suddenly became acutely aware of the fact that I couldn't breathe. I felt like someone had turned a switch off in my head and then turned it on; it was like my autonomic nervous system had been turned on and off for a moment. All of this translated into a pressing notion in my brain that my heart and my breathing were going to stop and that I had no control over them.

"I sat up straight in bed, gasping for breath, and sat there for a few minutes. The level of panic and anxiety rose and I was certain that I was going to die. I thought my throat was closing up, and I began wondering if it would be possible for a person to perform a tracheotomy on herself. Oh God, I thought—I don't want to die!

"I don't know how I did it, but I managed to get to the phone and call a doctor. I called 911 and told them I thought I was dying. The medics arrived and put sensors on me. My heart was going crazy and my blood pressure, normally low, was going way up. They determined that I was *not* having a heart attack, but still I totally panicked and felt disoriented. It was almost like vertigo: I was unsteady on my feet and everything looked weird to me. When I got to the hospital, I felt like I was looking through a fish-eye lens. I didn't quite know where I was, or who I was, but I was fairly certain of my imminent death.

"The diagnosis was a full-blown anxiety attack. The blood workup they did indicated that there was no allergic response. I got a shot of Benadryl and was driven home by paramedics. I eventually returned to normal, but not for several days. During the attack, I didn't think about my rancor or the central problem—

hating to have to write the article. The compelling issue was my death. I was absolutely stunned that my body would do such a thing. I have had no such attacks since then.

"Still, I'm worried that it could happen again. I'm scared that my body will go completely awry, and that my concentration and functioning will go out the window. The entire experience has made me quite wary of myself and my behavior. I don't completely trust myself anymore."

By the time of examination, Tina felt well again. Examination revealed no obvious CVS dysfunctioning.

- ☐ Were all of Tina's concentration and related symptoms triggered entirely by Type I and/or II anxiety mechanisms?
- ☐ Does not the absence of CVS findings support this assumption?
- ☐ Might the CVS be impaired without obvious findings—as occurs in approximately 10 percent of cases?

With luck, Tina will continue to do fine and we'll never know. But it is important to recognize the limitations of our diagnostic abilities for some cases and situations.

If you have seen a glimpse of yourself or a loved one in any of these first ten chapters, I encourage you to turn to the pages that follow. You will not only find a logical explanation of the problems that may have been mystifying you all your life, but you will also find solid information that will prove that you, too, can be helped.

CHAPTER XI

ADD and the Inner Ear

You have now met scores of my patients who suffer from Type III ADD—in other words, their concentration problems are due to an inner-ear dysfunction. As you read of their experiences, did you wonder how a tiny structure, located deep within the ear, could possibly account for their behavioral and academic disturbances? Throughout this chapter, we will explore the anatomical complex that is responsible for the myriad symptoms associated with ADD. But first, let's take a crash course in human biology, beginning with a brief look at how the central nervous system (CNS) is organized and how it controls body posture and muscular movements.

Like a computer that is constantly being fed data, your brain—the prime mover behind your ability to stand up straight, keep your balance, and coordinate your bodily movements—constantly receives an enormous stream of information from sensory nerves throughout the body. Consider the sensory nerves involved with vision, for example. Let's say you're going to walk a straight line from one end of your living room to the other. As you do so—assuming you keep your eyes open—your optic nerves transmit messages to the brain about your body's motion and position and help keep you on a level course. But if you covered your eyes, thus depriving your optic nerves (and your brain) of vital sensory information, and tried again to saunter along that imaginary straight line, you'd veer off your course and probably stumble into chairs, walls, or people.

Although there's no question that our sense of sight is at the forefront of conscious awareness, it is not the only source of information necessary to keep us in balance and in control of our body position. If it were, then people who are blind would not be able to walk and maintain normal posture, nor would sighted people, when blindfolded, be able to sit and stand properly and perform any number of complex motor activities such as dribbling a basketball, playing the piano, or skipping rope. In fact, there are a variety of sensory systems other than vision that provide the brain with important information that allows for the maintenance of balance and posture.

If you've ever spun around in circles and then stopped quickly, you've no doubt experienced a feeling of great dizziness and of disorientation with your surroundings. The sensory system that creates these feelings is located deep within your ear in an area called the inner ear. It is usually referred to as the *vestibular apparatus*, or balance mechanism, and it consists of several thin fluid-filled canals and sacs that are lined with tiny hairs which arise from nerve cells called *neurons*.

Each time you move your head and change its position, the fluid in the canals shifts and causes those tiny hairs to bend. When this happens, the neurons fire off electrical signals to the brain, which provide it with information about the angle of your head and how the rest of your body is positioned in relation to it. Based on this information, your brain stimulates the muscles of your body to react in such a way that you continue to stand upright. If your brain did not receive this vestibular information, it's likely that every time you leaned your head to one side, you'd have trouble keeping your balance.

It's important to note that your vestibular and visual systems often work together to provide balance and proper posture. When your brain receives messages from the neurons in the inner ear, it can instruct your eyes to change their position in relation to the objects in your visual field while your body is in motion. Because of this working partnership, you're able to keep a fixed gaze on your friend while you move toward her.

As you walk toward your friend, other complex and crucial sensory systems are hard at work sending messages to your brain. One of these is called the *proprioceptive system*, a network of sensors located in the ligaments and other soft tissues of all your joints. Whether you're moving or standing still, these sensors send information to the brain about what your joints are doing at any particular moment and where they're positioned in relation to the rest of your body.

Other sensors within the body provide *tactile data*, or information about touch. For example, such sensors within the skin of your feet send messages to your brain that tell it whether you're standing on a surface that is flat, inclined, stationary, or moving.

You'd think the circuitry of the brain would be overloaded by the time it had processed all this complex data. Not so! In fact, the brain has the ability to pack even more information into its data bank from yet another elaborate group of sensors—the body's *motor control system*. This sends and receives messages related to the degree of stretch and tension each muscle in the body is experiencing.

When you're reaching for an apple, for instance, your brain sends a message to the muscles of your arm that says in effect, "Muscles, you must reach six inches in order to get to that apple." Your muscles receive this message and begin to extend themselves; then they send back a message to the brain that says, "Is this far enough?" Your brain now uses this information to fine-tune the reach until the hand finally grasps the apple.

Although this motor control and sensory information is not a part of the apparatus that is concerned with detecting body position, the information it provides is crucial to the brain's ability to direct the muscle activity responsible for holding the body upright and in balance.

All of the information transmitted by these various sensory systems is received, processed, and integrated by the central nervous system in phenomenal quantities with incredible speed. As you walk down the street, engrossed in a pleasant daydream, the central nervous system is working at a fever pitch to maintain posture, balance, and smooth, efficient walking.

Now that you have a rough idea of how the central nervous system works, let us focus more closely on the inner ear, for it is here that we will find the key to Attention Deficit Disorder. Known technically as the *cerebellar-vestibular system*, or CVS, our inner-ear system is made up of two components: the part of the brain known as the cerebellum, and the tiny canals and fluid-filled sacs that comprise the vestibular system.

To understand the cerebellum and its role in modulating sensory motor information, I'd like to share with you a wonderfully descriptive passage from an article entitled "The Cerebellum" (*Scientific American*, 1958), written by R. S. Snider:

> In the back of our skulls, perched upon the brain stem under the overarching mantle of the great hemispheres of the cerebrum, is a baseball-sized, bean-shaped lump of gray and white brain tissue. This is the cerebellum, the "lesser brain." In contrast to the cerebrum, where men have sought and found the centers of so many vital mental activities, the cerebellum remains a region of subtle and tantalizing mystery, its function hidden from investigators. . . . Its elusive signals have begun to tell us that, while the cerebellum itself directs no body functions, it operates as monitor and coordinator of the brain's other centers and as mediator between them and the body. . . . One is tempted to see the cerebellum as the great "modulator" of nervous function . . . In the meantime we have to contend with the possibility that the cerebellum is involved in still more diverse aspects of the nervous system. It becomes increasingly evident that if "integration" is a major function of this organ, trips into the realm of mental disease may cross its boundaries more frequently than the guards in sanitariums suspect.

Much has been learned since Snider published those words. In fact, we now know that the cerebellum performs three important functions: (1) it is responsible for the management of voluntary and involuntary muscle activity; (2) it administers all motor responses dictated by the cerebrum; and (3) it integrates and processes virtually all of the sensory information transmitted to the brain from the millions of sensory receptors located throughout the human body.

The other component of the CVS is the so-called inner ear, which is located deep within the skull, behind and slightly below the eyeball. There, we find (1) the snail-shaped cochlea, the sound-analyzing mechanism of the ear, and (2) the vestibular organs: three semicircular canals that run along the length of the cochlea, and two fluid-filled sacs. Known as the "organs of balance," the canals react to body movement and the sacs respond to the pull of gravity; together, they inform the cerebellum about changes in the position of the head. If they are damaged or diseased, they send too many or too few impulses to the brain. Such miscommunications usually result in problems related to equilibrium, balance, even our intuitive sense of direction.

Obviously, the cerebellum and the vestibular system form an extremely complex communications network. Together, they act as the sensory-motor processing center of the brain, where all information—including light and sound in all existing wavelengths, motion (internal and external), gravitational (electromagnetic) energy, air pressure, chemicals (external and internal), odors, tastes, textures, etc.—converges and is filtered, integrated, coordinated, and controlled. Acting as an intermediary, the CVS also processes and modulates light, sound, motion, taste, touch, smell, gravity, temperature, barometric pressure, chemicals, direction, balance, time—even our position in space. Moreover, it controls all the motor instructions the brain wishes to send to the various parts of the body. Hence, the CVS is responsible for all functions related to movement, including our ability to walk, cry, breathe, make love, and play sports.

As you might have guessed, the relationship between the components of the CVS is so intimate that it is often difficult to determine where the work of the cerebellum ends and that of the vestibular system begins. In fact, they are so enmeshed in each other's business that one is tempted to compare them to a supercomputer—like "software," the vestibular system supplies sensory information, while the "hardware" of the cerebellum orchestrates, processes, and converts millions of bits of information into motor instructions at any given moment.

To begin to understand how a dysfunction in the CVS can cause the symptoms of ADD, let us take the supercomputer analogy a step further. You're probably aware that the "brain" of a computer is made up of tiny printed circuit boards designed to transmit electrical current. Because each circuit is designed to control one function, we can say that the circuits process information in a highly compartmentalized, circuit-specific fashion. In the CVS, information processing occurs in much the same way: a separate circuit is responsible for the processing of each and every different type of sensory and motor information.[1] For example, within the area of the CVS that is responsible for processing all motion-related information, there are individual circuits that process different types of motion. In other words, one circuit may be processing counter-clockwise motion while another processes clockwise motion, and still another processes vertical motion, and so on. Interestingly, groups of circuits work together as well: one group processes the quality of motion triggered by a car, another the motion of a boat, and so forth.

Not only can the circuits work alone and in groups, but they can also function independently of one another. Thus, a disturbance or dysfunction in one circuit may have little or no effect on the performance of another, regardless of the similarity of the information they are processing. This explains why, for example, some individuals may get motion-sick from vertical motion—when an elevator drops suddenly—but not from the clockwise motion that occurs on an amusement ride such as the whip. It also explains why an individual may get carsick but not airsick.

Despite their diverse capabilities, all CVS circuits are interconnected so that the inner-ear system can function as a unit. Together, they become an integrated whole. This integration accounts for what I call the "spillover" effect: if you've learned, for example, to tolerate the horizontal motion caused by the side-to-side rocking of a boat, you may also become resistant to the disturbing effects of vertical motion without having been conditioned to do so. Integration also accounts for "linkage" of circuits—a condition that occurs when an individual is oversensitive to most forms of motion rather than just one particular form.

Because the concept of CVS integration is crucial to our understanding of ADD, let me offer another analogy by which we may understand it. Imagine that the CVS is like a telephone switch-

---

[1]Scientists know this to be true, because by plotting the electrical activity of the cerebellum, they've been able to map the specific areas that control the various sensory-motor functions.

board. Because everything on the switchboard is interconnected, damage to the system can take many forms. Consider the following possibilities:

SWITCHBOARD MALFUNCTION	CVS MALFUNCTION
One telephone number	One CV circuit—horizontal motion, for example
Two adjacent numbers	Two CV circuits—horizontal *and* vertical motion
Two nonadjacent numbers	Two CV circuits—horizontal motion and ultraviolet light
Entire section	All motion-processing circuits
Entire switchboard	All sensory-processing circuits

Via the switchboard analogy, you've seen that malfunctioning within the circuitry of the CVS can take myriad forms. Similarly, the *repair* of various circuits can cause diverse effects as well. Damage or repairs to one section of the CVS may affect just that section, other sections, or the entire CVS. It all depends upon the nature and extent of the dysfunction. We will see many examples of linkage, spillover, and circuit-specific dysfunction as we examine the many facets of ADD in greater detail.

One final note before leaving this section. Over the years, while attempting to describe the highly complicated CVS to patients and others, I have been asked to try to give as many simple analogies as possible so that people can be certain that they understand the mechanisms that characterize ADD. On the assumption that you may feel that way, too, I'd like to offer the reader five additional ways of describing the CVS:

(1) It acts like a guided missile, piloting our eyes, hands, feet, and various mental and physical functions in time and space.
(2) It acts like the vertical and horizontal knobs on a television

set, fine-tuning all motor responses (voluntary and involuntary) leaving the brain, and all sensory responses entering the brain.

(3) It is a compass system. It reflexively tells us spatial relationships such as right and left, up and down, and front and back.

(4) It acts as a timing mechanism, setting rhythms to motor tasks and governing your ability—or inability—to tell time or to sense time.

(5) It is interconnected to all other vital brain centers via feedback circuits and neurotransmitters—including the alerting and concentration/activity modulating systems.

It is also important to mention that any combination of the inner-ear mechanisms discussed in this chapter may be impaired. And that this primary impairment may secondarily interfere with or disrupt the functioning of a host of other vital brain systems and centers with which it is interconnected. In a similar fashion, the CVS may be secondarily destabilized by primary impairments in other centers, such as those characterizing Type IV ADD. Moreover, any mechanism may be compensated for, or even over-compensated for. What this suggests is that every symptom of ADD—from distractibility and impulsivity to problems with reading, writing, and math—can be viewed as the result of opposing forces, dysfunctioning and compensatory. By understanding this concept, we can more easily see why some patients are distractible but not impulsive, for example, and why others are poor spellers but excellent readers.

In the next chapter, we'll examine how a breakdown in any of the mechanisms discussed above can independently, or collectively, account for the symptoms of Attention Deficit Disorder.

CHAPTER XII

Understanding the Symptoms and Inner-Ear Mechanisms of ADD

As you will recall from the previous chapter, the cerebellar-vestibular system (CVS)—your inner-ear system—is the information-processing center of the brain. Specifically, it constantly performs the following functions:

☐ The CVS is our sensory processor. It filters and fine-tunes all *sensory information* entering the brain—light, sound, motion, gravitational (electromagnetic) energy, chemical information, air pressure, etc. Therefore, it is responsible for coordinating, controlling, and fine-tuning our vision, hearing, balance, sense of direction, sense of motion, sense of altitude and depth, sense of smell, anxiety level, and so forth.

☐ The CVS is our motor processor. It coordinates, controls, and fine-tunes all *motor information* leaving the brain. Therefore, it is responsible for guiding and coordinating our eyes, head, hands, feet, limbs, etc., as well as our various mental and physical functions (voluntary and involuntary) in time and space.

With those functions in mind, I would now like to examine all the symptoms and behavior patterns of ADD that you've read about in this book. The information in this section is based on a sample of several thousand people with ADD—the largest such sample ever recorded and analyzed. You should also know that:

☐ All the symptoms were painstakingly collected and studied for years before their true meaning and significance were recognized.

☐ All the symptoms have been analyzed to determine the underlying mechanism(s) responsible for their creation.

☐ All the symptoms were statistically analyzed so that their relative incidence and frequency were determined in large ADD samples.

☐ Each and every exceptional, atypical, and unexpected finding has been studied and analyzed with the same intensity given to symptoms that occur typically or frequently.

As you will see, the categories that I have discussed below are not mutually exclusive. In other words, there is considerable overlap among the mechanisms of ADD. For example, the CVS processes that are responsible for difficulties of balance and coordination can also account for problems in reading, writing, and math; those related to memory may also be responsible for phobias and related mental and behavior disorders, and so forth.

BALANCE AND COORDINATION

The majority of patients you've met so far have some degree of difficulty with balance and coordination. For Karl, a high-school dropout, an inability to work with his hands got him into trouble in shop class. After his accident, Jerry, the research scientist, had trouble walking and talking smoothly. Carla, a graphic artist, told me she often bumped into walls; as a child, she rarely made it across the living room without stumbling. Why do many people with ADD have a tendency to be uncoordinated? As you'll recall, the inner ear regulates all balance and coordination mechanisms; therefore, an inner-ear dysfunction will frequently result in some delay or disturbance of these mechanisms. Some adults and children with ADD seem "klutzy" or clumsy. Others seem accident-prone and often bruise themselves, giving rise to erroneous suspicions that they have been abused. Even bed-wetting and soiling can be indicative of ADD—poorly coordinated motor control may result in over-relaxation of the involuntary sphincter muscles, for example.

Like Jackie, who often jokes that she "can't chew gum and walk at the same time," many individuals with Type III ADD cannot perform more than one task at a time. If they must do two or more things simultaneously, the circuitry of their CNS becomes overloaded. It is incapable of interpreting multiple visual and/or auditory inputs. This results in sensory scrambling, a condition in which the brain cannot coordinate multiple motor tasks without the benefit of extreme compensatory concentration efforts. And there are just not enough concentration reserves in ADD subjects to divide up among several sensory-motor tasks—and still function adequately. Stated another way, in the presence of a CVS impairment, the reflexive, automatic processes of selective attention and sensory-motor-based selective intention are impaired. As noted in earlier chapters, this results in a decomposition or falling apart of vital subfunctions. As a result, intense conscious efforts are required for compensation to occur. And it's easier to compensate for one task or function at a time. Is it any wonder that when simultaneously riding a bike and talking to a friend, Jackie felt "wobbly" and couldn't control the bike?

When an inner-ear dysfunction is present, the neurons—which are stimulated by the tiny, bending hairs in the vestibular canals and sacs—may *misfire*, providing inaccurate information to the cerebellum. When this happens, other balance and coordination problems may occur, including dizziness, fainting spells, delayed walking as an infant, spastic movements, poor aptitude for sports, a tendency to fall, head tilting—even postural reading preferences such as lying on the floor. Many patients who insist on crouching over their work, or reading in a prone position, are criticized by peers for being eccentric or "weird." Upon examination, it becomes clear that they are merely attempting to keep their balance. Without knowing why, they are trying to compensate for a dysfunction of their CVS.

It's important to note that *any* of the balance and coordination problems discussed above—like all other symptoms of Type III ADD—can be compensated for, or even overcompensated for. Therefore, they are not always noticeable. One can partially overcome poor hand-eye coordination by practicing or rehearsing. Dizziness while reading can be reduced by occasional rest periods, by reading in an unconventional position, or by intense efforts at compensatory concentration. A wide variety of research has shown that ocular fixation and concentration (e.g., sitting in the front seat of a car and driving) dampens or reduces vestibular sensitivity and reactivity—and thus results in decreased dizziness, motion sickness, imbalance, and related inner-ear symptoms. Jerry partially compensated for his balance problems by moving slowly and by using furniture to steady himself. Alan, the contractor from California who had trouble dialing the phone, purchased a programmable unit that did his dialing for him. In many cases, patients' tenacity, determination, and old-fashioned stubbornness come to the fore, allowing them to overcome their difficulties.

HYPERACTIVITY, OVERACTIVITY, AND IMPULSIVITY

Just as the inner ear fine-tunes all motor activity, so, too, does it modulate the body's energy levels. When not functioning properly, the inner ear can cause many of the symptoms you've seen in earlier chapters: various levels of hyperactivity, impulsivity, overactivity—even hypoactive or decreased activity—as well as fluctuations between these different states. When excess activity is the predominant symptom, a person is said to have ADD-H—i.e., Attention Deficit Disorder with Hyperactivity.[1] In some cases, abnormal activity levels of ADD-H patients can be seen at an early age: pregnant mothers have reported that the fetuses in their wombs "climbed all over the place." In other instances, ADD-H occurs rather late in life. After an inner-ear infection, Debbie L. recalled that she had "become hyperactive for extended periods of time. This results in insomnia, and sometimes I won't calm down enough to sleep for twenty-four to forty-eight hours."

To understand the inner-ear mechanism as it relates to abnormal activity, let's briefly review a few case histories:

[1]It is often extremely difficult to determine whether abnormal activity is indeed the most pronounced symptom arising from ADD.

—When at home, Jeremy W. acted like a "little Ford tractor—he went ninety miles an hour, and his mouth never hushed," explained his mother. Yet when he got to school, he became nonresponsive or hypoactive; often, he said nothing at all in the classroom environment.

—Young Beth was always a fidgeter. Said her mother, "If she's reading a book, her feet are tapping a mile a minute, she's fiddling with her hair, and she's either whistling or humming her favorite song. I wish she could harness all that energy and put it into learning."

—Josh, the young boy whose impaired tuning mechanism and auditory filter caused him to hear even the slightest sounds, was also described by his teacher as a whirlwind of unfocused activity. Restless, irritable, and easily frustrated, he'd "fly off the handle" at the slightest provocation or for no apparent reason at all.

—According to his teacher, Allen B. has a short fuse. "If there's a fight, Allen has usually started it. It's not as if he plans to get into trouble, he simply responds to situations impulsively. . . . It's almost as if he can't control his impulses. He rarely looks before he leaps." In other words, various sensory-motor and related mental signals are improperly modulated, inhibited, or slowed, leaving inadequate time for adaptive checks and balances—reasoning and reflection—to occur.

The above patients illustrate several important facts about ADD. Persons who have it may exhibit varying types of activity at different levels of intensity in certain environments. For example, Jeremy's speech function became excessive at home, but not at school; other patients find that the reverse is true. Some patients experience a revving up of bodily activity—squirming, fidgeting, and toe-tapping are common examples. Still others become overactive or impulsive only when frustration triggers anxiety. Interestingly, when patients of this latter type are in stress-free or nonthreatening environments, they may calm down appreciably and be able to function at a "normal" pace. Indeed, many a patient who acts like a whirling dervish in a classroom of thirty will find that he or she is transformed into a serene, unflappable student when working alone with a tutor.

What accounts for the excessive activity levels and the impulsivity sometimes seen in anxious patients with ADD? If you have ever studied biology, you probably learned that your body possesses a built-in alarm system. Popularly known as the "fight or flight" response, the system is your body's reaction to a known danger, such as a man with a rifle, a house on fire, or extreme emotional stress. What you didn't learn is that many of the symptoms associated with fight or flight are also the body's response to other dangers we're not even conscious of: sensory flooding, sensory deprivation, or sensory scrambling. All three of these sensory effects put severe physiological stress on your cerebellum and vestibular apparatus, and each one, or a combination, creates the same result: an internal state of alarm.

If we liken the inner-ear system, or CVS, to a network of filters that control the flow of sensory information entering the brain, we can better understand how *sensory overload* contributes to excess activity. When they are impaired, one or more of the filters of your CVS will develop holes or perforations. If the spillage through the holes is severe, the brain may be overwhelmed by a flood of sensory information. Just as you might react with panic or fear to being deluged by water, your brain responds to this torrent of information by tripping the fight or flight alarm. Besieged by an excess amount of data, the brain sends signals to your body that result in stimulation, anxiety, fear, even total panic. Think back to Josh for a moment. Knowing that his CVS was already in turmoil due to tuning and filtering difficulties related to hearing, is it so surprising that the slightest provocation—perhaps the introduction of additional sounds from his teacher's voice—could make him irritable and restless and cause him to fly into a rage? Now recall Allen's behavior: should we be astonished that when, for example, he is accidentally bumped by another student—adding yet another "jolt" of sensory information to his overloaded CVS—he gets into a fight?

But what about Jeremy? Aware of his CVS problems, which have been mentioned in an earlier chapter, wouldn't you expect him to be overactive at school, where there is an overabundance of sensory information? It must be remembered that the brain triggers an alarm that provides us with two choices: fight or *flight*. At school—a potentially intimidating environment—Jeremy responds by fleeing; his system is clutched by fear and, hence, he becomes hypoactive and even nonresponsive. Depending upon the individual, fight or flight may be the response of choice.

When the inner-ear system is impaired, the sensory filters may be misshapen—they may be gnarled or too bulky to allow for a continuous flow of information to the brain. Such misshapen filters become clogged with data, resulting in sensory shortage or *sensory deprivation*. Sometimes the deprivation is so great that the brain is literally "starved" of vital information. In addition, the inner-ear system can scramble incoming sensory information in much the same way as an AM/FM stereo tuner can scramble electrical signals. When *sensory scrambling* occurs, the brain cannot use the information being fed to it by the various sensory systems of the body. Both of these conditions can trip the flight or fight alarm, bringing on anxiety, fear, or panic attacks and causing the victim to feel compelled to escape his or her environment. In many cases, the escape tactics require an excessive amount of activity.

How do these theories explain Margaret's behavior? Margaret often tried to fill up short periods of time with multiple activities. Frenetically, she would read, listen to music, call a friend, watch TV, try to help her mother, all within minutes. During these jampacked moments, she would exhibit extraneous movements—toe tapping, hair twisting, humming. Clearly, Beth was "fighting" against sensory deprivation and scrambling by trying to supply her system with new—and hopefully more pleasant—sensory stimuli. As you might have guessed, other patients will respond to their conditions by fleeing. In these cases, individuals become totally panicked and exhibit other traits associated with hyperactivity: children may race around a room; adults may feel compelled to do many tasks simultaneously.

You may have read that hyperactivity or overactivity disappear by puberty and that medications are no longer needed or helpful afterward. Although this assumption is true for some individuals with ADD, it is by no means valid for all. Many ADD-H children will act out their frustrations and develop into explosive, impulsive, drifting, antisocial, driven young or older adults. They still require active medical and psychological treatment, even as adults.

To provide a proper diagnosis, clinicians must get detailed reports from as many "observers" as possible, including parents, teachers, peers, and others who see the child or adult on a regular basis. Clinicians who provide a diagnosis of ADD-H based on a single office visit with a patient tend to miss behavioral patterns that are seen in other contexts. The reason? Many patients—even youngsters—can often will themselves to display "proper" behavior in the setting of a doctor's office.

CONCENTRATION AND DISTRACTIBILITY PROBLEMS

As you have seen thus far, many patients with ADD *appear* to have short attention spans:

- After an inner-ear infection, twenty-four-year-old Debbie said, "I've lost my ability to focus on one thought at a time. My mind jumps around from one subject to another."
- When I was interviewing Jackie, her eyes darted from me to items elsewhere in the room. If I asked her to explain something, she seemed unable to stick with the discussion, preferring instead to comment on the model of the brain atop my desk.
- Fourteen-year-old Margaret jumped from one task to another: in the span of a half hour, she'd try to read a book, play her tape cassette, watch TV, call a girlfriend, and help her mother bake cookies.

Upon close examination, all these individuals—and many others you've met so far—do not necessarily have short attention spans. In fact, their concentration is disturbed or fragmented by drifting sensory input. Because their sensory-motor processor is in such a state of chaos, they are forced to abandon even simple tasks after a brief period of time. To compensate, they expend tremendous amounts of *extra* concentration effort; when that happens, burn-out or fatigue rapidly ensues. Carla, a graphic artist, stated: "I feel exhausted all the time because I have to concentrate so hard on stupid things. By evening, I've completely run out of steam. It's like there's too much pressure on me." The pressure, of course, was exerted by her malfunctioning CVS and a need to compensate via the use of excessive concentration energy.

When our CVS is functioning normally, we can rest our concentration mechanisms while adequately performing many tasks on a "reflex" level. Unfortunately, many individuals with Type III ADD cannot relax or rest these mechanisms—they must constantly be on full alert and vigilant. When they let down their guard, they pay the price—their focus wanders, they appear "spacy," they act and perform inappropriately and may even blurt out seemingly nonsensical statements. As you will recall, Jack, the editor, had a tendency to lose "complete control of myself . . . I tend to say the first thing that comes to my mind."

The compensatory or perseverative vigilance required by people with ADD results in "overconcentration," a condition that can cause a variety of other symptoms, including headaches, a feeling of "fogginess," anxiety, fainting spells, and blocking. When any of these symptoms occur, the victim has a difficult time concentrating on the task at hand. Recall Albert F., the salesman who dreaded reading "dry" reports: "I get nervous," he told me. "My palms sweat and my heart races. . . . I feel light-headed . . . dizzy. Eventually, I can't focus on the reading; I can only focus on me."

As the fine-tuner of sensory information, your inner-ear system filters auditory or sound input. When a malfunction occurs, this input may drift or be garbled. The situation is not unlike what happens when your AM/FM tuner is affected by interference—the words or music you were listening to may suddenly vacillate in pitch, loudness, or clarity, for example, or different radio stations may converge on one channel, causing sound clutter. What's the result of the drifting and scrambled input caused by an impaired inner ear? Distractibility, misunderstanding, and confusion, as well as sporadic or delayed comprehension, blending of foreground and background noises, oversensitivity or undersensitivity to sounds (all sound or specific noises), and a variety of other hearing-related symptoms.

If the inner-ear system is malfunctioning, you may be unable to shut out irrelevant sensory information. Josh, from Chapter Five, responded to every "little" noise—a pin dropping or a bird flying by. No wonder his teacher wrote, "If I'm talking to him and there's noise in the background, he's a goner. He seems to tune me out . . . and tune the noise in." Over-response to sound and/or inadequate filtering can also cause distractibility problems. Explained Josh's teacher, "I've seen him hold his ears . . . when an ambulance or fire truck goes by." Needless to say, the sound of a siren would command Josh's attention more than the sound of his teacher's voice. Caused by a malfunctioning inner ear, such problems do not usually disappear with age; they can continue with a vengeance into adulthood. Recall Josh's forty-eight-year-old father—because his CVS circuitry produced sound clutter, he had to shout at parties "in order to hear himself think." When surrounded by people in a restaurant, Jane L., the registered nurse, had "trouble hearing what my friends are saying. All the sounds blur together."

Individuals who suffer from auditory drift often appear to be inattentive—they tend to respond slowly to questions and often compensate by stalling for time. Remember Carla, a graphic artist, who experienced severe difficulties with balance and coordination. Her husband thought she had a hearing problem because, she explained, "When he says something to me, I almost always have to say 'pardon?' or have him repeat himself." Yet Carla knew she wasn't really "hard of hearing." Said she, "By pretending that I didn't hear him the first time . . . I'm giving myself extra time to figure out what he's saying." She needed extra auditory processing time.

Many people with ADD also need extra time to figure out what's been written, be it text or numerals. As you might have guessed, the culprit in these cases is a malfunctioning CVS or, more specifically, a poor eye-tracking mechanism that causes faulty visual input. To understand how such a mechanism can interfere with concentration, we must now look at problems related to specific academic skills.

READING AND SPELLING

Because the CVS guides our eyes and coordinates their movements, a disorder in the system may deflect the eyes while they
attempt to reflexively and automatically focus on and track letters,
words, and sentences while we read. What are the consequences?
One's eyes do not track properly, which can result in omission or
insertion of letters, words, or entire sentences; improper tracking
can also result in change in word size, background streaking, or
compression and/or expansion of letters, words, or sentences.
Sometimes, written material may seem to jump and move about
the page, or blur—in Jerry's case, when he came to the end of
a line in a magazine, he had trouble finding the beginning of the
next line. At other times, the eyes will retarget the same word
or phrase over and over again, a condition called ocular perseveration. Obviously, any of these problems can lead to poor concentration and confusion, as well as compensatory blinking and
squinting, finger pointing, slow reading, and seemingly peculiar
movements of the head. Although motion sometimes facilitates
inner-ear-based functions in some with ADD, the opposite effect
may occur with others. The outcome depends on whether the
system is motion-deprived or -overloaded.

Quite often—as in the case of Jackie and others you've met
throughout this book—the reading process becomes an unpleas-
ant, tiring chore. Patients become fatigued, feel dizzy, complain
of double vision, develop headaches, or report feeling "sick" when
confronted with the written word. In these situations, many individuals are accused of making excuses when, in fact, they are
accurately describing—albeit unknowingly—how their malfunctioning CVS is making them feel.

If the inner-ear system is not working properly, visual input may
drift or become scrambled. In fact, if the drift is 180 degrees,
reversals may occur. You'll recall that even though she knew a
word was spelled d-o-g, Jackie invariably spelled it g-o-d. Jeremy
W. amazed his teacher by recalling the letters of the alphabet forward and backward—yet he couldn't tell her whether Z was at
the beginning of the alphabet or at the end. Such transpositions
of and confusion over letters are common symptoms of ADD,

although many individuals tend to reverse words, entire sentences, and numbers as well. Simple arithmetic becomes a baffling exercise to one who confuses 21 with 12, 131 with 311. Even telling time—is it 1:30 or 3:10?—is a struggle to a person with a malfunctioning CVS.

MATHEMATICS

Although mathematical dysfunctioning in ADD can be caused by transpositions of numbers, columns, and computation signs, it is often experienced as an uncertain *memory* for computational facts, requiring compensatory finger or mental counting. In fact, so necessary is finger counting for some patients, they literally cannot compute even simple addition problems without using their hands. For many patients, addition and subtraction cause the most difficulty. For others, problems arise when learning the multiplication tables; the facts of multiplication are learned and then rapidly forgotten unless reinforced by almost continuous repetition. Interestingly, some people with ADD experience more difficulty with one multiplication table than with others. For example, some will have difficulty with the eights, while with others it may be the nines. These variations highlight the fact that each specific math function and even subfunction is processed by way of its own corresponding circuit; thus simple circuits may be impaired while more complicated processing occurs with ease.

Many patients have told me that they understand the rudiments of a mathematical discipline because they learned the basics *in a lecture format*—i.e., they heard the information. Unfortunately, when they *look* at equations or angles, reversal and scrambling errors result in misreading, miswriting, and misremembering number sequences.

What about Jackie's problems with making or counting change? It appears that in some but not all individuals with ADD, their calculation channels became blurred at an early age. In later life, anxiety resulted in their avoiding situations that would have led to compensation. As a result of this insight, I realized that some people with ADD blur out the ability to remember concepts, just as others readily blur out the ability to remember hard facts. In other words, some individuals with ADD know the meaning of money; they just cannot easily recall the significant operational steps required to use it or make change. The resulting anxiety and embarrassment lead to secondary conceptual difficulties, including money phobias, even math blocks.

WRITING

Remember Josh's brother, Bob Jr.? "All of his homework is sloppy," his mother told me, "especially writing assignments." And what about Jeremy W., the "Jekyll and Hyde child" whose writing, described by his mother, was "illegible—a mess"? Inner-ear-related coordination problems can make it difficult for an individual to guide a pen across a piece of paper, resulting in discombobulated, illegible, uneven, or infantile handwriting. In many cases, improperly balanced muscle tone is the culprit.[2] More often than not, however, illegibility and sloppiness related to written work are caused by a malfunction in the CVS motor processor. When impaired, it may misinterpret the sensory information being sent to it. Hence, it loses its ability to accurately coordinate hand and limb movements. For this reason, many people with Type III ADD have difficulty performing relatively simple motor tasks, such as tying shoelaces, buttoning, zipping, and using utensils. Moreover, it is not uncommon for individuals to have problems learning how to skip, hop, jump rope, or dance because rhythm may also be affected.

It should be pointed out that not every motor function and reflex is misguided in persons with ADD. If you recall Alan, the contractor, you'll remember that he spoke of having "golden hands," and of having an aptitude for mechanical tasks. Jackie, who kept a daily

---

[2]Poor muscle tone can also cause or intensify symptoms such as flat feet, toeing-in or toeing-out, knock-knees, strabismus ("lazy-eye"), or double-jointedness. Intermittent muscle-tone disturbances—especially when triggered by anxiety—may result in "jelly legs."

diary, jotted down her notes with almost calligraphic beauty. Such examples clearly indicate that each specific motor function or task has its own specific wavelength or circuit on or by which it is processed. This is true of sensory functioning as well. Each piece of information entering the brain is processed with circuit-specificity. Thus, some input functions may be impaired while others remain well within the realm of normalcy. Still other functions may be categorized in the gifted range.

MEMORY

As we have seen, specific patterns and types of memory instability play a vital role in reading, writing, spelling, and mathematical delays. Yet it must be realized that for people with ADD, memory is not an all-or-nothing function. One can have a poor memory for visual and word recall while having a superb memory for phonetics, and one can easily learn addition and subtraction facts while experiencing extreme frustration when attempting to learn and retain the multiplication tables. Based on this insight, it is clear that in the CVS, each and every piece of information is processed, stored, and retrieved independently of other memory functions. Each and every person with ADD will therefore be characterized by a unique quality and pattern of memory functioning versus dysfunctioning.

To understand this point, consider some of the patients you've met so far. Do you remember Alan? If he went to the kitchen for a glass of milk, by the time he got there, he forgot what he came to get. Alan also had trouble recalling telephone numbers. During a "panic attack" that occurred while taking an exam, Jeremy couldn't remember how to compute equations. Marion D., a physician, couldn't recall patients' names and had occasional trouble remembering medical procedures. Young Jeremy W. couldn't remember that both his parents had helped redecorate his room. Jackie had problems with important dates, even simple daily tasks. After his accident, Jerry couldn't remember names and/or faces. After her inner-ear infection, Debbie also forgot names; she also "drew blanks in spelling" and had trouble finding the appropriate word needed to express a thought. Other young patients have had problems learning or retaining the names of colors and shapes, the letters of the alphabet, directions, or days of the week and months of the year in order. The list could go on and on.

Intriguingly, some patients have difficulty erasing information from their memories. Individuals with this problem cannot forget something, even if it is wrong. As a result, they often continue to make the same errors throughout their lives. Someone with this trait might be able to spell new, multisyllabic words with ease but continue to misspell simple words—using *their* instead of *they're*, for example—that they mislearned during childhood. Others find that mislearned motor skills present problems: one of my patients continued to have difficulty tying his shoes even into adulthood, though he was extremely skilled at mechanical tasks such as fixing broken watches. Again, we see that the CVS circuits respond in specific ways: one function may be impaired, while others operate with efficiency.

If your inner ear—your sensory processor—is malfunctioning, you may also experience the perseveration exhibited by the eyes when they fix on something or return to it like a needle on a scratched record. To understand this, recall Josh, the young boy in Chapter Five. His teacher wrote, "He seems so tuned into things that he 'gets stuck' in or on them. For example, if he's writing something, he may continue to write the same sentence over and over again until he's off the page and onto the desk. Or if he's playing with a ball in the school yard, he'll keep bouncing it again and again in a compulsive sort of way." This broken-record effect appears in a wide variety of behavior patterns related to inner-ear dysfunction. The eye becomes stuck to a word, the pen to a letter, the mind to a thought or action. Moreover, the patterns can be affected positively by compensating, or negatively by circumstances such as fatigue, infection, or trauma. At times memory traces have been subconsciously imprinted and stored—but there are retrieval problems. This can be clearly and dramatically shown when treated patients suddenly recognize and spell words they apparently didn't know before—without any additional tutoring or learning.

SENSE OF DIRECTION, SENSE OF TIME

You will recall that your CVS is like a compass system. Via the fluid-filled sacs and canals of the vestibular apparatus, it reflexively indicates spatial relationships such as right and left, up and down, front and back. If the CVS apparatus is not working properly, patients become confused and sometimes resort to devising compensatory methods for right and left. For example, some patients wear a ring or watch on one hand, while others recall which hand has a scar or was broken or was used to pledge allegiance.

Your compass system directs all body functions: sensory, motor, speech, thought, even biophysical patterns. One sequence may be misdirected or scrambled while another remains unaffected, or is compensated for and appears unaffected. Some patients become easily confused about where they're going and how to get there, while others, through compensatory techniques, develop especially keen directional skills. Two examples illustrate this point: Josh's father could "get lost just going around the block," his wife told me. Yet Jerry's spatial difficulties occurred *only* when he was driving the car; when friends asked him for the best route to take, he was able to use a road map to give flawless directions.

The inner ear is also a pacemaker imparting time and rhythm to various sensory and motor skills. Some patients who lack the rhythm supplied by the CVS do poorly in sports, or cannot dance or talk without stuttering. This same rhythm may be impaired while reading—thus some refer to themselves as "reading stutterers." Others have difficulty playing a musical instrument (unless they use compensatory techniques such as toe-tapping or playing near a metronome.) Moreover, a dysfunctioning inner-ear system may result in difficulty or delay in sensing time. Such a problem can cause the "insatiability" referred to in Chapter Eight: a minute seemed like an hour to fourteen-year-old Margaret, whose dysfunctional sense of time caused her to need instant gratification. In a similar way, twelve-year-old Scott, whose favorite phrase seemed to be "I want," moved from one item or activity to the next without pause. Feeling that time stretched out endlessly—and unbearably—before him, Scott tried to shorten the hours of his day by filling them with as many things and events as possible.

Because of a poor sense of time, some individuals with ADD have difficulty making time projections as well. Recall Sally K., whose husband told me she "confused past and present events and memories. She can tell the time with her wristwatch, but cannot figure out what time it will be in ten minutes." For other patients, the time involved with traveling causes problems. How long will it take to get from point A to point B? If you have Type III ADD, you may be compulsively late or early because your malfunctioning CVS interferes with your frame of reference for point A and/or B.

Although some individuals with ADD can intuitively measure time spans down to split seconds, they still may have trouble deciphering an ordinary watch. As you might have guessed, malfunctions in CVS circuitry manifest themselves in a variety of ways: one person may have difficulty recalling numerals, while another may be stumped by hand representation—i.e., which hands tell minutes and which tell hours. Still others get confused by concepts such as clockwise and counterclockwise, or before and after.

To compensate for their difficulties telling time, a number of my patients have purchased digital watches. Although such watches have been a great help for many with ADD, they have presented difficulties for others. If you'll recall what has been said about "transposition" problems caused by a dysfunctional CVS, you can understand why: 7:15 may easily be misread as 7:51 or any reversal combination thereof.

SPEECH AND GRAMMAR

Josh's older brother began stammering and slurring his words at the age of fourteen; only when he reached adolescence did each word become a "giant hurdle" he couldn't overcome. What accounts for these and other speech problems found in some patients with ADD? As discussed, the inner-ear system—your internal clock—imparts timing and rhythm to various motor tasks. If your speech timing is off, you may stutter, or exhibit other dysrhythmic speech patterns. Poor speech timing can also result in rapid speech or unusually slow, slurred, monotonous speech that lacks modulation or inflection. Among people with ADD, the internal "clock" may slow down or speed up at an early age, or it may run smoothly for years and then rather suddenly become dysfunctional.

The most common speech disturbances found among those with ADD are input and output speech lags. In the presence of drifting sound input, many individuals will hear the sound and not know its meaning until some time later. If the sound sequence coming into the brain drifts, it will take the thinking brain several seconds or even minutes to compensate for the disturbance. Patients like Carla frequently ask "What?" or "Come again?" Such reflex responses allow the patient time to compensate for drifting input and to eventually know what has been said. Unfortunately, however, the reflex response technique can lead to misunderstandings. Carla's husband thought she was hard of hearing. Explained Stephen B., "People sometimes think I'm not listening—because while they're speaking I'm still trying to understand what they said previously."

If the motor speech responses drift, or if there are impaired word memory or concentration mechanisms, then there will be a lag between the intention to say something and the actual motor speech response. After his accident, and even after sessions with a speech therapist, Jerry knew what he wanted to say, "but the words just wouldn't come out. I spoke slowly, hesitantly, and erratically." His thinking brain had to compensate for underlying impairments in CVS-based or reflexive sequential speech functioning. In some cases, memory disturbances for word and thought recall may so complicate the spontaneous speech flow that people with ADD develop "loose," rambling, and disjointed speaking styles. As Debbie L. explained it, "If I'm in a conversation when these word blocks occur, I get embarrassed, pause while searching for the right words, then make excuses for not completing the thought while I furiously try to grasp the elusive word that seems to be right on the tip of my tongue. Usually by then, I've rambled off the subject."

What about the slips of the tongue that Alan, the building contractor, experienced? For example, intending to say "socket," he inadvertently said "sprocket" instead. And what about the use of "bad" verbal grammar that plagued Jack, the editor, and Sally K., the college-educated housewife? Why did their speech have a rambling quality to it, and why did they sometimes resort to inappropriate word choices such as "ain't"? Directional disturbances in the circuitry of the CVS frequently affect speech processing and result in word and even thought reversals. For this reason, some people with ADD are prone to so-called Freudian slips, saying words out of sequence, using inappropriate words, reversing directions such as up and down, and even mistakenly choosing inadequate grammatical expressions.

Not all individuals with ADD will have speech disturbances. When they do, their problems vary in intensity and quality; oftentimes, their speech difficulties are subtle and are elicited only upon careful questioning.

PHOBIAS AND RELATED MENTAL AND BEHAVIORAL DISORDERS

Now that you have studied the ADD case material presented thus far, it should be obvious that people with ADD have difficulty processing motion input and are therefore prone to motion-related phobias—fears of moving elevators, escalators, cars, planes, trains, buses, carnival rides, crowds, etc. Because imbalance mechanisms result from a dysfunctioning inner ear, these people may also experience fears of heights, bridges, even walking.

They also have problems processing and filtering sound—some hear too much, others too little. Josh tuned in to irrelevant sounds and often complained of excessive noise levels—he'd cover his ears when he heard a siren or thunder. Many such individuals develop sound-related phobias because they literally cannot filter out excessive noise. Jane L. is a registered nurse. Due to her malfunctioning inner ear, which caused auditory distractibility problems, or difficulty filtering out background noise, group conversations "all blurred together." As a result, she had trouble hearing what her friends had to say. "I get embarrassed and feel stupid in these situations," she told me, "and I avoid them whenever possible." Is it any wonder Jane developed a phobia related to restaurants?

In addition, because the scanning mechanisms of such individuals periodically become fixed or stuck to sensory impressions, thoughts, and motor events, they are prone to obsessive-compulsive or perseverated symptoms. In a sense, thoughts are perseverated in much the same way as a word on a page is perseverated. When the mind gets stuck on a thought (an obsession), the result is a "broken-needle" behavior pattern (a compulsion), such as the need to touch something, move something, or do something over and over again. Joan S., the schoolteacher, provides a good example of perseverated thinking. Before leaving for work every morning, she explained, "I run back to the apartment several times to make sure I've turned off the lights, or the iron or toaster. If I don't recheck things, I'll feel upset all day long." Like many people with ADD, Joan had a physiologically based inability to suppress a recurring thought, which resulted in a need to act on that thought repeatedly. In addition, her memory was faulty. As a result, she was driven to check, recheck, and then check again—never knowing or remembering with certainty whether she had completed a vital task. No wonder these individuals are characterized by doubts and indecisiveness!

As you recall, one of the functions of the inner-ear system is to control and regulate motion-related mechanisms. Therefore, any inner-ear dysfunction and resulting anxiety may predispose some people with ADD to rapid and long-lasting anxiety buildups and anxiety states. When Sally K. became nervous, she would "get dizzy, nauseous, say the room is spinning and have to hold on to something or someone." her husband explained. "This often happens in crowds or when she has to deal with people who intimidate her." Because of a defective inner-ear system, Sally did indeed suffer from anxiety or "panic attacks," and as a result, she developed a phobia related to crowds.

What other phobias may develop because of a dysfunctioning inner-ear system? Some individuals with ADD develop compass-related phobias—they fear new places and thus avoid traveling. If you're wondering why, ask yourself this: If one's sense of direction and memory for direction are significantly impaired, isn't it reasonable to want to avoid straying into new or disorienting situations?

Patients with ADD sometimes develop school phobias; in these cases, the phobia represents an unconscious attempt to avoid the emotionally devastating and humiliating feelings of stupidity triggered by academic frustration.

We can also add to our list agoraphobia—the imbalance mechanism makes individuals feel dizzy when crossing an unfamiliar or wide-open space. Remember how Jerry felt off balance and "would trip over any little thing" that was in his path? It should now become clear why he said, "I became quite fearful of any place where I was apt to fall. . . . I wouldn't even try to walk down the block alone."

By now, you may be wondering whether all phobic behavior among people with ADD is caused by a dysfunctional inner-ear system. The answer is "not quite." Certainly there are those individuals who develop "realistic" phobias (Type I)—their problems occur after traumatic exposure to a real and present danger. Others develop "neurotic" phobias (Type II), which are related to some repressed childhood trauma (usually sexual and/or aggressive in nature) and are triggered by some symbolic reminder of that trauma during a current emotional conflict. Yet my research indicates that the realistic and neurotic mechanisms together account for less than 10 percent of all phobic behavior among people with ADD; the other *90 percent* is inner-ear-related (Type III)!

Now that I have provided you with a qualitative analysis of the wide-ranging symptoms characterizing ADD or ADD-H, it is important to offer a reminder: A person with an impaired inner-ear system may experience varying degrees of any or all of the symptoms presented in this chapter, especially since most of the symptoms can be veiled by a variety of compensatory techniques. Moreover, the appearance, disappearance, or intensification of symptoms, as well as the many possible variations and combinations of symptoms, may be affected by fatigue, allergies, dyes, toxins, metabolic and chemical disorders, mononucleosis, ear infections, concussions, or any other factor that can destabilize the inner-ear system. With that in mind, now take a look at your answers to the self-test that appeared in Chapter Two. How many questions did you answer with a "yes"?

If you suspect that you or a loved one may be suffering from Type III ADD, you are probably wondering: Can I be helped? In the pages that follow, you'll meet individuals who have been successfully treated with medication and behavioral techniques. As you will see, many of them have attained a personal level of total concentration. Hopefully, their stories will convince you that you can, too!

CHAPTER XIII

Responses to Medication

Throughout this book, I have mentioned that special medications can be extremely helpful in alleviating—or in some cases, eliminating—many of the symptoms of ADD. In this chapter, I will discuss specifically what those medications are, how they work, and how I determine the best dosages. Along the way, I will also answer many of the questions you may have had about medication: Are there dangerous, long-lasting side effects? What short-term side effects are there? What do I tell my patients before they start medical treatment? How long do patients have to remain on medication?

Before answering those questions, however, I would like to share with you a series of progress reports that contain the observations and insights of parents and patients. As you read them, keep in mind that approximately *80 percent* of my patients experience such responses with the treatment program I am currently using in my practice. Hopefully, as new medications come on the horizon, the success rate will be even greater.

TYPICAL RESPONSES

Josh

Of all the patients you've read about so far, perhaps Josh is the one you remember the best. At the beginning of Chapter Five, I posed this question: Why can't Josh concentrate? As you might have guessed, the answer to the question was relatively simple. He was suffering from an inner-ear dysfunction. After he was placed on a medication regimen for several months, his mother wrote:

"I never thought I would be writing this letter. It seemed impossible to even hope that a small amount of medication could help Josh, much less perform such a miracle—but that is what has happened! I can't believe we once worried that he might be mentally retarded. . . . he's doing fantastically well! He calmed down almost immediately after being put on Ritalin and the other medications you prescribed. He can stay with a task for long stretches of time now; he doesn't burn out the way he used to. His temper also seems to be more in control; no more flying off the handle! It's just such a relief for my husband and me!

"A couple of weeks after being on the medication, something remarkable happened that I want to share with you. We were all sitting and watching TV. Josh seemed really interested in the program—I think if I'd have waved my hand in front of his face, he wouldn't have seen it! Then his brother walked into the room and asked Josh if he wanted to play a computer game. Instead of being easily distracted by his brother, and jumping up and running out of the room, he very calmly said, 'Shhhh . . . Not right now. Maybe when I'm finished here,' and he returned to watching the program . . . very intently! That may not seem remarkable to you, Dr. Levinson, but to us, it meant that Josh has finally learned to focus on one thing at a time! This new-found ability is also operating at school. His teachers say he can stick with a subject as long as other kids do. For us, that's nothing short of miraculous.

"P.S. As you probably know, I still haven't been able to convince my husband or my other son to visit you and talk about their concentration problems. But now that they're seeing Josh improve so much, I wouldn't be surprised if they change their minds in the very near future. I hope so!"

Jeffrey

Jeffrey, a young man who described "blanking out" episodes, recently wrote to me of his progress since taking medication:

"The first and most noticeable change is the removal of a sense of 'strain' in my head. This is difficult to describe, but the medication definitely seems to be having a considerable calming effect. Everything is just easier and more natural to do, without anxiety and effort. Without excessive concentration to force things in and out of my head. In other words, I don't have to concentrate as hard to get things done, on the one hand, and I can concentrate for much longer periods without fatiguing or distraction on the other. In fact, I feel more awake and alert at the end of a day's work now than I did prior to the medications.

"My handwriting has certainly improved. I do much better at maintaining horizontal lines on unlined paper, with much less of a tendency to shift from lower case to upper case at random as I write. I can perform coordinated physical activity with both hands much more readily than before; I can shuffle and deal a deck of cards with ease, for instance. I have a much better sense of 'spatial location,' too. I feel a 3-D awareness now, especially when driving. I am much less prone to mental fatigue at the end of the day. Overall, there is still room for improvement, particularly in self-confidence, but I have a definite sense of progress, and am confident that the process will continue."

Six months after he wrote the above letter, Jeffrey sent me another progress report:

"I am very satisfied with my progress to date. I have felt and noticed continuing improvement in a variety of areas, which include improved concentration and alertness, decreased distractions, even with anxiety; increased general awareness of surroundings; ability to follow what is going on around me; improved coordination, especially in terms of handwriting and shuffling/dealing cards, or working at my computer terminal (typing in data is much faster now).

"More good news—in terms of *socializing*, I have much greater confidence in my views and abilities, with willingness to defend them. Now, I'm much more likely to engage in casual conversation, and am much more in control of my life and decisions."

Ellen

Ellen is a fourth-grader who had complained of severe difficulties with concentration, distractibility, impulsivity, and restlessness associated with dizziness throughout her young life. Because of the dizziness, words blurred on the page, and Ellen had extreme difficulty writing.

After Ellen was placed on medication, her mother noted the following improvements:

"What a change we've seen in Ellen! She no longer suffers from dizzy spells. And she can keep her mind on her work at school, without constant fidgeting and distractibility. You may remember that we told you that her teacher reported that Ellen had been prone to these symptoms as well as rocking her head back and forth and stuttering on occasion. All these symptoms have virtually disappeared in the six months she's been on medication. Schoolwork no longer frustrates her. As she has more successes, she feels good about herself. Would you believe this? The other day, she actually told me she was looking forward to doing her homework! And when we read together, she often interrupts and asks, 'Mommy, can I try it?' And she will, in a new tireless and determined way. As far as I'm concerned, medication has given us a brand-new Ellen!"

Lana

Lana, a forty-seven-year-old housewife, wrote to me two months after she began taking medication:

"I am happy to say my energy level is up. I feel more confident, enough so that I decided to go back to college and finish my bachelor's degree that was started many years ago. Now, I not only feel capable (I have a 3.9 GPA to maintain!) but I'm doing it. It's difficult—only because I want to learn everything, do everything, and my time doesn't permit that. But I am taking physiology. And for me it is so complex that in the past I would have had to rewrite everything in my own words to be able to concentrate and memorize. It is much easier to concentrate on my tasks. I used to have trouble staying awake while reading. But now I study physiology for *hours* at a time without frustration, fatigue, 'burn-out' or distractions (unless I have to stop for some reason). Without the medication I couldn't do this—I'd really be struggling! I am able to stay focused on schoolwork and ignore other things if it's necessary (housework, etc.). My speech is improving, too. I am not so tense about speaking and my words flow better. Recall is better, too. My written spelling is not as much improved as I would like. *I know the spelling, have always been good at it*—I just keep skipping letters when I write! I am more relaxed than I used to be, have more energy to do important things. I can even read while riding in a bus or car. Hallelujah!

"The 'world out there' doesn't feel so difficult as it did before. Now I feel more confident than I had before. And I want to get into something I love—and really put a lot into it *and* get a lot out of it!"

Norman

Fifty-year-old Norman is Lana's husband. Norman began taking medication in January of 1989. Here is an excerpt from his progress report, written in June:

"All my life I have suffered from both severe concentration and completion problems, including anxiety culminating in panic attacks, as well as a fear of heights. I am now calm! Fearless! I concentrate for endless periods, without fatigue, frustration, and self-accusations. And things just naturally get done without endless diversions and procrastinations. My temper is better, too. My tolerance is infinitely improved. And I'm not so impulsive. I just don't say and do things without thinking first anymore. It's like doing and thinking go together now, welded. Before, it seemed they were separate and had little to do with one another. It is as if I have been set free. I am comfortable (comfortable! imagine that!) discussing in detail my medical history with family and acquaintances. My sense of shame is gone.

"Dr. Levinson, *I am convinced most alcoholics and many with criminal traits would benefit immeasurably from inner-ear treatment.* Since I have been on medication my inner craving or appetite for a glass of wine is gone. It's as if that part of me has passed away. It is my conviction that society cannot afford not to test every person and to make available medications when needed. As you can see, I am very hopeful for my continued excellent progress."

Nathan

After eleven-year-old Nathan had been on medication for one week, his mother wrote the following progress report:
"We noticed changes right away. Nathan started doing his homework and didn't get bored, distracted, tired, or frustrated. Prior to medication he wasn't paying attention at school and invariably was reported to be restless, daydreaming, and even out of control. Now he's gone up two grades in school. In science, he never got higher than a *C-*; now he's getting *B +*. His reading grades were always in the *D* range—they're *B +*, too. On a scale of one to ten, math has improved to about nine. He used to say he could hear everybody talking at once. Lately, he's not so distractible—he hears more foreground activity and less background. He's also improved socially. He's much more likely to wait his turn on the playground and let the other kids go first. Before, he was impatient and completely impulsive, acting on what he felt rather than what he thought. I've also noticed that he can recall facts much more easily than he used to, even in subjects he's not interested in. That's *very new* for Nathan"

Anthony

Within three months of beginning medication, Anthony, thirty-two, sent the following letter:
"After taking medication for a few weeks, I've found that my concentration span has increased beyond my wildest expectations. In fact, I never knew how bad I was until things improved. Now, I'm amazed at how 'well' I did before with so little. Before, I'd get down on

myself something awful. Now I'm calmer. Not so restless. And not driven to drift from thing to thing and person to person. I can actually stick with just one thing until I'm finished with it. Before, I'd start ten things and finish zero.

"Words on a page don't seem to jump around as much as they used to. And the letters don't reverse themselves anymore. As a result, my interest and concentration in reading has increased. And I'm more relaxed when I do it. Also, *what* I read seems to stay in my head longer. I'm focused, and neither driven to distractions nor looking for them. They've suddenly disappeared!

"It used to be that I could not understand basic algebra. Now I can. I always used to get confused about left and right. Now they're as different as night and day. I also have a much better sense of direction, and that's a godsend. And as I said, my attention span is so much improved. I'm now able to keep my mind on a subject, and I feel I can remember things about it better.

"One thing really surprised me about the medication: I no longer slur my words, and I don't hesitate as much when speaking. With all these improvements, I don't feel stupid anymore. And I don't fly off the handle at every little thing. Because I feel more confident, I'm spending more time socializing with peers. And I don't have to hide anymore!"

Marsha

In a recent progress report, twenty-six-year-old Marsha described how medications affect her:

"Last week, I went to my MBA finance graduate-school night class and didn't take my medication. What a disaster! I was completely disorganized again, and hyper. Really, really hyper! My mind, body, and words began racing again. But not in any coordinated and integrated manner. My mind and concentration were as disheveled as my dress and writing. In fact, my tutor, who attends class with me, had to help me decipher and recopy my notes. And he told me how foggy, sleepy, and distracted I seemed.

"Well, tonight I took my medication before going to class. What a difference! My tutor commented afterward what a dramatic difference he saw in one week. He was surprised at how accurate, organized, and thorough I and my notes were. How effectively I participated in class. And how I asked the professor pertinent questions to clarify the lecture. I felt wonderful!

"Just last week, I left class feeling despondent and discouraged. Tonight I left feeling terrific and looking forward to maybe another *A* this semester."

Steven

For most of his life, Steven, fifty-seven, had trouble concentrating, preventing distractions, and completing tasks. He also was frustrated by difficulties with spelling, reading, and memory. Now on medication, Steven reports:

"Although I expected some improvement in my concentration, I was not prepared for the intensity and span of the changes I noted. It is just amazing. I never really thought my '3 *R*'s' and my spelling would ever change. Certainly not my memory.

"I've read more books (with help of tapes) than I've ever read before. Also, I don't have to go back and read over what I've just read as often as I did two years ago. My writing seems naturally straighter and more readable. And spelling is becoming more fluent. I make fewer mistakes. I'm still having trouble with mathematics, but there's progress. And I'm really pleased with my memory improvements: I can remember names of books and authors and titles. The names of the wives of my business customers are remembered with ease."

Michael

Twenty-four-year-old Michael, a university student, has taken prescribed medications for roughly one year. He describes his progress as follows:

"Distractions are gone. Even my crazy daydreaming—to the point where I didn't even hear people talking! All of them! So now I can really concentrate and finish things. I'm also calmer, less restless. And not so impulse-prone.

"My ability to read has also improved. And I have become interested in different intellectual areas because of all these improvements. My ability to write and put together meaningful compositions has increased. I have begun to decrease my use of printing while increasing my use of cursive writing. I am using periods, commas, colons, and semicolons more in my writing. And I am now using more words, and my writing speed has increased. I also find it easier to grasp the meaning of new concepts, not only in mathematics but also in other fields. I also feel more at ease talking because I can think of the words and thoughts to say. Before, I'd get lost between my inner and outer distractions as well as my difficulties remembering words and thoughts. It used to be all but impossible to carry on an intelligent and truthful conversation.

"Before treatment, I would begin many of my days with either dizziness, headache, or nausea. This feeling would last until noontime. Since being on medication, I no longer experience these symptoms, except when I forget to take my medication for a few days. I also have increased feelings of internal steadiness because I now feel that I am not going to lose my balance."

Ryan

The mother of six-year-old Ryan describes in detail the "before and after" effect of medication on her son:

"We've been through a nightmare, but thanks to you we feel hopeful about our son. Before Ryan was put on medication, he was by anyone's standards a little, impulse-ridden monster. At one point, we thought he was schizophrenic. He was very, very hyper and high-strung. And he would get frustrated very easily. He couldn't deal with anything! He'd cling to me constantly, but would fight with his sister and push his dad away. His driven behavior was downright scary at times. At the age of two, for instance, he got hold of a butcher knife, then pushed a chair up to the kitchen counter, hopped on the microwave, and got up onto the fridge, where he found a bowl of oranges and began stabbing them with the knife! Another time, he grabbed a 'childproof' bottle of medication my daughter was taking and managed to rip it open; he drank the whole bottle! We tried to get him to vomit it up, but he didn't. And that was the only night in his life that he slept through the night.

"And as you know, he had no concentration span to speak of. And everything and anything unimportant and dangerous would distract and direct him. All my relatives and neighbors used to tell me that I was just too lenient with him, that I wasn't disciplining him enough. But whatever I tried—spanking, putting him in his room—wouldn't faze him. He'd throw fits if I put him into a corner. Sometimes, if I was alone with him, he could be really sweet. But at other times, he wouldn't let me cuddle him or read to him. It was like we were dealing with two different children. And neither one of them could be disciplined—or learn from discipline. In fact, it actually made him worse.

"Now that he's been on medication for six months, he's much better than he ever was—and than I secretly feared he'd ever be. In fact, he has just said, 'Gee, Mom, I don't feel *mean* anymore.' He's not *mad or aggressive*. And he doesn't hit and fight with his sister for no apparent reason. And he doesn't cling to me anymore. If we're at a shopping mall, he skips out in front of me and sings. This is a happy child! At school, he's participating more and more. His teachers now love him. That's a first. And they claim he's now focused and attentive. Before, they literally told me he was hopeless and should be put either in an institution or special school. Maybe it was just for the teacher's well-being? But they were right, too!

"Before medication, he could never look anybody in the eye. Now he makes eye contact all the time. In the past, if his teacher called on him, he would drop his head down on the desk. Now he responds. And doesn't get nervous if he doesn't know the answer to a question.

"Interestingly, you can tell when the medication has worn off—he becomes loud and obnoxious. When this happens, he'll come to me and say he needs his medicine. We're relieved to know he has ADD. And to know, finally, that he can be helped. Thank you so much!

"And I almost forgot: He started reading. And his writing and speech are much better, too. But these improvements are secondary to me. I was willing to settle for his being illiterate. But his prior behavior and attitude were frightening—and dangerous. There's just no way he could have made it through life without seriously hurting someone—or getting hurt!"

At this point, you may have the feeling that medication is something of a panacea for ADD. You've read of its "miraculous" powers, of its ability to virtually change the personality of the person who is taking it. The fog lifts. Concentration is enhanced in time and span. Distractibility is minimized or eliminated. Impulsivity and activity levels are normalized. And mood and anxiety levels stabilize. Memory improves. The poor student becomes an achiever. Although these and other positive changes do occur via medication, they do not take place for all patients, nor do they always occur in such a dramatic fashion. Indeed, in some cases, the therapeutic effect of medications appears to decrease with time or when use is interrupted. It is as if the body develops a tolerance or resistance to the medications, rendering them ineffective. Of course, this phenomenon occurs with many medications, not just the ones I use for the treatment of ADD.

Unfortunately, there is no way to predict how you, as an individual, will respond to any of the medications listed below. But there are steps you can take to ensure that you will find the medication or combination of medications that work best for you:

1. First and foremost, do not experiment with these or any other medications on your own. Even though many can be acquired over the counter, that does not mean you should take their purchase lightly. All medicines, however simple, may have side effects—sometimes serious—particularly when taken in improper does or at the same time as other medications.
2. Work willingly *with your doctor*; over a period of time, he or she may have to "experiment" with types of medications and dosages before finding the one medication or combination that works best for you. Remember—only an experienced physician is qualified to monitor your response to medication and to predict the benefits and/or side effects that can follow from medical use of given drugs and vitamins, or any combination of vitamins, chemicals, or medications, in light of a given

patient's height, weight, general physical condition, and sensitivity to chemical substances.

3. Try to be patient during the trial-and-error stage of finding the right medication. As I mentioned earlier, not all individuals attain positive results immediately. As you begin treatment, expect *gradual* changes, rather than radical ones. Also be aware that some persons will develop a tolerance or resistance to certain medications. If this occurs, do not give up hope—for every four or five medications, there will be one that works for you.

WHAT MEDICATIONS ARE HELPFUL IN TREATING ADD?

In treating persons with ADD, I have found that a wide range of chemical structures can prove helpful, including antimotion-sickness medications, antihistamines, stimulants, antidepressants, and vitamins. They act as "fine-tuners" of the inner-ear system, and the chemical structure of each one appears to fine-tune a specific pattern of sensorimotor channels, much like a guided missile strikes a targeted area. Because of this specificity, I often find that *combinations* of these chemicals will result in the best possible response. For example, in a recent study involving one hundred children, I discovered that a combination of antihistamines *and* stimulants brought about a positive response in 88.9 percent of patients with ADD-like symptoms.

CVS Stabilizing Medications and Chemicals Found Helpful

Chemical Name	Brand Name
Stimulants	
Methylphenidate	Ritalin
Dextroamphetamine	Dexedrine
Pemoline	Cylert
Pseudoephedrine	Sudafed
Methamphetamine	Desoxyn
Phenmetrazine	Preludin
Phentermine	Eutonyl

Antidepressants

Tricyclics

Imipramine hydrochloride	Tofranil
Amitriptyline hydrochloride	Elavil
Desipramine	Norpramin

Monoamine Oxidase Inhibitors (MAOIs)*

Isocarboxazid	Marplan
Phenelzine	Nardil
Tranylcypromanine	Parnate
Pargyline	Eutonyl

Phenothiazines

Thiroizadine	Mellaril

Serotonine Uptake Inhibitors

Fluoxetine	Prozac

Antimotion-Sickness Medications

Meclizine hydrochloride	Antivert
Cyclizine hydrochloride or lactate	Marezine
Dimenhydrinate	Dramamine
Piracetam (Not in use in US)	Nootropil

Antihistamines with CVS-Stabilizing Properties

Diphenhydramine hydrochloride	Benadryl
Brompheniramine maleate	
Phenylephrine hydrochloride	Dimetapp
Phenylpropanolamine hydrochloride	

Other Drugs

Ergoloid mesylates	Hydergine
Deanol Acetominobenzoate	Deaner

Vitaminlike Substances

Vitamin B Complex
Gingerroot
Niacin
B-6
B-12
Lecithin or Choline

162

*Antipanic Medications***

Diazepam	Valium
Alprazolam	Xanax
Lovazepam	Ativan

* The MAOI's are used primarily for adults.
** The antipanic medications—including the B-blockers—were shown to be CVS stabilizers, thus explaining their efficacy with vertigo and related symptoms, especially those due to CVS-determined anxiety disorders.

HOW DO I DETERMINE THE BEST DOSES?

If your doctor has prescribed medications for you in the past, you may have noticed that he used the *Physician's Desk Reference* or another manual to assist him, and that he took into account your age and weight when calculating the dosage he wanted you to take. While such techniques are critical to proper treatment with certain medications, my clinical experience has indicated that with medications used for the treatment of ADD, the therapeutic dosages often have little relationship to such factors as age and weight. Indeed, I have found that each patient has his or her own sensitivity and reactivity to the medications listed above—in other words, a personal threshold. As a result, a "sensitive" adult may need only one-eighth the recommended dosage, whereas a child may benefit from twice the average dosage. This difference among patients underscores an important point: No one should experiment with dosages unless under the supervision of a qualified physician.

I have found that recommended dosages are usually too high for half my patients and not high enough for the other half. For this reason, I start all patients on approximately one-quarter of the average therapeutic dosage and then observe their responses. Depending on the results, I may lower or increase the medication.

HOW DO THESE MEDICATIONS WORK?

Although scientists have spent years trying to figure out how these medications work, no one to date has unraveled their mysterious nature. What's important, though, is that they *do* work. Acting like chemical "fine-tuners," they readjust impaired inner-ear and related mechanisms and allow sensory input and motor output to become better tuned, sequenced, and coordinated.

Do these medications cure an inner-ear disturbance? Unfortunately, the answer is no—at present, there are no medications or surgical procedures that are capable of accomplishing that feat. Instead—and this is certainly good news—these medications seem to *teach* the brain how to permanently compensate for the underlying disturbance.

COULD THIS BE A "PLACEBO" EFFECT?

Stimulant and antidepressant medications have been previously proven pharmacologically effective for ADD subjects in double-blind scientific studies by a wide variety of researchers. To date, these very same double-blind studies have not yet been performed for the antimotion-sickness medications. However, for many, many reasons, it appears clear that the therapeutic effect of all three categories of medication are "real" for the most part rather than just due to wishful thinking. As you've seen in the many case histories presented thus far, the improvements are as real and as specific as the patients themselves.

Most of my ADD patients have been from pillar to post in search of help. They have tried every type of therapy imaginable. They have tried every type of medication imaginable. But no matter how desperate these patients are, nothing helped.

Yes, these patients have always wanted to get better. They have always hoped that each type of treatment they tried would rid them of their symptoms. And they would have been thrilled by any improvements—even those caused by a placebo. Yet few lasting improvements were seen.

So why do these other types of treatment so often fail while the medications I prescribe continually bring about such clear-cut improvements? Clearly it is not because of placebo effects. Otherwise such improvements would have been noted with other treatments as well (and all medications would work for all patients). The antimotion-sickness and related CVS-stabilizing medications work because they do something no other type of treatment does: they treat the inner-ear system, the physiological root of ADD.

HOW LONG DO PATIENTS HAVE TO REMAIN ON MEDICATION?

It would be wonderful—and cost-effective—if ADD patients could take medication for only a week and respond favorably forever after, but such is not the case. Most patients need to stay on medication anywhere from one to four years. Of course, depending on how one metabolizes the medication, the period of treatment can vary in duration. Some patients require short periods of treatment, others require longer periods. In any case, after one to four years of treatment, 80 percent of my successfully treated patients have continued to do as well off the medication as they did on it.

ARE THERE SHORT-TERM SIDE EFFECTS?

For some patients, the medications I prescribe cause no side effects whatsoever. But for others, medical treatment may result in short-term fatigue, irritability, moodiness, and even intensification of various inner-ear-related symptoms. By reducing or discontinuing certain of the dosages, however, all of these side effects can be readily reversed. If you do experience a problem—which usually indicates the dosage is too high or that it is inappropriate for you as an individual—make sure to let your doctor know immediately. No side effects should be tolerated!

WHAT ABOUT DANGEROUS LONG-LASTING SIDE EFFECTS?

The medications I have used to treat inner-ear dysfunctions for the past twenty-five years have been around for many, many years. They have been used safely for other conditions without any observable or recorded irreversible side effects. That is not to say that the wrong dosage, or treatment without a doctor's supervision, cannot result in moodiness, tiredness, irritability, and even intensification of ADD symptoms. Such problems can occur, but they can be minimized or avoided if low dosages are administered by a physician and if patients are treated sensibly and carefully observed. In cases where long-term use causes immunity, the doctor need only make a slight change in medication to "restart" a favorable response.

WHAT SHOULD DOCTORS TELL PATIENTS BEFORE THEY START MEDICAL TREATMENT?

As you know, nothing in life is without cost or risk, however great or small. Medications may cause side effects and thus entail a certain risk, whereas untreated symptoms can and do cause emotional (and sometimes physical) damage and pain. Thus, one should weigh the alternatives before agreeing to treatment. No one should be *told* what to do. All patients and doctors should discuss the possible advantages of treatment before a decision is made.

When I present the facts of treatment to my patients, I may tell them what I would do, or have done, in treating members of my own family. I also discuss alternative therapies for ADD that have been found to be helpful. (These are detailed in Chapter Sixteen). But most important, I tell them to think things out for themselves and to do whatever they feel is correct for them. After all, clinicians and experts are only professionally responsible for the well-being of their patients. Patients are totally responsible for themselves. Therefore, they must be aware of the pain and consequences of professional errors and unknowns.

I respect patients who raise questions and express different opinions. And I work with them to the extent that I can, in the manner I would like my colleagues to work with me and with members of my own family. All patients with ADD need and deserve this kind of respect and attention.

Throughout my twenty-five years of clinical practice, I have found that patients are often skeptical when they hear that they, too, can be helped. This is a very natural reaction, and it should not be ignored. In fact, to help patients gain confidence in my work and in the treatments I am currently using, I will often put them in touch with patients who have responded favorably to treatment. Toward that end, I now urge you to turn to the next two chapters, where you'll meet many more patients who've been helped via medication. Listen carefully to their stories. Weigh the advantages of treatment against the disadvantages. Then decide for yourself whether you're ready and willing to achieve your own personal level of total concentration.

CHAPTER XIV

Transformations: More Responses to Medication

"Whatever you can do or dream you can, begin it."

Goethe

A.J.C.

Within the realm of big business, pressure is sometimes just a way of life. But for A.J.C., a victim of ADD who spent years managing 150 people and $250 million in goods annually for a huge health and beauty aids corporation, the strain of doing business couldn't be shrugged off—indeed, it threatened to overcome him. "For me, doing that job required triple work. Because I couldn't concentrate on any one thing for any length of time, I had to have four or five projects going so that I could drift from one to another and eventually get them done. It's not like I enjoyed this 'jumping game'—I couldn't function without it. As soon as I'd be stuck with any one project too long—like a half hour at a clip—I'd get bored, irritable, and restless. Even angry. And I'd be prone to impulsive decisions, just to get away. It's almost like a form of claustrophobia, but different somehow.

"And to avoid the distractions of others, I'd set up my own. That's why I needed so many projects going on simultaneously. In this way I sort of controlled the direction my mind and energies would drift to and back.

"Superficially, I acted like one of those movielike business tycoons. But inside I was devastated. I knew what I was doing, even if no one else did. And I had to perform appropriately in all my projects. They thought I was just a hyper-workaholic. Well I may have been hyper, but I had to keep myself so busy or else I would not get anything done at all. I was working far harder than I wanted, harder than was expected of me. And I had enough experience to know that I'd burn out or up sooner or later.

"When you have a tendency to reverse numbers, as I did, and you're working with a twenty-four-million-dollar budget, you've got to double-check and triple-check your numbers. I developed my own fail-safe way of catching mistakes, but I paid the price: due to the strain of having to overconcentrate, I developed an ulcer that put me in the hospital for twenty-two days. Eventually, I simply had to quit the job."

Reversing numbers wasn't A.J.C.'s only problem. "When reading, words used to jump off the page. And I would see ahead—two or three words ahead—instead of where I should have been. And thus words were reversed and skipped over. It's not that I was illiterate (I graduated from high school and had two years of college under my belt), it's just that reading was such a chore. It gave me a headache! Needless to say, schoolwork turned me off. I couldn't do algebra to save my life. And the best I ever did in school was get 'gentleman's C's. I'd cram for exams and stay in studying for a week straight. But by the time I'd get to an exam, all the information had disappeared!

"When I had to travel, I used to have this great anxiety and fear of getting lost. I had right and left problems, and a very bad sense of direction. If I had to go to Bayside in Queens, I might just as well wind up at the Empire State Building in New York City. My friends used to joke that I could get lost in a revolving door. I grew very dependent upon my wife—she's the best copilot in the world!

"I've also had severe mood swings, like being on an emotional roller coaster. I had anxiety attacks at work, and sometimes thought I was having a heart attack. Every day on the job was pressure, lots of deadlines, prices, lots of personnel to deal with. I guess I handled it fairly well. I became director of operations at one point. But deep inside I always knew I was pulling one over on them. I felt so stupid—and I had to work so hard just to stay on top of things!"

That was a year ago. Recently, A.J.C. talked with me about

what his life has been like since taking medication. What follows is an excerpt from that conversation:

"My mind is now clear and calm, not driven from job to job and distracted by all and sundry events. *I am focused.* And I can spend as much time on any given project as I need without being forced to tackle four or five others in succession. I'm still energetic, just not as hyper as before. In other words, I am physically calm as well as mentally calm.

"Even my personal life is different. My wife claims I can spend more time with her and be closer than ever before. I didn't notice that so much. But it sounds possible, since it is similar to what has been going on at work.

"Reading used to be a chore; now it's an enjoyment. Since taking medication, I can't stop reading. It's like I'm addicted to books! This change started shortly after I visited your office. And seven or eight months later, I was averaging a book a month. In one four-week period, I sat down and read an average of four hundred pages a day. My comprehension and understanding are excellent and my concentration is unbelievable! My recall is sometimes still a little vague. But now that I'm on Sudafed, it's better. We've fine-tuned the medication and I'm on the lowest dosages . . . and it still works great! Reading is like a gift. I can knock off eighty or ninety pages in an hour. I'm even reading on my lunch hours.

"My teacher used to say I just couldn't 'click' with math. Now I mess around with it on my own and don't have too much of a problem. I'm even playing around with logic and statistics now. It's like learning it all over! But now, it stays in my head. I can decipher what I'm doing, and it's a nice feeling. Before, I couldn't even read a ruler, particularly when I got up to the sixteenths. Now, I figure dimensions all the time. And it comes to me very easily. Before, I used to have to ask my associate.

"I've seen a difference in my ability to manage, too. I'm totally different in that area. In fact, on my last job—the one I took after recovering from my ulcer—my bosses thought I was the greatest thing since sliced bread. That job folded for financial reasons, so now I'm cranking up my *own* business. I'm doing great at it and expect to triple or quadruple my salary in the near future.

"As for my directional problems, they're gone. Now I can read a map. And if someone says meet me here or there, whether it's north or south or west or east, I can do it. Even if I hear directions wrong, I can figure it out. My success rate isn't always great, but it's certainly in the high eighties.

"I used to slur my words . . . I used to say 'it's ssssnowing outssside.' It's not that I was a stutterer. But I would lose total recollection of the word I wanted to use. And it would sound like I was giving someone the raspberries! Now, I don't hold back—I'm very outspoken, in fact. And what I say makes sense. It's easy!

"Taking medication is my secret. Nobody but my family knows about it. It's something I'll take to my grave. You performed a miracle on me, and I have no complaints whatsoever. My only regret is that I wish that this had been caught at a younger age. If this could have been caught at six or seven years old, maybe I would have taken a different career path, maybe in the medical field, which I've always been interested in. Perhaps I would have become vice-president of my former company. As I look back on the work I did, I think if I had to do it now, it would be a piece of cake!"

Gary

What is it like to experience a "living hell"—and then return to life again? Gary, a forty-year-old restaurant manager, recently shared his views during a telephone interview. His story provides a striking picture of his life before and after medical treatment.

"I've spent my entire life living a lie. I always knew there was something wrong with me. But just exactly what that something was, I was never sure. I guess I just always felt like I was stupid. And for a time, I was convinced that I was mentally retarded. But I managed to keep this weird thing a secret from my family and friends . . . until about four years ago. It was then that I was forced to come out of the closet.

"When I look back, it seems I was successful for a few reasons. I was hyperenergetic on the one hand and needed to work day and night or I couldn't sleep. And as it was, I really needed only a few hours to feel fully charged again in the morning. Secondly, I drove myself to achieve, no matter what it took of me and out of me. I had to prove to others—really myself—I wasn't dumb. Plus, I learned as a kid how to get by with the little I had. I was sort of street-wise—knew angles and shortcuts and developed a 'con' that fooled people into thinking I was smarter than I felt, than I really was.

"I always took or got jobs where I'd manage large numbers of people and things on my feet—never a desk job.

"As long as I was active, busy, moving and talking, nothing was too much for me. But sit me down and I was finished. There was no way I could concentrate while sitting still, forced to look or think about one stupid thing at a time. That's when I would get restless. And my mind would start daydreaming and looking around for something else to do. . . . You see, I couldn't read or write or spell . . . or anything. And sitting at a desk made things worse. I need action to function. Even if it's playing cards or gambling, where I'm using my hands and talking and interacting with a number of people at the same time.

"While I was dating this really beautiful ballet dancer, we used to meet with her friends every Tuesday night to play games like poker or Monopoly. One night, we played Trivial Pursuit. And when it came my turn to read, I said, 'Oh, I guess I forgot my glasses,' and handed the card to somebody else. My girlfriend looked at me with a funny expression on her face. She knew very well that I didn't wear glasses. Everyone else was staring at me, too. And all I could do was just sit there, red in the face. But secretly, I was relieved that the rest of them seemed to believe me.

"The next week, we got together again to finish the game. And pretty soon it was my turn to read again. I knew it was all over for me. The charade would have to come to an end now. Since I knew most of these people pretty well and was tired of lying to them, I just put the card down on the table and said, 'I'm really sorry, I'm really stupid. I can't read . . . or write.'

"Everybody was so shocked! They said, 'My god, how can that be? Every game we play, you always end up winning the second time we play it.' So I explained to them that I can memorize anything I hear and even things I see—I just can't read. Like if we're playing poker, I can remember which cards people pick up or throw down, so I can have a pretty good idea of how to play my hand. It's a technique that's saved me from a lot of embarrassment over the years.

"After that night, my friends all got together and confronted me. They said, 'Have you ever been checked out for having dyslexia?' I said, 'What's dyslexia?' Eventually, I was tested at a special-education class at the local college. And sure enough, they said I had dyslexia and ADD, too, because I was also hyper and inattentive. So I was enrolled in a class with mostly Down's Syndrome adults who were really like little kids. They'd throw spitballs at each other and write stupid love letters all the time. The class just wasn't for me! It was like being in elementary school.

"I got pretty discouraged, so I tried another specialist. He taught a form of meditation where you try to think in another place in your mind, which works if you can keep your thoughts and yourself in that place. But I had real trouble with it. *I have a hard time concentrating on anything for more than a few minutes or so.* After spending fifteen hundred dollars, I realized that this wasn't getting me anywhere."

Exasperated by failure, Gary was about to give up. Luckily, a caring relative took steps to get him the help he needed. Below, Gary explains the unexpected turn of events that helped turn his life around:

"About a year ago, my in-laws paid us a visit. At the time, I had trouble getting along with my father-in-law. He's very much an intellectual, always analyzing things, always asking questions. Well, I had a hard time keeping up with him. And so I would often cut him short and sometimes would even ignore him. After a few days, they announced they were leaving—and I figured it was because of me.

"Apparently, after they left, my father-in-law spent every spare minute in the library, trying to figure out what was wrong with me. And how he could help. He knew I was dyslexic. And I guess he thought he could find some new information that might help me. He finally picked up a copy of *Smart But Feeling Dumb* and a book on ADD, and read both of them. Then he called at two in the morning and said to my wife, 'Gary has to read these books.

You don't know what he's been going through.' So I ran out and got the books and definitely saw myself. Every page had part of me on it.

"When I took one of Dr. Levinson's tests (the 3-D Optical Scanner), where you're supposed to see several elephants moving slowly on the screen, I only saw one. My wife was there with me. And she told me she saw *seven* elephants. At that moment, I think my wife finally was able to understand what I was seeing. My eyes could only focus on one thing at a time. I literally only saw one elephant! Then I took a half a tablet of Meclizine—chewed it right there in the office. And when I looked again at the screen, it started getting clearer and brighter right away! I began to see more than one elephant! And my mind and concentration cleared, too. I immediately felt a little calmer, less restless.

"I didn't really understand how much my seeing improved until we came back to California from New York. We were coming across the Golden Gate Bridge into Sausalito and I looked at a sign and I saw 'E X I T' and I said to my wife, 'The sign says *EXIT*.' And she said, 'Of course it does.' Then I said, 'But I can see the *whole* word!' I never realized that before I was seeing only one letter at a time, and that my eyes moved from one letter to the next without seeing anything else—even a single word!

"After my first week on medication, I found that my job was so much easier! Managing eighty people, sitting down and listening to their problems, keeping track of things at the restaurant, even little details—they're so much easier to handle. I don't read novels or anything. But I read two or three newspapers a day, plus business reports. Reading feels very good—I feel like I've always known how!

"I still need to build my confidence. I have a very low opinion of myself, and that's going to take some time to get over. But the other day, I felt like a whole person. It was okay to be me. It came as a sudden rush! And recently I met with a real-estate friend of mine whom I hadn't seen in ten years. He said, 'My God, have you changed! Your self-confidence is unreal!' I don't see that yet. But I guess other people are noticing a difference.

"I think if I'd gotten the right help a lot earlier in life, I might have done a lot more with my life. Maybe made millions of dollars.

But at least now I *know* what's wrong. And what can be done about it. In fact, since taking medication I've made some business decisions that will eventually help me change careers: I now own three homes and hope to get into real estate. Now I know I can go out and take some risks. I can see things clearly at last!"

Jeremy

When Jeremy came to my office for testing, he appeared as a "Jekyll and Hyde" child. He was overactive, distracted, impulsive at home, unresponsive at school, and dyscoordinated. He also had enormous difficulty with reading. In third grade, he couldn't read a kindergarten primer. After his parents spent $25,000 on various types of "learning treatments," and despite a 123 IQ, he remained nearly uneducable and unruly, and suffered from severe memory lapses.

Two years have passed since my initial visit with Jeremy. Recently, Jeremy's mother described the effects of medication on her son:

"Since being on medication, Jeremy is like a different child. Seldom does a week go by that somebody doesn't call me about him. Parents and teachers ask me: 'What did you do? How did you get him help?' It's amazing. I have seen absolutely no adverse changes. All the changes have been good.

"His learning-disability teacher is amazed at the constant leaps and bounds he's made. For the 1987-1988 school year his math pretest score was first grade, seven months; at the end of 1988, his posttest is third grade, six months. And all that happened in just eight short months. He recently got a $C+$ in spelling. And the rest of his subjects are all A's and B's! Last year, he was three grade levels behind in English, science, and reading. Today, he's on grade level. And he hasn't had any private tutors or gone to any learning centers. He's done it on his own!

"The first three weeks after starting medication, when he'd come home from school, we just sat there laughing. Things were so much clearer for him! 'Why didn't I understand that before?' he'd say. Before medication, we spent lots of afternoons just crying over homework, trying to pound it in and get through it. I had to *physically* force him to do it. Now he does it alone, automatically, rapidly. Now he's a happy ten-year-old kid. The difference in Jeremy is like daylight and dark. Dr. Levinson, you're our knight in shining armor!

"We have survived. I see the light at the end of the tunnel. But the best part is that Jeremy sees it as well. I'll admit, we were skeptical about drug therapy. Our family members had criticized us. And so did the school system. But we had reached the point where we had tried everything else and had nothing to lose. So we figured, 'What's the worst that can happen? If the side effects are bad, we can stop it as fast as we started.' To date, there have been no bad side effects. All the effects have been good and great.

"And the best of all is that he's now a 'together' kid, and 'with it.' His mood is steady, happy. And he's calm and collected about his schoolwork, his dress, and even his room. He is no longer disorganized. And I hate to say it, but he's not a 'mess' anymore. His mind and body are at the same place at the same time. He's no longer klutzy and accident-prone. And not so high-strung and defensive . . . He's normal!"

Pete

From an early age, Pete, thirty-nine, had experienced concentration, distractibility, and memory problems, number and letter reversals, and difficulty with directions such as left and right. During my first interview with him, he told me, "When I was in school, there was always a fuzziness about me. Other kids used to call me 'spacy.' In the sixties, everyone assumed I was on drugs. But it was just that I was naturally a spacehead. I daydreamed a lot, couldn't focus in on things very well. My mind was always in a cloud, drifting all over and distracted by everything."

Fortunately, these symptoms of ADD did not deter him from becoming quite successful in business. Today he is manufacturing director for a large footwear company. However, he was tired of having to "overachieve" in order to stay on par with friends and peers. "I just figured I wasn't as smart as other people. And so

I had to be a little more creative and ingenious than my friends. I managed to do all right in school by overachieving. And I've succeeded in business because I push myself to an extraordinary extent."

A year ago, Pete was transferred to a foreign country to head up a new manufacturing division for his company. "It was a great challenge for me. And I was excited to go. But when I got there, I found I couldn't learn the language, no matter how I tried to. My 'problem' had finally caught up with me."

During a trip east, Peter sought help at my clinic. Following diagnostic evaluation, he was placed on medication. He recently described how medication affected him:

"At first, I felt terrific for about a half an hour. But then I got tremendous headaches. So I reduced the doses. After trying some of the combinations you suggested, things started stabilizing. And I'm now feeling very good. My work has improved incredibly. And I've just signed up for a language course. I'm not afraid anymore!

"My concentration has increased by more than 20 percent. I can focus much better on a problem. Everything's clearer. I can solve problems more quickly and have more time to do other things. Before, everything was sort of fuzzy. And I'd have to push myself, exert extra effort and concentration in order to get things done. Now, instead of finding an alternative route, I can do things directly. Myself!

"My memory has improved by at least 10 percent. I used to always have to write things down so I could be sure of what I had to do. Now I can just remember. If someone tells me a phone number, I know it. I don't have to write it down. It's a nice luxury not to have to have my 'props.' Before, if I lost my notes, I'd become frantic and I'd waste so much time worrying about where I put them. Now I know I'll remember things.

"My productivity has improved, too. Before medication, it would take me two hours to compose a letter to a supplier or customer. Now I can do the same letter in an hour or so, depending on the difficulty of the subject matter. And the letter is better, besides. It's focused and gets to the point instead of rambling! I'm getting things done 15 percent faster. Instead of writing five letters a day, I can produce seven or eight. Everything's going better. Everything seems easier now.

"Meetings go much more smoothly for me. I'm more efficient. I used to bring so much stress upon myself because of my inefficiencies. Now I can go directly to a problem. Let me give you an example. We have a weekly staff meeting. In the past, it would take me hours and hours of preparation before I'd go into one of these meetings. I'd be worried, wouldn't be able to sleep at night, and spent hours of preparation time on it. For our last meeting, I got the whole thing done in forty-five minutes. And the meeting was more powerful and productive than it's ever been. I have so much more confidence in myself. It's like being on *cloud nine*!

"Even my golf game has improved. I've come down from a 15 handicap to a 10. It's because I can focus better. Golf is a game of concentration, you know. I've won more tournaments, too. I used to win six out of seven. Now I'm winning nine out of ten.

"Since I've been taking medication, my peers have noticed a difference. I'm more demanding than before, in a good, positive way. And people are living up to my demands. The reports are coming out better. I'm getting quicker responses from suppliers. And faster responses on decisions from people within the company. My staff was always capable of really performing, but they needed me to bring out the best in them. Now I'm capable of doing that. In fact, it would not be an exaggeration to say that my new-found efficiency can be translated into dollars and cents: I'm worth $200,000 a year. And I'm 15 percent more efficient—which means an increase in productivity of roughly $30,000!"

Pete was not overstating the case when he said peers were noticing a difference in his behavior. Two of his employees volunteered the following information:

"I have joked with Pete that he is driving me up the wall," said his secretary of six years. "Now that he's taking medication, he catches all of my mistakes! Before, he used to let things go. . . . He'd be hesitant to correct me. Now if something is wrong, he'll tell us right out. He's more direct and to the point, and has a better philosophy. He livens us all up and keeps us on our toes. He is much more confident now, and doesn't lose his temper as much as he did before. He's able to joke around more, and doesn't take himself as seriously. Before, he didn't organize me very well, and things weren't always done on time. Now he gives more exact directions and prioritizes things better. He was always a good boss. But now he's even better."

"Pete was always well prepared for meetings," explains a company executive, "but he's really organized now. He has more information at his fingertips. He projects a better image in meetings—he's friendlier, more outgoing, more confident. As a result, meetings are more organized and focused. The big difference I see is that he can organize his thoughts better when speaking or when writing a letter. Before, he might reverse things. But not now. And he's 100 percent more confident, poised, and knowledgeable. He's in control!"

Laura

Forty-eight-year-old Laura recalls that she "never felt as good as other kids in school. . . . I never felt equal. I felt that I had a flaw, a failing, something that was going to hold me down forever." In fact, Laura's only "flaw" was a dysfunctional inner-ear system. Her condition manifested itself in a variety of symptoms, including "a general inability to concentrate without innumerable distractions . . . math blocks . . . out-of-control stress, an inability to follow directions . . . on the job, and an overwhelming desire to stay close to home because that's the only place where I didn't feel like a second-class citizen."

A year ago, Laura's diagnostic tests revealed the presence of Type III ADD. I immediately placed her on a regimen of medication. Here's just a sample of the successes she has experienced since that time:

"When I first started on medication, I felt 'draggy' for a couple of days. But then my dosage was lowered and I noticed improvement pretty much right away. I feel *so* good! I'm handling stress in ways I never thought possible. In a stressful situation, prior to medication, I'd become completely inattentive, disorganized, anxious, and sweaty. Sweat would literally run down my sides. I'm so calm now, I don't even use deodorant.

"I used to want to stay at home and be a housewife—home was my center, the only place I felt under control. Now I've re-enrolled in college, with hopes of becoming a marriage counselor. I'm even taking courses like physiology and biology. And I can handle whatever math is required, even statistics!

"During class, I really notice a difference when I'm on my medication. It's like having a zoom lens—you can zoom in close and see and concentrate on things clearly. I can hear my professor's words loud and clear now, all her words, her inflections, and her meaning. I can take it all in and assimilate it. When I'm not on medication, it's like the lens pulls back. I can't hear or see as clearly and I miss things. And I hear distracting sounds as loudly as my teacher's voice, so that at times it all sounds scrambled, blurred out.

"Now I have energy that lasts until bedtime. I'm up at five-thirty. And I'm doing exercise to keep my weight down. During the day, I can study for about six hours straight and still feel wonderful.

"Before, I didn't enjoy the process of reading. I couldn't focus on the difficult parts long enough to get it. In fact, I used to have to paraphrase every line by writing it out in order to focus on it. Now I'm able to focus on a specific activity or interest and stay with it without distractions pulling me away. When I was at home, I was constantly doing a dozen different things at the same time; it was hard to stay with one thing. Now it's much easier to stick with something. Anything—even things I dislike.

"It's kind of funny. I used to always apologize for myself, and usually felt down about myself. I blamed a lot of things on my first husband, who was always putting me down. But now that I've been on medication and look back on my life, I realize that chickens usually pick on the weakest in the barnyard. Maybe my husband was just targeting my weak spot—ADD—and taking advantage of it."

Ned

Ned, a mortgage loan officer, has "battled with negative feelings about myself for the past twenty years." Diagnosed six months ago as having Type III ADD, he told me he couldn't remember a time in his life when he "felt 'okay'—I was apologetic about everything: I was always spacy, out of it, dizzy, distracted, just plain different. My memory was poor. Seasickness was common. I didn't have a muscular body. And I was clumsy in sports. Fainting episodes and panic attacks were common. And I had severe stage fright, too. Reading was difficult, just too stressful. I've spent my entire life in a defensive position to avoid making a fool out of myself."

How has Ned responded to medication? I recently received the following progress report from him:

"I've been on the medications for two and a half months now, and I'm finding that I am a changed person. My attitude's a lot healthier now. I'm much more self-assured and feel physically calm. I feel so good that I sometimes wonder, 'Gee, is this really me?' I'm much more verbal. In fact, I have become sort of a spokesperson for a change at our company. I'm going into meetings with ideas and proposals, and have had no anxiety or panic attacks. I seem to know what I want to say and say it without losing my words, thoughts, and focus.

"I feel solidly grounded, mentally and physically. The 'fog' is gone. And my thoughts feel crystal-clear, sharp rather than fuzzy and nebulous. That's why I feel more secure talking.

"I can now actually hold a thought sequence in my mind, consider it, and decide what should be said, all automatically. Before, all this was an impossible effort, and no amount of extra pushing and concentration helped. All the effort just frustrated me. The more I concentrated, the bigger a headache I got. I either functioned impulsively or not at all. Now it's completely different.

"I am no longer burdened with recurring doubts that fragment and distract me from whatever I want to do—or think about. In fact, my mind was burdened from two directions—doubts from within and distractions from without. Now all these crazy distractions are gone.

"My relationship with my wife has even improved. Just tonight, she came home tired and didn't have a good day, and she started taking things out on me. In the past, my feelings would have been hurt and I would have gotten very upset. Instead, I just told her very calmly that I didn't want to talk with her until she had cooled off and was more rested. She didn't like that and flew out the door in a rage. If that had happened six months ago, I probably wouldn't have let her out the door. I'd have been apologetic and in a panic to create peace at any price. Tonight, though, I felt confident that I'd behaved properly. I was honest with her in a nonthreatening way. And I felt 'okay' doing it. That's a real change for me.

"I used to hate reading. . . . In fact, there was a period of about seven or eight years when I didn't read any newspapers or magazines. Now I'm doing a lot of reading. Every day, I cut out articles from the daily paper related to business or personal interests. I even have started a clipping file.

"Work's been very busy. I have three times as many accounts as I did last year, but I'm handling them very well, thank you. What I find is that words are coming up to the surface that previously weren't available to me. Even saying 'thank you' in that context is a difference. I'm more self-assured. Also, an element of humor has come into certain business situations. In the past, I took things *very* seriously. Now I can laugh! I really feel that I've come into my own."

NONMEDICATION ALTERNATIVES

While medication can be extremely beneficial, it is not the only way to overcome concentration-related difficulties. As noted earlier, depending upon the type of concentration mechanisms impaired, psychological counseling may be beneficial; for others, behavior modification techniques may prove helpful. In such cases, your doctor can probably recommended a professional who is qualified to assist you in those areas.

What else can you do—right now? In the final section of this book, we'll explore a number of techniques that can enhance your powers of concentration on a day-to-day basis. In Chapter Seventeen, we'll take a look at ways that youngsters with ADD can be helped to function more effectively at home and at school. And you'll learn what educational institutions are doing to help boost concentration. In Chapter Eighteen, we'll focus on methods that *everyone* can use for reducing stress and increasing energy at home, at school, or in the office. In Chapter Twenty, you'll discover how visualization and imaging can help enhance concentration. And in Chapter Nineteen, you'll find tips for improving memory. Armed with these therapeutic tools,

☐ you can win the battle against concentration disorders and the resulting mental, physical, and occupational chaos that interferes with everyday life, and

☐ you will be well on your way to reaching your own level of *Total Concentration.*

Chapter XV

Free of the Monster at Last!

Ann B. is an intellectually gifted twenty-eight-year-old who compensated for the concentration, distractibility, overactivity, and impulsivity symptoms that characterized her ADD, eventually becoming a pharmacist.

As a child she was poorly coordinated and experienced difficulty distinguishing right from left as well as remembering the alphabet in sequence. Spelling was difficult, and still is. Reading was always in the above-average range but required compensatory gyroscopic and focusing maneuvers, i.e., near-point focusing to minimize fixation and tracking difficulties as well as head tilting and specific body positions to minimize her experiencing the print as slanted. In other words, Ann had typical ADD and dyslexic or LD symptoms.

At the age of sixteen, following a "cold," Ann suddenly developed panic attacks as well as a slew of unexplainable fears/phobias. These symptoms were associated with "stuffy ears," dizziness, and intensified feelings of imbalance and dyscoordination. In addition, her typical, previously compensated ADD symptoms were reactivated from two apparent directions:

1) destabilized inner-ear functioning following her "cold"; and
2) distractions and preoccupations resulting from her severe anxiety symptoms.

Moreover, Ann's anxiety symptoms appeared derived from two sources:

1) inner-ear dysfunctioning; and
2) realistic intensifications of her difficulty coping.

To illustrate all of these points, I will let Ann describe:

1) all her symptoms as she experienced them; and
2) her favorable responses to medications used for subjects having ADD as well as dyslexic and anxiety symptoms.

A POEM

Although Ann wrote this poem following her dramatic improvement and recovery, I feel it worthwhile to begin her case with it. In a sense, this poem symbolically represents the end of her illness and a new beginning:

To live life with a passion is to experience it
        to its fullest extent.
To not be afraid to reach out and learn more,
        even if it means it will take you
        further from those you love.
To look deeper inside and explore oneself,
        even if it means facing the reality
        of who you are or what motivates you.

To move ahead and follow your instincts,
        even if it means going against popular
        opinion or what you were once taught.
To have the courage and insight to find a golden opportunity
        for growth in each of life's experiences,
        even if it means giving up old ways of
        judging situations.
It means taking a chance, looking inside, finding the
        unique and beautiful person that you are and
        allowing it to evolve to its fullest potential.

FREE OF THE MONSTER, AT LAST!

Many patients with ADD struggle inwardly with feelings of humiliation, fear, hopelessness, and anger for many, many years. In a majority of referred cases, the consequences of the disorder touch every facet of their lives. In her own words, Ann B. describes how her life was nearly ruined by the symptoms of ADD, and how she became free of the "monster."

"I was in a high-school typing class in October of 1976 and feeling ill with a head cold. Suddenly I experienced my first panic attack. I felt awful! My ears were plugged, and I had a feeling of vertigo. While sitting at the typewriter, I began to feel lightheaded. I didn't feel hot, the way you do when you're going to faint, but just whirly and off balance. Putting my head between my knees just made everything worse. Before I knew it, I was paralyzed with fear. I couldn't move. I couldn't look to my right or left. I couldn't even turn my head. If I did, my dizziness intensified and I felt like I was falling. I can remember it like it was yesterday—the beginning of a nightmare that lasted for twelve years!

"It was at that time that a veil of fear descended over me. All of a sudden, living day to day became an exercise in determination and strength. Going to school, church, the hairdresser, basketball games, filled me with terror and anxiety. I told no one, but somewhere deep down inside I secretly believed that I was going crazy.

"I had no sense of balance. I couldn't sit in chairs at school unless they had backs and arms. Sitting on a stool took more coordination than I had. Every day I panicked—in lunchrooms, while taking exams, everywhere! When the panic would come, I'd have to leave the room. I got a feeling of being closed in, that I was choking and going to die. Claustrophobic! Then the room would start shifting and my heart would start beating. I felt like I was being swept up in a vortex. Bright lights and big classrooms made it worse.

"The fear became like a monster, living within me. I tried desperately to explain away the monster, even reason with it. I was so scared all of the time, tense, anxious. Concentration on reality-based events became impossible. I hated both reading and school—I'd look at a book and get overwhelmed. Even though I was a poor student, I tested extremely gifted. So the guidance counselor concluded my academic symptoms and restless behavior were of a deliberate nature. She brought my parents in and said my behavior was atrocious, my grades were poor, that I was disruptive, inattentive, and deliberately hyperactive.

"I was so humiliated in front of my immigrant parents! To try to get me to change, they punished me. I couldn't go out of the house. I never was allowed to date. I became a prisoner in my own home. When all this happened, I tried to reason with the monster again. I vowed to be good, *very good*.

"While I was in college, I developed a photographic memory. But I still couldn't remember numbers and spell correctly. . . . I'd force myself to study for eight hours straight without stopping, because I thought that if I was perfectly good at school, all these feelings of panic and whirliness would go away. As a result, I became very compulsive, feeling that if I were perfect I'd feel better. If I didn't get 100 percent on an exam, I felt I would die. All my attempts were in vain, however; the monster stayed. I screamed, cried, prayed, pleaded with God, but the fear remained. I reached out to those around me, but they could not understand my fear. So I stopped talking, stopped reaching out, and did what I was told. I built a second life, went through all the usual motions of living, all the while resentment building inside of me. Resentment and anger because the monster would not leave. And I would frequently become dizzy and panicky with no warning at all. I had lost control!

"My life was a living hell. I don't think I was ever as close to committing suicide as I was then. While working for a pharmaceutical company, I would go to my desk and try to read my reports. But I couldn't do it. The words seemed blurry, moving and difficult to focus and concentrate on. Distractions were everywhere. And it took all my control not to impulsively jump from task to task—to just get them over with. I think my compulsive need to be good and perfect held these impulses in check. Strange, but one symptom seemed to mask the effect or appearance of another.

"I felt like I was rocking on a boat all the time! It really seemed like it was a physical thing. I'd get up and go to the lab bench and would lean against it for support, but I'd still feel dizzy and couldn't do the experiment. My timing was off, too. I couldn't finish a step before I'd have to sit back down at my desk. So I tended to procrastinate—which in turn made me frustrated, angry, and guilty. I desperately needed to function perfectly.

"The monster was preventing me from doing my work! If I had to use the computer, I'd have to stand up and hold on to the table for support. I'd shift from leg to leg, or would put my nose right down on the keyboard. And that would help. If I tried sitting down in a chair, I felt like I was falling over. As a result, the only way I could read was by lying on the floor. And the only way I could write was if I bent over and put my nose to the paper. That way I seemed better able to concentrate and visually compensate for my poor writing coordination and sense of imbalance when sitting. Staring and concentrating on my writing and the paper actually lessened my dizziness. I felt like a hunchback! And eventually I developed a spinal curvature, too.

"Even my intimate relationships were threatening. I feared the other person would eventually find out my secret and stop loving me. And that he would tell me I was crazy, reinforcing what my family had been telling me for years. I secretly hoped I would find a person who would understand me so well that the monster would vanish. I went from relationship to relationship feeling empty and lost inside, unable to feel connected with anyone.

"I kept a journal during those years. Perhaps one of my entries will help explain what I was feeling. I wrote: 'It is very scary being alone—painful and scary—almost like falling into a large abyss and not being able to find anything to grasp on to. It is as if I need some stability. And no matter how hard I search or where I turn I can't seem to find it. I need arms to hold me. And I need to sit on someone's knee and tell them how lonely and scared I really feel. Someone to direct, guide me, and console me. I need a mother or a parent—not what I have. In my heart I yearn for and dream of a warm cozy place to go where the world is safe and secure. Where I can go and be loved for who I am and nurtured and hugged, where I can have guidance and smiles. I guess what I really want is a family. I have people, but the pain is so intense that they bring me no comfort. I want to cry out for all the anguish my heart has felt, all the aloneness I have wallowed in. This pain is deep and intense, searing through me and ripping out my heart in its fatal grip.'

"An exacerbation of symptoms occurred after the death of my mother. Perhaps the most devastating result of this was that I had to quit my job in research. I had not given in to my fears for twelve years. And now the scenario that I had secretly feared was unraveling. I was totally out of control. Fluorescent lighting in the labs evoked a feeling of disorientation. And merely standing gave me a sensation of falling through space. I felt even more defeated, humiliated, and crazy. I cried constantly. I couldn't move forward or backward. My concentration, distractibility, and reading got worse. And so did my dizziness and sense of imbalance.

"Here's another journal entry, written for a psychologist who asked me to 'write through' a panic attack I had at work. 'I go to the lab bench and try to work, panic. I run back to the other lab bench, panic. I go to my desk, anxiety. I try to think of a new experiment, enjoy it, no I hate it. I cannot think of anything new. Been doing the same experiment for over a year. I feel trapped, closed in. The sterile environment chokes me. I run down the hall, panic envelops me. I clutch my clipboard for safety. I bolt up the stairs to the warm soft comfort of the library. In a few moments I feel guilty. I must go back down. As I walk along the corridors, the walls seem to close in on me. God help me, I hate it here. The white walls, the white floors, no feeling just an empty coldness. It scares me. Makes me want to run to someone and feel their warmth and caring. I've made it back down to the lab area. My legs are shaking. I shake—like a leaf. Oh please, someone get me out of here. I cannot talk to anyone. If I do they will see my fear. I cannot work. I hate it—someone help me get out. I feel like a trapped animal. I can't produce like a robot any longer. Turn off those white lights, do away with those sterile white floors. Give me feeling, give me warmth. My God, don't let me perish.'

"After I quit my job, I also left my fiance, thinking that would help. My whole future hung in limbo. How could I marry if I was afraid of being in church because I'd pass out? Have a family if I was afraid of being pregnant? Take care of myself if I was afraid of going to the supermarket? I had reached the end of the line. The monster had taken away my freedom of choice and made the decision for me.

"Fortunately, my therapist recommended that I see a clinical ecologist. The physician found numerous vitamin and mineral deficiencies, a long-standing yeast infection, and hypothyroidism. He treated me. And almost immediately, the panic attacks decreased in severity. My depression and horrible mood swings also subsided. *But something still remained.* There was a piece of the puzzle still missing. I still had difficulty standing in church, going to certain shopping malls and large, brightly lit supermarkets. I had trouble using the computer at work and would frequently feel sort of disoriented.

"At that point, I was accepted to graduate school. I had taken the necessary undergraduate courses to prepare me for my studies. Because of my desire to achieve, I had performed extremely well, and I was looking forward to school. Imagine my horror when I arrived at school only to realize that I could not walk down the corridor without experiencing anxiety! I could not stand the lights. It felt as if the walls were closing in on me. What could I tell my friends and family? I told them, as well as tried to convince myself, that I had changed my mind. I dropped out of graduate school. Once again, I felt humiliated and defeated. And I was worried that I would eventually be reduced to somebody living in bed all day. I had a constant fear that I would become a bag lady.

"It was around this time that I was browsing in a bookstore and stumbled upon Dr. Levinson's book, *Phobia Free.* The information about the inner ear astounded me, to say the least. I wondered: Is it possible that the monster will go away forever?

"When I met with Dr. Levinson, and after I underwent testing at his office, he told me that I was suffering from a severe inner-ear dysfunction. He immediately prescribed a combination of medications and vitamins. It has been ten weeks since the initiation of treatment. In that time I have blossomed. The fun and excitement that I have experienced in the past few weeks stands out vividly in comparison to the harsh realities that I have faced for the past twelve years. The changes are too numerous to even mention. I feel a centeredness and an inner peace that I haven't experienced since I was a very young child.

"Where do I begin? I have since spoken to several relatives who have filled me in on some enlightening aspects of my childhood. Apparently, I was unable to distinguish between my left hand and my right for many years. I remembered utilizing a birthmark on my left hand as a reference point. And to recall the left-hand birthmark I made up a little jingle.

"I had a difficult time learning the alphabet and how to spell my name. I remembered using a visual type of memorization in an effort to learn. I would picture what the alphabet looked like on my little desk and print my name from that picture. I had difficulty tying my shoes. And to this day I cannot spell. I developed some remarkable coping techniques. I would read with my chin on the book. And I would write with my head lying sideways on my desk. In an effort to concentrate, I would tilt my head severely to the right. And I would use a very quiet space, with absolutely no distractions.

"I didn't learn to ride a bicycle until after my younger brother had. Since treatment, I now bicycle a lot. And I am able to ride much faster because I don't have the sensation of falling over the front of the handlebars. Sports were extremely frustrating. I always had the feeling that the ball was going to hit me in the face, so I stayed away from all sports activities. Skiing was particularly frustrating, because I felt as though I was always going to fall forward when I went down the hill. And as an adult I have trouble cooking and coordinating a dinner so that all the dishes are ready at the same time.

"My piano teacher to this day commends me on my perseverance in learning how to play. I always felt as though I was going to fall off the piano bench. And I could never get my fingers to coordinate with the music I was reading. Additionally, I had difficulty timing the music. Even counting out loud would not help. It's just that I couldn't coordinate and integrate multiple steps at the same time. Each thing I did required *all* my effort and concentration. And as soon as I had to subdivide my concentration, the whole task would fall apart—no matter how hard I would push myself and how loudly I would talk to myself inwardly.

"Needless to say, everything has now improved immensely. I can read while sitting in a chair or standing. Concentration and distractibility no longer are problems. I feel calm and relaxed, no longer driven and restless or hyper. And not so prone to jump in and out of things. No longer do I have these herky-jerky 'impulsions.'

"I listen intently with my head straight, my shoulders back, and my spine straight. I walk properly and stand with the weight distributed evenly throughout the bottoms of my feet.

"My writing has improved, and I can keep my head a comfortable distance away from the paper. And best of all, I can write in a straight line. I ride my bicycle fast (even down hills). And when the bike tour is finished, I am able to walk without feeling motion-sick. I've started to play piano again, as well as tennis.

"My personality has become amazingly calm. My roommate is astounded at what you have done for me! More than a few times a day I am taken aback by the profoundness of it all. My body and personality feel new, almost alien to me. I can tolerate stress. I can fill prescriptions, manage a crew of people, work ten hours, go home, and walk for an hour—all on less sleep than I have required in ages. My restless sleep and terrorizing dreams are gone. Instead, my dreams are both calm and pleasant.

"I no longer work compulsively, trying to run away from my anxiety. Gone is the bargaining with God, the fruitless searches, the endless reading and analyzing in an effort to still the turmoil within my body. Nor do I have to find a deep psychoanalytic reason for why the room shifts or why I cannot stand in church. I actually thought my dizziness in church was caused by a deep-seated fear of God. Now I know there was a physical reason for it. There's nothing *Freudian* about an inner-ear problem! On medication, I am able to sit through a church service!

"Gone is the feeling of helplessness. I am able to make a commitment and follow through without distractions and procrastination. I can plan in advance without worrying how I will feel that day. I can command respect from my family and friends. And I can walk away from those who don't like me without precipitating a panic attack and having to run back for help (only to have someone say that I am crazy). I have my dignity now.

"My impulsivity and mood swings are gone. I am able to make a decision and stick with it. I have become very organized and competent. I am no longer the victim of constant aggressive or hostile thoughts. I am able to let go of the past and live in the present. All this has happened in just a few weeks. I'm free of the painful memories of things my dad did, like locking me in my room. Instead of not being able to let go of old thoughts and memories, I can hardly remember them! They don't seem important now. All the events which had terrorized me during my childhood seem to have receded into the back of my mind and out of my present day-to-day consciousness.

"Last week I went to the mall and walked through it feeling calm and cool, even looking out over the balcony! I can even walk quickly now. Ordinarily, I would have had to stop every five or ten feet to recapture my balance and reorient myself. Until recently, I could not look at clothes without holding on to the rack, change in the dressing room without feeling the walls were going to close in on me, or walk without the aid of the shopping cart. Now all these symptoms are gone!

"This past weekend was remarkable. I volunteered to work at my church festival. Here I was, working in a huge gymnasium that was brightly lit with fluorescent lights and packed with five hundred people. Working at a steady and fast pace was simple as pie. And I'm calm as a cucumber! I also came to realize that I'm not as sensitive to oxygen changes in crowded, stuffy stores and planes as before. That's why I don't have to avoid them, or run away.

"Then, to top it all off, I went out dancing with all my friends. Greek dancing involves moving in a circular motion at a fast pace with small dance steps. Last year all this was impossible. Walking just a few feet inside the room terrorized me, and after it was all over I just went home all alone and cried. This time it was all sheer pleasure.

"The small wonders range anywhere from being able to ride in elevators, walk up and down stairways, and go up tall buildings and enjoy the New York skyline, to tilting back in a hairdresser's chair, going shopping alone, and making some major changes in my life.

"Finally, the most wonderful news of all. In the past couple of months, I have resumed communication with my ex-fiance. Since I have become fully functional I can go on with my life. We are considering a December wedding. I plan on walking down the aisle with confidence. No longer am I afraid of the church and the altar. At the reception, I hope to kick up my heels and dance, twirling 'round and round' lots of times!

"It's kind of funny, though. I've mixed emotions about my 'recovery' from my life in hell. A letter I wrote to a dear friend shortly after visiting Dr. Levinson will explain it best.

"'Dear Peter, Perhaps you were the only one who held my hand and helped me through this whole ordeal. For twelve years I have searched for an answer to these feelings of fear and anxiety that I've had. Now that I'm so stable I must admit that it feels kind of empty—I've never had any other emotions besides fear.

"'Because of all this I was forced to compensate and grow intellectually. But deep down inside I remained like a small child, forever searching for some sort of stability from the outside to stop the panic. I feel emotionally stunted because I've spent all my time fighting an internal monster. For people like me, without treatment, a childlike concept of security seems to be all we can hope for in a marriage or a relationship. Like children, we just want someone to provide the basics—food, home, clothes, etc.

"'My attempts to find inner peace have taken me on journeys away from home and resulted in changes in careers, hobbies, and expectations. I've read every piece of philosophy from Sartre to Camus to St. Augustine, gone back to college, even turned down eleven marriage proposals!

"'Had it not been for this illness, I probably would never have pushed myself to grow and explore. The medication I take stabilizes my personality and gives me a freedom to move about. I have a sense of peace I've never felt in my life. Still, a part of me feels sad, as well as joyous.

"'In a way, it's like when Gus [an old boyfriend] tells me that you can never appreciate money until you experience poverty. Well, you never really, really want to go out until you're forced to stay in.

"'One who has not experienced a disorder like mine can never understand the past twelve years of my life. I had the spirit of a bird. But my mind and I were trapped in a sick body. What would my life had been like if I had married Glenn? Would I have gone skiing in Austria? Would I have taken the scholarship to grad school?

"'All those times I stayed home, all those opportunities missed because I had to play it safe. Any small change in emotions or environment would make me panic.

"'Well, at least I had my fantasy life. I dreamed of all that I couldn't do. In my dreams I was a pianist. I flew in airplanes, I skied the Alps. In real life, I played the wrong notes, never made turns in an airplane at angles sharper than 180 degrees, and fell down the slopes in Vermont.

"'The fantasies saved me, though. In all my dreams I had control. I felt well. No panic.'"

Chapter XVI

A Primer For Parents and Teachers: What *You* Can Do to Help the ADD Child

Throughout this book, you've met scores of my patients who've been helped via antimotion-sickness medications and/or stimulants. In fact, so much copy has been devoted to the subject of medication that you might now have the feeling that it is the best and *only* remedy for the concentration and distractibility problems we have associated with ADD. For many patients, this is certainly true—medication alleviates most or all of their symptoms, and they require no additional psychological or educational treatment. That does not mean, however, that psychological counseling and/or special classes for learning problems can't be beneficial. Indeed, for many individuals with ADD, "outside help" from psychologists and special education teachers is an absolute necessity; it can provide them with techniques and tools for dealing with the mental and emotional scars that may remain even after successful medical treatment has been undertaken.

Talk with your doctor about counseling—he or she can determine whether the services of a psychologist or psychiatrist should be enlisted and can provide you with either a personal recommendation or the phone number of a referral organization. Discuss educational concerns with your child's guidance counselor or individual teachers—they can supply you with information about testing, special classes, private tutors, or learning programs that may help your child.

But don't stop there. Help for the ADD patient should *not* be limited to the psychologist's office or the resource room at school. There are things you can do *right now* to help your child. In this chapter, we'll explore a number of techniques for managing the ADD youngster at home and at school.

WHERE TO START? DEMYSTIFY ADD

Space cadet. Dummy. Airhead. Has your child ever used these and other derogatory terms to describe himself or herself? Have your child's classmates whispered the words behind his back? Perhaps as a child, you yourself knew the pain such labels could bring. Feeling hopeless and strangely "abnormal," the children with ADD often live life on the fringe. In their minds they're outcasts and in reality they're outsiders; is it any wonder that many ADD children have a negative sense of self and extremely low self-esteem?

The most important service parents can perform is to explain to ADD children that they are *not* spacy or dumb or lazy or stupid, but rather that they have a simple *physical* problem that is causing them to have difficulties in school, at home, or in personal relationships. What's the best way to do this? Since young children may have difficulty understanding references to the CVS or inner-ear system, I often recommend that parents use a simple, easy-to-understand analogy: that the child is like a television set whose internal "tuner" doesn't function quite properly, and that sometimes the tuner causes things to become fuzzy, and so forth. When children are placed on medication, parents should explain that the pills act as "fine-tuners," able to reduce or erase fuzziness or to help bring things into clearer focus.

Once the child grasps the concept, he or she should be encouraged to add his own interpretations. Indeed, many of my youthful ADD patients have strengthened the TV analogy and provided parents with new insights by adding their own personal touches. When his tuner wasn't working properly, said one boy, it was capable of "turning up the volume of voices" around him and "mixing them up"—an apt way of describing auditory overload and scrambling. After being placed on medication, another youngster told his mother that his tuner now seemed to be able to "control how fast other people talked—it slowed them down." In actuality, of course, the medication enhanced this youngster's ability to listen and understand.

APPROACHES TO HOME MANAGEMENT

Whether they're on medication or not, *all* ADD children need understanding and encouragement in order to overcome and deal with their behavioral and academic problems. This requires a great deal of patience on the part of parents, since total recovery may take months, even years. Nevertheless, there are a number of coping techniques, listed below, that parents can use to help them over many of the hurdles:

☐ When parents don't see immediate improvements, they may tend to blame the child—or themselves. They believe that if the child "tried harder," or if they themselves were "better" parents, the child would quickly be transformed into a model youngster. Don't fall into this dangerous trap! If your child had diabetes, for example, would you punish him because he didn't get well overnight? Would you blame yourself because he didn't recover immediately? Of course you wouldn't, because you know that diabetes is a physical problem. Remember: ADD is caused by a physical problem, too. Just as children need to understand this important fact, so do parents—particularly those who feel compelled to blame themselves or their child when positive results don't occur on the spot.

☐ As a parent, you know all too well that the symptoms of ADD can radiate in a thousand different directions. Feeling overwhelmed by this fact, you may have an urge to try to "fix everything at once." My advice to parents is simple: Take things one day at a time, and deal with one problem at a time. To help her sort out which problem was most important to deal with, one patient's mother devised a technique whereby she assigned a numerical value to her child's various problems. As she explained it, "Bobby had lots of problems, so I sat down and tried to narrow them down. I tried to figure out which four troubled us the most. He fought with his little sister every chance he got. He threw tantrums every time he didn't get his way. He left his room messy all the time, despite repeated warnings. And, last but not least, his table manners were atrocious—he fiddled with his silverware and played with his food until, sometimes, we'd have to send him to his room. At the time, I wanted to do something about all these problems, but soon realized that was impossible. So I asked myself: 'On a scale of one to ten, which problem is causing the most trouble, and which one should we deal with *now*?' Once I started labeling, it became easy to sort things out. The tantrums were most disruptive to the *entire* family, so I labeled that a ten. Fights with sister—which could be somewhat controlled by separating the kids—got a five. The table manners got a three, and the messy room got a one. The number system helped put things in perspective. Right now we're dealing primarily with the tantrums and how to stop them. Once we get that worked out, I think we'll *all* be calmer and in a better position to work on the other things."

◻ A number of parents I've talked with have had great success entering into "contractual agreements" with their children. Working together to create this written document, families start with a goal, however small it might be. For example: "We want Billy to finish his math assignments this week." Then write down what's required to achieve the goal: "Billy will work for a half an hour each night on his math problems. He will not be allowed to watch television until he has finished the math problems. When he's completed his assignment, he'll show it to Mom or Dad for checking." Such contracts usually include a reward—if Billy meets his obligations, then his parents will allow him to watch his favorite television program. After writing up the agreement, all parties sign it.

◻ If you want your child to do well at the three R's and all phases of life, try managing his home environment with the three S's: Specifics, Structure, and Sensitivity. Let's look at each of these a bit closer:

Specifics

Give your child clear messages. If you want him to clean his room, explain what that means: making the bed? picking up toys? sweeping the floor? or all of the above? When you praise your child, let her know *what* she did: "You behaved great today" is vague, whereas "You sat so quietly and were so friendly to me while we were in the car today. I was very proud of you" gets to the heart of the matter. When criticizing, the same rule applies. "You're a bad boy" is ambiguous, whereas, "I'm disappointed that you threw your toy at me . . . that was very childish" is more to the point.

Structure

All children need structure to their lives, but ADD children probably need more of it. Set up daily routines that are manageable for the child—including times for getting out of bed, having breakfast, doing homework, playing, etc. Having structure doesn't mean inflexibility, however. Remember, children, like adults, have their own inner time clocks: some children are early risers, others are night owls. Moreover, some kids work better lying on the floor than sitting rigidly at a desk. The list could go on and on, but the point is this: Try to understand your child's learning style and create a structure around it. (For more information on learning styles, see Chapter Seventeen.)

Sensitivity

For a child with attention deficits, life can seem like riding on a merry-go-round that's gotten off track—it's not much fun, and it seems like you can't control which way it goes. Be sensitive to the difficulties your child is experiencing. Be patient. Give plenty of praise when it's warranted, and when you criticize, make it constructive. Perhaps most important, listen to your child. Let him or her express his concerns and feelings about himself, his behavior, his schoolwork, and his relationships with family and friends. How is he feeling today? What was bugging her last night? Simple questions often pave the way to understanding complex problems—as long as somebody is there to listen.

COPING WITH SCHOOLWORK

Whether you're a parent or a teacher, you've probably had plenty of opportunities to watch the ADD child trying to study. What have you observed? That instead of sitting down to the task, pencil in hand and paper at the ready, the child spends an inordinate amount of time fiddling around? That he or she becomes distracted by irrelevant objects? That the youngster can't find the needed textbook, or discovers that her notebook was left in her locker? All of these activities—which drive parents and teachers up the wall and prevent ADD children from completing tasks— point to one problem: *lack of organization.* What can be done? In the classroom and in the study room at home, children with attention deficits need to build their organizational skills. What follows are some suggestions which were developed by parents and teachers of several of my ADD patients:

☐ *How to avoid the "I can't remember the assignment" syndrome.* At the beginning of the school year, the child, his parents, and his teachers should sit down together to devise a simple "homework reminder book." Start with a blank notebook or tablet, and section off several pages for each class, labeling each section as math, spelling, English, and so forth. Each day of class, the child (or the teacher) should write down the assignment for the next day and should note whether the textbook should be taken home. The child needs to know that he is responsible for taking the reminder book home and for bringing it back to school each day.

☐ *Does your child continually misplace his textbook?* Many teachers and parents recommend buying two sets of a textbook. One copy stays at home, the other remains at school. The beauty of this idea is that when the child "owns" the book, he can feel free to make notes in it—an important organizational skill that will be discussed in greater detail later on.

☐ *Organize a home work station for the child.* Ideally, a youngster should have a private, quiet study area to call his own (preferably one that is *not* a bedroom full of distractions). If this isn't possible, attempt to cordon off space in the bedroom or another area and make it the "office." After furnishing it with a desk, proper lighting, and a comfortable chair, make sure the office is well-stocked with supplies: paper, pencils, pens, erasers, etc. If children feel they can concentrate with soft radio music in the background—and can demonstrate that it is not an interference—I see no reason to deny them a radio in their office. As for the television, I think "out of sight, out of mind" is the best policy.

☐ *Education shouldn't stop in the schoolroom. Promote a "learning atmosphere" throughout the house.* You don't need a formal library; simply keep quality books and magazines around for those times when the child does not have homework to do. Games like Junior Scrabble, Trivial Pursuit, even the simple board game Memory can help keep kids interested in learning. You may even want to consider subscribing to publications like *Weekly Reader,* or purchasing crossword or word-scramble workbooks; they're designed to make learning fun.

WHO'S THE BEST TUTOR?

For youngsters with ADD, just keeping up with classwork can seem like an insurmountable obstacle. Hence, many children with ADD require tutoring to help them in certain subjects such as math or spelling, or to help them with study skills in general. This fact brings up an important question: Who should do the tutoring—the parent or a competent outsider?

Having talked with hundreds of parents on this subject, I have come to the conclusion that it is the rare parent indeed who succeeds in tutoring his or her own child. In many cases, the dynamics of interpersonal relationships are such that neither the child nor the parent can really focus on the subject at hand. Thus, I feel the most efficient—and least frustrating—way to handle the need for a tutor is simply to hire one, preferably a person who (1) understands attention deficits, (2) takes an interest in your child, and (3) is competent to tutor the particular subject matter. Your role as parent can be that of a facilitator—you provide your child and the tutor with a workable schedule, comfortable work space, proper study materials, and plenty of encouragement.

GUIDELINES FOR TEACHERS

Teachers who deal with ADD children have one thing in common: they need an arsenal of techniques to help these special students succeed in the classroom setting. What follows is a list of helpful suggestions, which were developed by teachers who have worked with many of my patients. Some of the ideas can apply to home management as well.

☐ First and foremost, get to know the ADD child and let him or her get to know you. Establishing a rapport and a trusting relationship with the child sets the foundation for a successful school experience.

☐ In today's overcrowded classrooms, it's difficult to provide youngsters with ADD the special attention they need, so make sure to give these children front-row seats. By being in close proximity with students, the teacher can easily (and subtly) supervise study time, and the student has fewer distractions to deal with, plus easy access to the teacher.

☐ Since the typical ADD student comes to the classroom filled with anxiety and, perhaps, battered self-esteem, one should not exacerbate these problems. Be firm, but fair. Avoid harsh criticism in front of peers. When problems arise in the classroom—and they surely will—have a plan for handling them. For example, several teachers have recommended using hand signals (discussed in advance with the child) for times when the child gets out of line. Said one such instructor, "When John starts daydreaming, or when he acts out impulsively, I touch my nose with my index finger. He alone sees the signal, and usually responds by stopping the inappropriate behavior. So far, this technique and variations of it work well with ADD students—in a subtle, nonconfrontive way, you can let students know they're off base, and you don't have to call attention to it in front of their peers. It also helps build rapport—now John and I have 'our little secret.'"

☐ Many youngsters with ADD will have a tendency to be over-active or hyperactive. Few would deny that these kids have lots of pent-up energy! Instead of fighting against it, try turning a hindrance into a help—let the child run errands; make him responsible for tacking items on the bulletin board; ask him to sharpen the pencils or pass out the books. Such tasks are good for the child's self-esteem, and they help defuse all that excess vigor.

☐ A number of teachers suggest setting up biweekly "talk sessions" during which there's time to discuss schoolwork, behavior, goals, and objectives. Most important, the meetings should be designed for two-way communication. Avoid a teacher monologue—let the child express his or her concerns and feelings, too. NOTE: As an aid to discussing behavior and overall performance, teachers may wish to use "The Concentration Box" mentioned in the next chapter.

☐ During talk sessions and regular classroom time, take note of activities that the child excels at. Then give him ample opportunity to "exercise his expertise," as one teacher put it. Many educators still make time for a "show and tell" hour, when students have an opportunity to demonstrate their skill in art, music, athletics, etc. I can't imagine a better way to build self-esteem and enhance self-worth!

☐ Although it's often difficult to achieve, *consistency* is a key to successful classroom management and home management as well. A fourth-grade teacher put it best: "Don't make promises you don't intend to or can't deliver. When you punish, be fair. If they don't get it perfect the first time, take a deep breath, give lots of encouragement, and let them try again. Everybody deserves a second chance."

A TEACHER SHARES HER SECRETS

Good organizational skills are crucial to peak performance in school. Here are several tips for enhancing organization in the classroom, submitted by a middle-school teacher who teaches a class called Study Skills:

"Kids with attention deficits need to become actively involved with their work, particularly in reading. That's why I recommend that parents *buy* class textbooks for their children—then they can mark up the material as much as they wish.

"I try to teach them how to underline or circle key words, using brightly colored flow pens. They make notes in the margin. Then they try to summarize the main ideas—on paper, to each other, and to me. I don't tell them that they're 'paraphrasing,' but that's really what they're doing. It not only helps them comprehend what they've read, it helps them remember it, too. Written summarizations help their writing skills, and the oral summaries help them with speech *and* with listening.

"When we read a short chapter, I work with them on outlining, too, using numerals and letters to develop main points and subpoints. This helps them develop logical thinking, and teaches sequencing of ideas. I also encourage kids to use their outlines when studying for exams—when they've got the information compacted in outline form, they're not so intimidated and they seem to be able to concentrate better.

"During lectures, I insist that students take notes, and I check their notes every day. Sometimes, before the lecture, I'll ask them to take notes on main *ideas*; at other times, I'll ask in advance that they write down certain details, such as all the colors mentioned, all the action verbs, all the names, etc. This helps them with selectivity, and helps them learn how to focus.

"No matter what we're doing in class, we use a technique I call 'chunking.' This simply means that we break up our tasks into smaller parts, so that kids are not intimidated by sheer volume. Instead of asking kids to try to read a five-page chapter, for example, I'll assign it in chunks—a few paragraphs at a time. Then, as a class, we discuss the main points of the chunk, and when everybody's got it, we move on to the next one. This helps kids feel like they're working together, and it reduces the anxiety that these kids feel when they're 'competing' with others to finish first. Finishing first is rarely the goal in my classes—we strive to understand the material, and try to enjoy the learning process."

WORK VERSUS PLAY

Thirteen-year-old Jack P. spends roughly seven hours at school. He's taking basic math (with a little pre-algebra thrown in), Latin, science, English, speech, and gym class. When he arrives home each day, his mother insists he begin work on his homework, a process that often takes two to three hours. After supper, Jack either meets with his math tutor (Tuesdays) or his Latin tutor (Thursdays), and on his "free" nights he is given permission to watch a one-hour program on television—as long as it's "educational." On Saturdays, Jack cleans his room and may baby-sit his younger sister, and on Sundays, after church and bible class, he helps his dad with chores. Sunday nights, Jack is free to chat with visiting relatives, then he's off to his room for—what else?—work on Monday's school assignments.

What's wrong with this picture? The answer, of course, is *no play time*! Everyone—children and adults included—needs leisure time, those marvelous moments when perhaps we do nothing but let our imaginations carry us far away, or when we really work up a sweat slam-dunking a basketball or become mesmerized by a fast-moving game of Pac-Man.

Leisure time can be particularly therapeutic for the youngster with ADD—in fact, for some, it is the *only* time of the day when they're doing something at which they can actually succeed! If your son does well at football, encourage him! If your daughter enjoys playing the drums, use earplugs and cheer her on! Remember, too, that play is an excellent defuser of tension and pent-up energy. Aware of that simple fact, a number of researchers across the country have instituted exercise programs for children with ADD. In their experiments, they've found that the "movers and shakers" outperform their nonexercising peers in attention span and in academic achievement!

If you're intrigued by the notion that exercise can improve the performance of kids with attention deficits, and want to know more about what researchers and educators are doing to help youngsters with concentration problems, turn to the next chapter. There, you'll find many fascinating techniques that can be adapted for use at school or in the home.

Chapter XVII

Not for Teachers Only: Techniques for Improving Attention

When I was a young schoolboy, my teachers seemed to have only two techniques for improving the attention spans of their students: they either (1) banged a ruler on the side of the lectern when we began to daydream, or (2) threatened to punish or fail us if we didn't focus our minds on the lesson before us. Luckily for students today, educators are far more creative at devising techniques for improving attention and concentration in the classroom.

In this chapter, you'll find a potpourri of ideas that can work for ADD and non-ADD individuals alike. Some of the recommendations are derived from scientific investigations, while others are personal and anecdotal. Yet all of them, I believe, are worthy of consideration. Although most of the techniques are designed for youngsters and classroom use, many could be adapted for use in the home and for adults as well.

UNDERSTANDING YOUR CHILD'S LEARNING STYLE: CRUCIAL TO SUCCESS

The mother of one of my patients recently told me that she was desperately worried about her son. Apparently, after reading an article in a newsmagazine, he'd begun ignoring the "rules for homework" that she'd set up for him. As she explained it, "He used to sit in a straight-back chair in my brightly lit office to do homework. Now he insists on curling up in a beanbag in a shadowy corner of the house. And lately he's been threatening to try to 'make a deal' with the principal of the school: since he likes sleeping late in the morning, he wants to see whether the principal will let him begin his classes at ten instead of eight. When I told him I thought he was crazy, he just smiled and said, 'Hey, Mom, educators all over the country are changing the way they think about teaching and learning. Isn't it time you did, too?'"

That young boy was correct—educators *are* rethinking the ways and means of learning, thanks in part to a research tool developed by the National Association of Secondary School Principals. Now in use at hundreds of schools across the country, the Learning Styles Profile is a 126-question learning-style assessment that zeroes in on a child's own style—and helps teachers and parents come up with new ways to help the child do better.[1] You may have already noticed some of these tendencies in your youngsters:

Mobility: Not unlike the movers and shakers you've met throughout this book, kids who are mobile learners need to move around and take R and R breaks when they're studying. Even a brief respite—getting up to get a Coke, or staring into a fish tank—may *help* keep attention focused.

Manipulation: Let's call them the "hands-on" kids—he likes tinkering with model airplane sets, she enjoys shaping clay. These learners need to become actively involved in learning. When they do, they have a better chance of comprehending and retaining information as well.

Pairing: Some youngsters actually do their best when working with a partner as opposed to being alone or in a larger group. When it's time for homework, parents of these kids may want to remember the old adage, "Two heads are better than one."

Informality: Like the boy above who loved slouching in a beanbag chair, the informal learner does well in unstructured circumstances. Does your child enjoy reading while lying on the floor? Does he or she really get "cooking" on homework in the late-night hours? Consider bending traditional rules to accommodate these youngsters.

Visual learners: Instead of constantly lecturing to these kids, give them things to look at. For example, take them to a live per-

---

[1] To find out more about the NASSP's Learning Styles Profile, send $5.00 (check or cashier's check) to the National Association of Secondary School Principals, 1904 Association Drive, Reston, Virginia 22091.

formance of a Noel Coward play instead of reading it to them; show that terrific PBS-TV nature show on insects during class; arrange for a field trip to the shore to study wildlife. They'll get excited about learning—and remember *more* of what they learn.

Another benefit of using the Learning Styles Profile: Teachers can identify which kids have problems with certain cognitive skills, such as analysis of information or memory. Once such problems are targeted, teachers *and* parents can work together to help correct them.

THE CONCENTRATION BOX

Imagine for a moment that you are an elementary-school teacher, with twenty youngsters sitting before you in the classroom. Your goal today and every day is to see to it that these kids—some of whom are already squirming in their seats—pay attention to their lessons. What can you do to help them?

If I suggested that you involve the children in a *fantasy,* you might well shake your head in disbelief. Isn't fantasizing akin to daydreaming? And isn't daydreaming the enemy of concentration? Educator Sylvia Brackett doesn't think so. In fact, as an elementary-school counselor in Haw River, North Carolina, Ms. Brackett has developed a technique called "The Concentration Box," a guided fantasy technique she believes can increase student attention spans and help build the capacity to concentrate. According to Ms. Brackett, teachers should follow these steps:

1. Sit in a circle with your students in a quiet area with few distractions. Using a calm voice, help the children relax with breathing exercises. An atmosphere of calmness and serenity is important for the success of this activity.
2. Once the group is relaxed, count slowly backward from ten to one. On the count of one all eyes are closed and the group prepares to listen.
3. Ask the children to imagine an empty box. The box may be any size, shape, or color. Each child examines his or her box, noting the top, sides, and bottom. Encourage kids to maintain the

image and not allow other thoughts to enter their minds. Then ask each child to imagine a door with a lock. Instruct them to open the door and allow the image of a witch to enter. (Any concrete image works well in this activity. Older students may imagine a favorite food, an animal, or a favorite story character.) Once the witch (or other image) is inside the box, each child closes and locks the door. Looking closely at the witch, the child notices the colors and textures of her hair, her hands, her clothes, and her shoes. Urge the children to concentrate carefully on each detail of the witch's appearance and actions. Ask them to direct the witch's actions. Remind the children periodically that even though other ideas may come knocking on the door, they should be kept outside the box.

After another minute or so, slowly bring the children out of the fantasy by counting from one to ten. During this time the door is unlocked, the witch flies away, and an image of the classroom is created.

According to Ms. Brackett, when this guided fantasy is used consistently, the result is usually a positive change in attention span and concentration. She says the Concentration Box also appears to help students retain number facts, spelling words, and other memorized facts. When used in counseling with an individual, she notes, the technique helps the counselee to focus more clearly on events that may pertain to his or her problem. Before engaging in the guided fantasy, says Ms. Brackett, "be aware of the attention span of the group you're working with. Activities with kindergarten through third-grade students should not last longer than twenty minutes," she advises, "but those with fourth- and fifth-graders can continue up to thirty minutes."

CAN EXERCISE BOOST CONCENTRATION IN THE CLASSROOM?

Absolutely, says William H. Evans, associate professor at the Department of Special Education, University of West Florida,

Pensacola. And the notion isn't exactly new. Dr. Evans and several other researchers began work in the mid-1980s on a study that they hoped would prove what ancient Greeks and famous authors such as Locke, Rousseau, Kant, and Jefferson had believed for centuries: that physical activity is an effective tool that could be used in schools to increase attention to work, alertness, mental functioning, academic performance, and good behavior. If a relationship between "physical exercise and a specific class of behavior" could be identified, suggested Dr. Evans, "a valuable therapeutic tool could become available."

First, Dr. Evans identified behaviors that would be desirable to change. His study involved six young boys who were labeled "emotionally disturbed"—each youngster had a history of severe conduct problems that included being removed from special-education resource rooms two or more times per week. After interviewing the boys' teachers, Dr. Evans also learned that all the subjects had serious and consistent problems with "talk-outs" (any verbalizations without teacher permission). They also had trouble completing math problems while in class and, more often than not, received behavior ratings of "poor" from their teachers. No doubt about it, these kids needed help. But *what* sort of exercise would help them?

Although the researchers used a rather complicated design for their study, we needn't concern ourselves here with its complexity. It is enough to say that each of Dr. Evans's subjects was told he had been chosen to participate in a jogging club. On various occasions, each child was taken from his classroom, brought to a quarter-mile track on the school grounds, and told to jog as long as he could for up to fifteen minutes. At other times—for the sake of scientific comparison—some kids participated in fifteen-minute touch football games, and others engaged in fifteen-minute periods of reading alone outside the classroom. After any of these sessions, a child would be returned to the classroom, where an observer kept track of the child's "talk-outs," the number of math problems completed, and his behavior in general.

What were the findings? After exercise, whether jogging or playing football, the students "talked-out" less often, notes Dr. Evans. They also completed more problems after exercising. And what about teacher ratings? "For all subjects the highest teacher ratings occurred during exercise conditions," says Dr. Evans. (As you might have guessed, the sedentary activity of reading did little to change behavior.)

But that's not all. The Evans study also revealed what the researchers called "an unexpected serendipitous finding—the noticeable decrease in number of absences during this investigation. Prior to the experiment, each student averaged approximately one absence per week. During the study . . . only one absence for the entire experimental group was registered."

Although Dr. Evans's specific findings have not been replicated, other researchers have found that at the very least, exercise can have a positive impact on one's psychological health. Certainly the notion that exercise may boost concentration is well worth "studying" on your own. Perhaps it's time you dusted off those Nikes!

AVOID THE "DISTRACTING CLASSROOM WALL" SYNDROME

Visiting a classroom not long ago, Dr. W. N. Creekmore, a professor of special education at Northeast Louisiana University at Monroe, was "struck with the vast amount of 'stuff' packed into it. All of the colors of the rainbow were there," he noted, "children's work was displayed throughout the room, and decorations from a time gone by still hung limply on the wall." Perhaps most disturbing to Dr. Creekmore was the presence, on the bulletin board, of "a 3-D turkey, whose head protruded at least two feet into the room. Work on the piece was fine, but the date of my observation was nowhere near Thanksgiving."

Sure, it's fun for kids to display their creations in the classroom—and such items *can* contain content for learning. But isn't it just as likely that these materials are potentially powerful distractors as well, particularly where children with special needs are concerned?

Dr. Creekmore thinks so. As he explains it, "When presenting a lesson, the professional educator is intent on introducing 'new' material for consumption and learning. For this to occur, the learner must direct his faculties to the auditory and visual stimuli presented by the teacher. However, instructional control is challenged when children can see and hear material which is not central to the lesson. A teacher who places distractors in a room must compete with them to gain and keep the attention of the learners. This situation sets up a scenario that is counterproductive if not downright silly."

How to solve the problem? Dr. Creekmore recommends that teachers use his "learning wall approach," which involves organizing the walls of the classroom to enhance acquisition, maintenance, and generalization of material presented to students. Here's what you need to do:

1. The chalkboard and at least one bulletin board are designated the "acquisition wall." Keep it devoid of material that competes with lessons. It should be available only for the introduction and understanding of material being taught to students *now.* According to Dr. Creekmore, side bulletin boards—if filled with materials pertinent to the central lesson—should be masked until such time as they are needed, to prevent competition with the lecture. After a lesson, all materials should be removed or masked again.

2. A "maintenance wall" should be located to the side of the acquisition wall in full view of all students in the room, says Dr. Creekmore. It should be clear of visual and physical obstructions so that students can approach it and interact with the materials. The wall should be designed for review, reorientation, and fuller understanding of previously taught lessons. It should include carefully chosen, appropriate materials to be used to enhance tenuous concepts taught in the initial acquisition lessons—flash cards, instructional bulletin boards, and support materials are good examples.

3. Create a "dynamic wall," preferably at the back of the classroom. For example, notes Dr. Creekmore, "this wall could hold our old friend the turkey (but only if he is in season), announcements, students' art/academic work, and 'helper charts.' The

wall is dynamic because it should always be changing and should not be used as a 'parking place' for displays, materials, and outdated decorations for which the teacher has found no other home."

According to Dr. Creekmore, "Some of today's classrooms present obstacles to the very learning they try to enhance." He believes the "learning wall approach" can help remove some of those obstacles, and that in turn may reduce some of the "confounding variables with which special educators must deal in an effort to teach the student with special needs."

WHAT *KIDS* CAN DO ABOUT HOMEWORK DISTRACTIONS

Have you ever wondered what *you* can do to help kids overcome distractions while they're doing their homework? Here's how one teacher approached the problem:

When students in his sixth-grade study skills unit complained that the class didn't address the problem of homework interruptions, Ron Benson, a middle-school teacher with the Williamsville Central School District in New York, decided to do something about it. Actually, he got his *students* to do something about it: he asked them to (1) identify their most troublesome homework interruptions; (2) determine the reasons for the interruptions; and (3) begin to find their own solutions to coping with distractions. As a result of his practical field study, Benson found that "students began to look more deeply at themselves and appreciate the fact that *they* had the power to solve at least part of their homework problems."

What insights might teachers, students, and parents gain from such a study? After interviewing ninety-three pupils from four sixth-grade classes, categorizing and rank-ordering their opinions, and discussing results with the youngsters, Mr. Benson discovered the following facts:

- The *telephone* ranked number one as the most troublesome homework distraction, said 52 percent of the students.
- *Television* came in a close second, according to 51 percent of those interviewed.
- The third most frequently mentioned distraction involved *family*: 40 percent of the pupils said that parents, brothers, and sisters walking in and out of the room, teasing, and asking questions, created a distraction.
- Fourth in line were *radios, stereos, and tape players*, a distraction noted by 37 percent of the students.
- 38 percent of the students said *general noise* created a distraction. Sources included vacuum cleaners, washing machines, sirens, doorbells, musical instruments, and hallway disturbances.
- 36 percent complained of *being tired*. Reasons for this included not sleeping because of thinking and worrying, being kept awake by noises, and feeling restless.
- 26 percent were distracted by *pets* wanting attention, barking or being noisy, climbing on furniture, and so on.
- 17 percent said they were negatively affected by *background yelling, conversations, and crying*. Specific distractions mentioned included company visits, family arguments, and the crying of small babies.

According to Mr. Benson, his students offered a variety of alternatives to deal with distractions, most of which required self-awareness, self-discipline, and parent support. Suggestions included:

- Parents should monitor the telephone and answer the door during study periods.
- Turn off appliances and control the volume of the television, radio, and stereo located near study areas.
- Remove brothers and sisters as well as pets when studying.
- Request that the family keep yelling and crying to a minimum during study periods.

What will *your* students come up with? For more information about how to set up your own field study, consult the article "Helping Pupils Overcome Homework Distractions," by Ron Benson. His article appeared in the April 1988 issue of *Clearing House.*

COMPUTER-ASSISTED INSTRUCTION: HELP OR HINDRANCE?

If you consider the fact that more than 31.1 million adults use computers at home, work, or school,[2] you realize not only that these mighty mites are here to stay, but also that your youngsters are likely to come face-to-face with a PC or two at school in the near future. That being the case, many parents wonder: Will computer-assisted instruction help or hinder my distractible child? As you will see, this is a difficult question to answer. But thanks to the efforts of researchers at the University of Iowa, new light is being shed on the subject.

When they designed their study, researchers Gail Fitzgerald, Landis Fick, and Richard Millich already knew a few facts about children who have attention difficulties. For example, from a review of scientific literature, they were aware that hyperactive children:

(1) appear to do better academically when allowed to proceed at a self- versus teacher-paced rate;
(2) work best under continuous reinforcement; and
(3) often receive feedback of a primarily negative nature.

Knowing that about kids with behavioral problems, the researchers then considered some of the pros and cons of computers in the classroom
On the positive side, they felt that the computer can be a patient

---

[2]Source: *The World Almanac and Book of Facts 1989.* Estimates refer to data obtained through 1984 by the Census Bureau, U.S. Commerce Department.

teacher and can be programmed to emit any type and schedule of reinforcement desired, without drawing the attention of the entire class to the child's repeated failures. The computer can also attractively present information and help the student focus attention on the critical elements of a lesson through graphics, color, and/or animation.

On the negative side, they felt that the same color, graphics, and animation that serve to attract the student's attention may also act as distractors, interfering with the student's attention. And for children without typing skills, the task may be so frustrating, time-consuming, and/or distracting as to impede the mastery of the task.

Which side would win out? Fitzgerald and her colleagues began a study that would compare computer-assisted instruction (CAI) with traditional instruction (TI; i.e., write-and-check) and a no-practice condition in the mastery of spelling words. Their subjects were nine elementary-age students who were considered to have attentional difficulties. Five new words were assigned for each of the three conditions for each of the five weeks of the study. At the end of each week of practice, a spelling test was given for the fifteen words.

And the winner was . . . CAI *and* TI were significantly more effective than no practice in helping the students learn to spell new words. That meant *there was no significant difference between CAI and TI* in helping students learn the words.

So what's the good news in all this? Plenty. First, the results indicate that it may be possible to make available teacher time for more individualized instruction by having children spend some time on the computer. Second, the researchers point out that CAI in addition to TI may be more effective than either one alone. Perhaps most important, they say, the results indicate that children noted for having problems sustaining attention *can* employ computer-assisted instruction to master spelling words at a level comparable to more traditional methods of instruction. That finding alone may relieve the anxiety of many parents!

CAN MUSIC ENHANCE ACADEMIC ACHIEVEMENT?

Your child, of course, would say yes. But what's the scientific view on this subject? Turn on the stereo, sit back, relax, and brace yourself for a surprise.

At the University of Southern Mississippi, educational researcher Charles W. Davidson wanted to find out whether easy-listening[3] background music played in the classroom could be used to increase the amount of time students spent working on academic tasks. To do this, he designed a study that involved twenty-six pupils—fifteen boys and eleven girls—in a fifth-grade science class. Throughout forty-two class sessions over a period of four months, he monitored the children's behavior during class sessions conducted with background music and without it. In fact, Davidson and his helpers recorded their observations *every three minutes* during all of these sessions to keep track of whether or not each child was "on-task." The content of instructions consisted of class discussions on plants, animals, the solar system, and so forth, followed by an assignment that involved writing answers to questions provided by the teacher or the textbook.

The results? According to Dr. Davidson, the use of easy-listening music *was* effective in increasing on-task performance. Intriguingly, the boys in the class made the biggest jumps. For example, two boys who on average spent 91 percent of their time working moved up the performance ladder to 98 percent when music was played in the background. (Music didn't affect girls as much, noted Dr. Davidson. The study showed that most girls stayed on task roughly 98 percent of the time whether music was played or not.)

One final observation, provided by Dr. Davidson: "During the course of collecting data, it was apparent that neither the teaching methods employed nor the total classroom environment differed greatly from those for other subjects in the middle grades. There-

[3]Dr. Davidson defines easy-listening music as having "traditional orchestration (with) a rich use of strings and winds." It is also "non-percussive in beat (and) more lushly orchestrated than pop music."

fore, it would seem that providing easy-listening background music in the classroom would be a plausible yet inexpensive technique for increasing the amount of time in which students are actively engaged in learning." (And to those who consider a 7 percent increase in on-task behavior unimpressive, I say: isn't a little progress better than none at all?)

SELF-MONITORING: A TECHNIQUE FOR DISTRACTIBLE STUDENTS

Open the door to Mr. Smith's seventh-grade English class, and what you'll observe is unbridled chaos: a few children seem to be wandering aimlessly throughout the room, while those who are seated constantly fiddle with pencils and pens, bother their neighbors, or sit in a daydreamy trance. Mr. Smith spends most of his time speaking sharply to the group: "Johnny! Finish your paragraph! Ellen, quit poking Jim and get back to your reading! Bobby! Stop fiddling with that eraser and do your report!"

Just down the hall from Mr. Smith, you'll find the classroom of Ms. Jones. Peek inside and observe the serenity within: all of the students are reading quietly. Occasionally, you'll hear the sound of a beep being emitted from a tape recorder. When this happens, the students quickly—and quietly—place a checkmark on a sheet of paper, then return to their reading. Ms. Jones sits calmly at the front of the room, a Cheshire-cat smile on her face.

What accounts for the palpably different atmospheres of these two classrooms? The answer is simple: Ms. Jones's students have been trained to use a technique called self-monitoring. When they hear the beep from the tape recorder, they ask themselves, "Was I paying attention?" and check "Yes" or "No" on a preprinted card. Developed by researchers at the University of Virginia Learning Disabilities Research Institute, it is a novel procedure for improving attention in students who are often referred to as "inattentive," "distractible," or "spacy."

In fact, according to Dr. Daniel P. Hallahan, one of the creators of the technique, "[Our] results show that when self-monitoring techniques were introduced, on-task behavior increased *34 percent* during handwriting and *41 percent* during math." Moreover, he says, "In the area of academic productivity, the number of words produced correctly in handwriting increased by *2.89 words per minute* . . . and the number of correct answers written in math increased by *9.88 problems per minute.*"

Although complete details about how to implement this unique program are available free from the researchers (see ordering information below), the basics are highlighted below:

Materials: You'll need a tape recorder, a cassette tape, and a sheet of paper or card for the student's records. When preparing the tape, use an Audiometer or a piano tone for the beeps, which should be recorded at random intervals from ten to ninety seconds apart. Self-monitoring cards should include student's name, the question "Was I paying attention?" and two rows of twenty or so boxes labeled "Yes" and "No."

Procedure: Before beginning, explain to students that you want them to be more attentive. You may involve your entire class, or just certain students who have behavioral and distractibility problems. Depending on the age of the students involved, teachers may wish to role-play instances that portray "paying attention" or "not paying attention." Then explain that one way to increase attention is to have a student keep track of when he or she is paying attention and when he or she is not. Show students the tape recorder and the self-monitoring cards and explain that every time the student hears a tone, he or she is to ask, "Was I paying attention when I heard the tone?" and mark the card appropriately. This training procedure should take approximately fifteen to twenty minutes. (Note: In the manual available to teachers, the researchers provide scripts to assist in explaining the program to students and also discuss observation techniques for teachers to use in evaluating the effectiveness of the program.)

Follow-up: After five or six days of practice, says Dr. Hallahan, students should be able to self-monitor without the tape recorder: at various times during a study session, they merely ask themselves whether they're paying attention and then mark the card. Eventually, the card can be removed as well. When students ask the crucial question, they need only whisper or think, "Yes, good job," or "No, I'd better start paying attention."

Is this a panacea for the distractible student? No, says Dr. Hallahan. But he and his colleagues consider it "a highly effective means of improving children's attention to tasks—and often their academic productivity, too." The technique takes minimal teacher time and is minimally disruptive to other students when used with small groups within the classroom.

For more information, send for *Improving Attention and Self-Monitoring: A Manual for Teachers* by Daniel Hallahan, John Lloyd, and Laura Stoller at the Learning Disabilities Research Institute, 405 Emmet Street, University of Virginia, Charlottesville, VA 22903. You'll receive a copy of the manual within four weeks.

In the meantime, I encourage you to turn to the final section of this book. There, you'll find even *more* ways for improving concentration—from methods for reducing stress, boosting stamina, and fighting boredom to techniques for enhancing memory and fine-tuning sports performance.

Chapter XVIII

Taking Control: How to Manage Stress, Fatigue, and Diet

John glances at his watch and gasps. Just a while ago it was two in the afternoon, and he had two more hours to finish that report. Now, suddenly, it's three-thirty. In thirty minutes, his boss will call him into his office so they can review it. There's no time to lose—his job hinges on this project, and it cannot be late!

Odds are, John *won't* finish on time. He's bleary-eyed and foggy-minded. Even with seven hours of sleep, he began his day exhausted. Now, as the clock ticks louder and louder, anxiety overtakes him. His palms begin to sweat, his heart pounds. Sharp pains claw at his neck and shoulders. He writes a sentence, then crosses it out. Nothing seems to make sense. He pops a couple of aspirins, gulps stale coffee, munches a handful of M&Ms, then lights another cigarette. Again, he tries to focus on the report, but can't. A feeling of light-headedness overtakes him. "Just concentrate!" he tells himself, hoping that somehow, some way, he can command himself to perform. Alas, the mind refuses to comply. Uptight and on edge, John sits frozen. The wooziness turns to nausea. "What's wrong with me?" he wonders. "Am I losing my mind?"

No, John is *not* losing his mind, but I think you'd agree he has certainly put himself in a vulnerable position. Like millions of Americans, he's suffering from the ravages of stress, fatigue, and a poor diet. Just as insidious as a dysfunctional inner-ear system, these three problems not only exacerbate the symptoms of people who have ADD, they can wreak havoc among non-ADD individuals as well.

What can you do to reduce stress and fatigue and in the process boost concentration? Can diet really make a difference? You'll find the answers in this chapter. Many of the ideas and methods have been developed by well-known psychologists, sports physiologists, nutritionists, and a host of scientists and researchers from around the country. Try their techniques. Put them into practice. Make them a part of your everyday life. If you do, you'll not only feel terrific, you'll also be at your peak—primed to take control of your powers of concentration.

SHORT-CIRCUITING STRESS

Everybody's experienced it but few can define it. Your grandmother may have called it "nerves," but today we refer to it as stress—the condition that costs U.S. industry $150 billion a year and afflicts millions of Americans every day of their lives. Under pressure to perform? On a tough deadline? Afraid of losing your job? Had a fight with your spouse? Forced to listen to noisy workmen for hours on end? Almost any situation has the potential for producing stress—your body's "fight or flight" response to what your mind perceives as a threat or challenge. And left unchecked, it can cause a host of mental and physical problems, from panic attacks, memory dysfunction, disorientation, and depression to high blood pressure, weight loss, weight gain, headaches, insomnia, indigestion, chest pain, heart attacks, ulcers, and colitis, just to name a few. Is it any wonder that a stressed-out person cannot concentrate?

Let's face it: no one can escape stress. But there are things you can do to keep the consequences of stress at a minimum. Take a deep breath, try to relax, and read on.

Learn How to Quantify Your Stress

Your blood pressure's rising and your head is pounding. You know you're stressed, but you don't know why. Probably just having a bad day, right? Wrong, says clinical psychologist Michael Uhes. There are specific *reasons* for why you're stressed. Find out what they are, says Dr. Uhes—director of the Human Performance Institute in Lakewood, Colorado—and you've taken the first step in combating stress.

During the first of ten sessions in his four-month stress-reduction program, Dr. Uhes and his staff teach clients how to quantify their stress on a scale of zero (a reflection of inner calm and serenity) to ten (being uptight, high-strung, as scared as they've ever been). Using the scale, participants keep a log to keep track of changes in their stress levels. Every time they notice a change, they must ask themselves two questions: (1) Where was I? and (2) What happened? From there, they're encouraged to delve deeper. Who said what? Did my level go up then? What happened next? What was I thinking?

According to Dr. Uhes, his technique enables clients to separate fiction from fact. Those who thought they were having a bad day or just feeling tense are now aware of their own personal stress triggers: seeing their boss's furrowed brow, catching a whiff of perfume on the crabby, competitive co-worker, hearing a rumor that five executives will be laid off, and so forth. The self-questioning provides answers. Eventually, what was vague becomes specific. Clients begin to see that the triggers are predictable—and controllable.

Teaching people to take control of stress isn't easy, but so far, Dr. Uhes appears to be making considerable headway with his clients. According to a report published in *Prevention*, "the frequency of headaches in the 300 people studied was down 58 percent, insomnia was down 66 percent, indigestion was down 41 percent, and low back pain was down 53 percent. Shoulder and neck pain went down 73 percent, chest pain (angina) 69 percent, and diastolic blood pressure dropped 12 points. Follow-up six months to two years later still showed significant drops." Figures for psychological changes were similar: In brief, the report stated that Dr. Uhes's clients "felt more joyful, satisfied, clear-headed, and tranquil, and less discouraged, angry, rushed, distracted, and frustrated."

Three Ways to Calm Your Mind

As you've just seen, Dr. Uhes's program helps clients to reduce many of the symptoms of stress. To achieve the results mentioned above, he also encourages them to relax their minds by repeating to themselves certain calming statements such as "I am completely calm" or "Move slowly, think slowly." In addition, he recommends another mind-calming technique called the count-down, which is based on breath meditation and takes a mere five minutes of your time. Why not try it right now?

First, close your eyes. Breathe easily and comfortably. Now begin to focus on the air coming in. As you breathe out, focus on the number five. Continue this in-and-out pattern for a bit, then lower the number to four, and so on until you get to one. Stay focused on one for roughly a minute, and while you do so, repeat one of the calming statements noted above. Keep the focus on your breathing for yet another minute, then count back up to five. With enough practice, notes Dr. Uhes, clients can utilize the technique when they're under fire at work, or in other potentially stressful environments. And don't hesitate to try it *before* you walk into a stress-filled situation—your next job interview or that speech you've been asked to give at the Rotary Club meeting.

A third way to calm the mind: Try behavioral rehearsal or "visualization," a technique often used by athletes (see Chapter Twenty). Instead of concentrating on the stress, imagine yourself calming down—perhaps under an umbrella at the beach. Focus on the soft breeze blowing, the sun shining. Contemplate how you're feeling. Use such thoughts to block out what's stressing you, then sit back and revel in the serenity you've created for yourself.

Develop Your Own Stress Strategy

Most experts agree: we can't escape stress, but we can learn to minimize its effects. One way is to plan ahead for it by developing your own coping strategies. You'll feel more in control, less vulnerable to stress when it occurs.

Practice time management: If you're always feeling stressed by deadlines, you just may need more time to get things done. "To bring immediate order to your life," advises Dr. Marilyn Liebrenz, a time management expert at George Washington University, "start establishing daily, weekly, monthly, and even yearly goals. Put them in some order of priority. Start out trying to pursue them—then watch where your time is really going. You'll find your-self wasting time on nonessentials, most likely—and by shifting that time to essentials, you'll reduce 'deadline stress' instantly."

Avoid procrastination: Instead of dodging tasks that seem over-whelming, says Dr. Liebrenz, attack such projects in small steps. "Putting them off will only make them more stressful to deal with. You'll worry about them continually at first, and find them insur-mountable later—and that's a double dose of stress." When possible, prioritize tasks using a scale of one to five or one to ten. Then start with number one and divide *it* into steps.

Get support from friends/family: So many of us were brought up to be self-reliant; we were taught to "do it yourself if you want it done right." It's just that sort of attitude that can lead to stress. Next time a job seems overwhelming, ask for assistance. If the prospect of giv-ing a speech has you in a tizzy, practice in front of a friend or family member. Best advice: Don't try to do everything yourself. Set rea-sonable goals and ask for help when you need it.

The quick-stretch technique: When various parts of your body become painfully tight due to stress, try stretching them loose. For example, if your shoulders tighten, just shrug them upward for five seconds, taking a deep breath in—then drop them down in an exag-gerated motion, with a deep breath out. Or, if you're feeling tension in your neck and shoulders, wrap your arms around yourself as if you were giving yourself a hug; squeeze and relax. Stress should lessen right away. Note: With enough practice, the quick stretch can become an automatic, *positive* response to stress.

The Exercise Connection

The good news: Almost any type of exercise can reduce stress. The bad news: Fewer than 10 percent of Americans over eighteen years old exercise regularly.[1] The reason? Perhaps it is because most types of exercise—such as jogging or playing tennis—strike us as being too much like work. That's why I recommend the sim-

---

[1]Quoted in *The New York Times*, November 3, 1989; Dr. Stephen Blair, Institute for Aerobics Research and the Cooper Clinic, Dallas, Texas.

plest exercise of all: *walking*. It's easy, it's cheap, it reduces stress. And there's an important added benefit. According to a recent study of 13,000 men and women, undertaken by the Institute for Aerobics Research and the Cooper Clinic in Dallas to discover how physical fitness was related to death rates, researchers found that even modest amounts of exercise—such as walking—can substantially reduce your chance of dying of heart disease, cancer, or other causes. In fact, notes Dr. Carl Caspersen of the Federal Centers for Disease Control in Atlanta, "You don't have to be a marathoner. You get much more benefit out of being just a bit more active. For example, going from sedentary to walking briskly for a half hour several days a week can drop your risk dramatically." So what are you waiting for?

Remember, walking is more than just exercise—it's good for your overall mental health. If you're feeling anxious or depressed, even a short, brisk walk can help take your mind off your troubles, and you'll return from your stroll feeling stronger and more able to deal with life's aggravations. In fact, researchers have found that brisk walking can increase the body's production of endorphins— natural opiates in the body that reduce pain and raise spirits.

To take advantage of the physical and psychological benefits of this wonderful form of exercise, start by taking a daily walk. To get the most out of the time you spend, however, make sure you're walking properly. According to Dr. Robert Sleight, executive director of the Walking Association in Tucson, Arizona, this means picking your feet up (no shuffling!), gently swinging your arms, and using your feet correctly. "Land on your heel and roll forward until you get to your toes," he says. "Then push off with your toes" so that they get exercise as well.

Before going out each day, try stretching exercises. Start each of the following exercises from the same position, lying flat on your back with arms at sides. You can do these on a bed or on the floor. Remember to alternate limbs when necessary.

For the legs and hips:

(1) Knee exercise: Tighten your kneecaps by pressing them into the mattress or floor, then relax.

(2) Straight leg raise: Bend your left knee with foot flat on the bed or floor. Keeping your right knee straight, raise right leg toward ceiling, then lower it slowly.

(3) Hip exercise: Bend left knee with foot flat on floor. With right leg straight, slide it across the floor—as far to the right as possible. Return leg to center.

For the ankles:

(1) Ankle pumps: Point toes downward, then toward the ceiling.

(2) Ankle circles: With heels on the floor or mattress, rotate foot clockwise; then counterclockwise. Use your big toe as a reference for twelve o'clock.

For the arms and shoulders:

(1) Shoulder flex: With arms at sides, slowly raise shoulders straight toward the ceiling, as high as possible, then gently lower them. This exercise may be done with only one arm at a time if you prefer.

(2) Shoulder exercise: Gently slide your arm out sideways until it is level with your shoulder, then slide arm back to your side.

Try these exercises on those days when you can't take a walk—they'll loosen you up, help keep you fit, and reduce stress, too.

The Power of Humor

Can you really laugh your troubles away? Probably not. But that doesn't mean you should rule out the power of laughter to defuse stress. In fact, a couple of psychologists—Rod Martin and Herbert Lefcourt—have measured its effects. Their findings, as reported in the *Journal of Personality and Social Psychology*: Humor is a splendid way to combat stress. What's more, individuals who can be fanciful are less apt to be tense, angry, depressed, and fatigued than are people who let gloom overtake them.

You can put more humor into your life in a variety of ways. Go to the movies, stock up on videos, and seek out films starring people like Steve Martin, Jerry Lewis, Eddie Murphy, Laurel and Hardy, or your favorite funny person. Find out where stand-up comedians appear in your local community, then invite a friend to join you. Spend some time in the library searching for humorous books that will make you chuckle. Watch for cartoons that make you giggle; then cut them out and save them. Perhaps most important: Don't take yourself so seriously. Laughing at oneself may be the best antistress medicine of all.

FATIGUE: HOW TO FIGHT BACK

Do you feel time flies by so fast during a day that you can't possibly complete your work and fulfill family obligations?

Do you gulp so much coffee throughout the day that your nerves feel jangled?

Does your alcohol consumption worry you?

Do you "run out of gas" by late afternoon?

After eight hours of sleep, do you still feel tired when the alarm goes off?

Do you feel that your powers of concentration are operating at half-throttle?

If you answered yes to some or all of these questions, you may be suffering from fatigue—that weary, fuzzy feeling we get when our bodies and minds have been sapped of energy. What can you do about it? Well, you can try to sort through and make sense of all the books and magazine articles currently available on the subject. Or—an infinitely preferable solution—you can get simple, logical, easy-to-follow advice from an expert who's made the subject of fatigue his life's work: Peter Miller, Ph.D., author of *The Hilton Head Executive Stamina Program* and director of the Hilton Head Health Institute.

According to Dr. Miller, the secret to fighting fatigue lies in your ability to maintain peak stamina. He offers a twelve-day program geared to teaching busy executives how to reach that peak. You're not an executive? That doesn't matter. Dr. Miller's techniques can still help you do what successful executives do. And that, says Dr. Miller, is to "maintain an endurance level that enables them to create and sustain a surge of high-powered energy, even after grueling hours of work and travel."

Derived from the Latin word *stamen*, meaning "thread of life spun by the Fates," stamina is essential for peak performance—and not just in athletes, says Dr. Miller. Whether you're a CEO on the fast track or a housewife on the treadmill, everyone needs stamina to excel on the job. Unfortunately, though, today's sedentary life-style and the typical desk-bound, meeting-packed workday sap energy by the hour. Compounding those problems is a lack of awareness: most people don't realize the reasons for their fatigue and are therefore ill prepared to conquer it. Then they try quick-fix solutions—the catnap or the coffee break—which do little good or are actually counterproductive.

In his book, Dr. Miller helps to demystify fatigue by providing readers with key reasons why it occurs:

(1) Despite all those well-meaning headlines about eating right, many people still don't eat the right stuff, he says. "They don't fuel the body's engine properly and the body loses energy. The main energizer for the body is glucose," he notes, "which provides the cells with energy—particularly the brain cells. We get glucose from carbohydrates; most importantly, complex carbohydrates—fruits and vegetables, grain-based foods like bread and cereal. Also the starches, potatoes, and pastas."

Take heed: If your morning routine includes a cup of coffee and a small glass of juice for breakfast, and then you don't eat lunch until two P.M., you're functioning well below peak stamina for more than half a day. (More information about diet, as it applies to those with ADD, can be found in the next section.)

(2) "People lose fluids throughout the day, and not just from sweating and urinating," notes Miller. Other reasons for dehydration: Many offices have low humidity, as do airplanes (you can lose up to two pounds of water during a 3.5 hour flight). Furthermore, coffee and other caffeinated drinks are diuretics—and thus rob the body of more fluids, further sapping energy.

(3) You have a fairly sedentary job. Yet you suffer from tired muscles. How can that be? Just sitting with a phone jammed in the crook of your neck or with your head and shoulders hunched over a computer keyboard can drain energy via static tension. "It's like having one foot on the accelerator and the other on the brake," Miller explains. "The tension is building and has no place to go."

(4) Boredom also saps energy. Having a case of the blahs is one thing, but a repetitious, unexciting daily routine, triggering the same, rutted brain-wave patterns, often results in a drifting of attention or fuzzy focus—the opposite of a creative burst of energy.

Can a nap help? "If your fatigue is mental, your body doesn't need a rest. It needs *more* stimulation," emphasizes Dr. Miller. "Nor does passive relaxation help muscle fatigue brought on by static tension."

What about the coffee break? "The worst thing ever invented for the workplace. It actually robs you of energy," says Dr. Miller. "Usually it's not just coffee, but also a sweet. Sure, the sugar in the simple carbohydrate will give you a quick boost, but thirty minutes later your energy will have dissipated." The coffee, too, provides but a quick fix, and in draining bodily fluids, provides no lasting stamina solution.

What does Dr. Miller recommend?

☐ Eat four meals a day—60 percent carbohydrates, no more than 15 percent protein, no more than 25 percent fat. (You'll find additional information on diet in the next section.)

☐ Instead of a coffee break, take a rest-in-motion break. His book spells out a twenty-minute, closed door routine comprised of deep breathing exercises to stretch and strengthen key muscles. "I schedule them as needed. Usually once in the morning and once in the afternoon," says Dr. Miller. "I just close my door and get away from everything. But even five minutes away from your desk, stretching or walking around your office, will help."

Studies bear him out, notably a Belgian experiment that randomly assigned employees of a manufacturing company to one of two rest groups. One group simply sat and rested during their ten-minute break. The other did mild calisthenics. The results? Those who'd been physically active tested far superior afterward. They showed better decision-making ability, better memory, better mental acuity.

☐ Replenish bodily fluids with a "stamina spritzer"—eight ounces of orange juice plus four ounces of carbonated water and ice. Fruit provides glucose, and the carbonation speeds the liquid into the bloodstream.

☐ Eat a "power snack"—a banana, an orange, or a box of raisins.

☐ To combat motivational fatigue, look for new challenges. "We find this type of fatigue most often in people whose sole reinforcement is their work situation. We generally tell them to explore new activities or hobbies," he says, adding that learning photography or how to play the piano seems to stimulate the whole body, and the new energy often transfers to the job.

☐ Take control of your own "thread of life," advises Miller. And that means treating yourself as well as you do *any* job.[2]

THE DIET CONNECTION

When my patients ask me about my views regarding the role of diet and its ability to improve concentration, I usually respond with two statements: (1) I am *not* a nutritionist or food scientist and therefore not an expert on the subject, but (2) based on interviews with patients and my own personal experience, I believe without a doubt that what we eat can greatly enhance *or* diminish our powers of concentration. That said, I would now like to discuss two "special" dietary regimes that I believe are worthy of consideration. The first applies specifically to individuals who have ADD;

[2]Adapted with permission from "Stamina Seminar," by John Grossman. Article appeared in *InnerCircle* magazine, Summer 1989; published by The Continental Corporation, edited by Nancy Schommer.)

the second, to adults who've been looking for a diet that will prime the mind for peak performance.

The Feingold Diet

Parents of children with ADD will no doubt have heard about the famous (some would say infamous) Feingold Diet. Developed by Ben F. Feingold, M.D., in the early 1970s, this approach to treating the symptoms of ADD (known then as hyperactivity) is based on Feingold's belief that specific substances in the diet may cause behavioral disturbances in some children. The culprits: artificial colorings, artificial flavorings, and certain preservatives with names as long as your arm—butylated hydroxyanisole (found in potato chips) is just one example.

Where do we find these hidden demons? Here's just a sample of the foods not permitted on the Feingold Diet: most commercial ice creams, flavored yogurt, bacon, hot dogs, margarine, chewing gum, most commercial candies, toothpaste, apples, tomatoes, many cheeses, all barbecued poultry, mustard, mayonnaise, cough drops, Lifesavers, frozen fish fillets, ham, luncheon meats, chocolate milk, prepared gravies, many prepared pickles, soda pop, diet drinks, even Kool-Aid.

The list is daunting. Sticking to the diet is a challenge. Yet according to Feingold, if you eliminate the above items—and scores of others—from the hyperactive kid's diet, you'll find that a host of symptoms will disappear, including sleeplessness, hyperactivity, aggressiveness, destructiveness, abusiveness, short attention span, and inability to concentrate for more than a few moments. According to Feingold, when treated with his special diet, *50 percent of hyperactive learning-disabled children achieve a "full response, while 75 percent can be removed from drug management."*

Sound too good to be true? Many critics think so, including the National Advisory Committee on Hyperkinesis and Food Additives, a group composed of behavioral and medical scientists. Skeptical of Feingold's claims, the committee spent five years examining Dr. Feingold's research from top to bottom and found it wanting for a variety of complicated reasons. The committee also examined *other* researchers' studies of the diet, to see whether Feingold's findings could be duplicated. After everything was said and done, the group produced its "Final Report to the Nutrition Foundation" in 1980, concluding quite forcefully that "there have been no instances of consistent, dramatic deterioration in behavior in hyperactive children challenged under double blind conditions, with artificial food colorings, and no significant improvement following treatment with the diet that removes these substances." Layperson's translation: Feingold's theory isn't worth the powder to blow it up with.

What happened when the media got hold of the committee's dim view of the Feingold hypothesis? No one knows for sure, but I suspect that, nationwide, many parents who read about it stopped administering the diet to their hyperactive children. Within my own clinical "neighborhood," however, I did not notice a marked decrease in enthusiasm for the diet in 1980 or in any year thereafter. Indeed, over the past ten years, I've observed that more and more patients are trying it. Perhaps most important, approximately 10 percent of my patients are experiencing favorable responses.

It is not my aim in this section to provide the reader with a full account of the Feingold Diet; that has already been done by Feingold himself in his books. Instead, my goal as a physician is merely to suggest to readers that the diet is *worth trying*. It cannot hurt your child, and may in fact help him or her. Isn't that reason enough to give it a try?

For specific details about the diet, I recommend that readers obtain a copy of Feingold's first book, *Why Your Child Is Hyperactive*. It explains his theories in depth and provides guidelines related to which foods are permitted on the diet and which are not. Once you've read that, you may wish to pick up a copy of *The Feingold Cookbook for Hyperactive Children*, co-authored by Feingold and his wife. There, you'll find recipes and a four-week menu, plus a "survival handbook" to help you administer the diet with ease. Finally, you may wish to contact The Feingold Foundation for Child Development, 1050 North Point Street, San Francisco, CA 94109. The organization works with parents who are looking for support and want information on permissible foods available in their geographical locations.

A Diet for Peak Performance

At the beginning of this section, I stated that I am not a nutritionist or a food scientist. Perhaps I should have added that I don't consider myself a reviewer of diets. Nevertheless, I want to recommend another dietary approach, this one discovered in a book written by a research scientist at M.I.T. It's easy to abide by, it's based on proven research, and—best of all—it has the potential to increase mental energy, enhance your enthusiasm, boost performance, and focus your mind. Impossible, you say? Reel in your skepticism and read on.

I first came across Dr. Judith Wurtman's book, *Managing Your Mind and Mood Through Food*, when one of my patients claimed her life had been changed after reading it. I picked up a copy, thumbed through a few pages, and found some rather astonishing statements. For example, Dr. Wurtman claimed that:

"You will learn how food can help you bounce back when mental lethargy or a loss of enthusiasm dampens your ability to get things done.

"You will learn how food can help you focus your mind when the situation calls for clear thinking and creative problem-solving.

"You will learn how food can help you ward off 'brain fatigue' so you can stay up late to finish a report or study for an exam, and still perform at your peak the following morning."

In short, wrote Dr. Wurtman, "you will learn how to use food to shift at will from a state of mind that works against you into one that works for you!" As skeptical as the next person—and just as hopeful that what I'd read was true—I finished the book and with no small amount of trepidation began the diet at once.

That was over a year ago. Since then I have become convinced that the diet does indeed work and that the theories on which it is based are sound. Briefly, the principles underlying this dietary regime are as follows:

- Inside the brain, messages are passed from cell to cell via chemicals called neurotransmitters. From the foods we eat, the brain manufactures three of these message carriers or mood modifiers: dopamine and norepinephrine, the "alertness chemicals," and serotonin, the "calming chemical."

- How to get more of the alertness chemicals? Eat foods that contain *protein* (including shellfish, fish, chicken, veal, very lean beef, dried peas and beans, lentils, tofu, and low-fat dairy products). They increase the production of dopamine and norepinephrine and thus increase alertness and have an energizing effect on your mind. According to Dr. Wurtman, three to four ounces of protein is enough to stimulate production of the chemicals.

- How to relax? When eaten alone, without protein, foods that contain *carbohydrates* (bread, pasta, potatoes, sweets like pie and ice cream) increase the production of serotonin, and thus have a calming, focusing effect. As little as one to one-and-a-half ounces of a carbohydrate food—a sweet or a starch—will increase the manufacture of serotonin.

- If you eat protein either alone or with a carbohydrate, you'll respond more quickly and with greater accuracy to mental challenges. "You'll be more alert," says Dr. Wurtman, "more motivated, more mentally energetic and 'up.'"

- If you eat carbohydrates alone, without protein, "you'll feel less stressed," she says, "less anxious, more focused and relaxed."

(Note: Wurtman believes vegetables are "food-mood neutral," but she encourages dieters to "eat them as often as possible." What about fruits? "They're good for you," she says, "but don't reach for an apple or orange when you want to feel more focused or less stressed. It won't work.")

Using the above guidelines, Dr. Wurtman has developed eating "strategies" for just about any occasion. My personal favorite: business meal guidelines. Preparing for an early-morning brainstorming session, or a lunch to discuss a complicated financial matter, or a dinner designed to get your employees to know each other better? Try Dr. Wurtman's rules, which apply to all work-related situations:

1. *Eat sparingly.* "Maximum mental performance during and after a working meal demands that you limit your calorie intake," she says. "Don't eat more than 400 calories at a working breakfast, and stay within the 500-600 calorie range at working lunches and dinner." (In the case of breakfast, it makes little difference whether you eat proteins or carbohydrates, says Dr. Wurtman. That's when their mind- and mood-modifying properties "are barely perceptible.")

2. *Don't arrive hungry.* "Never go to a business meal on an empty stomach," advises Dr. Wurtman. If you haven't eaten, have a snack—preferably yogurt, fruit, a cup of clear soup, or a bran muffin. "The idea . . . is not to fill up," she says, "but to eat just enough so that an hour or so later your mind won't be drawn to thoughts of food when you should be concentrating on the agenda of your working meal."

3. *Eat protein before carbohydrate.* The reason? When you start your meal with a carbohydrate which stimulates calming chemicals in the brain, advises Dr. Wurtman, "you will begin to feel benign and relaxed." Such feelings are not to your advantage in a business situation, she notes. "You want your mental antennae quivering and alert."

4. *Order "easy" food.* This rule has nothing to do with brain chemistry; it merely helps you concentrate on the agenda of your working meal. Dr. Wurtman's recommendation: "Don't choose foods that require tricky manipulation with a knife, fork or spoon; and above all, never try a new dish that you do not know how to eat. If you have to focus too hard on the physical act of eating, your attention will be sidetracked from the *real* business at hand."

5. *Avoid alcohol.* Sure, a cocktail or a glass of wine is initially stimulating, says Dr. Wurtman, but "the subsequent result of drinking more than a very small amount is *always sedation.*" Her rule regarding alcohol is simple: "Order a drink before dinner only if *not* ordering one would call undue attention to yourself or inhibit your dining partners. When it arrives, take only a single sip and put the glass down. By drinking no more than a sip . . . you'll be able to maintain your own mental alertness while that of others at your table may be ebbing."

Maybe business meals don't interest you. Not to worry—in her book, Dr. Wurtman covers many more subjects than that. In fact, I believe her book offers dietary help for just about everyone. Want suggestions for all-day, everyday "power" eating? Looking for answers to your questions about caffeine? Wondering how to eat for a winning presentation? Want more information about eating to ease stress? I believe you'll find the answers in *Managing Your Mind and Mood Through Food.* As Wurtman herself puts it, the diet "is not magic and wish fulfillment . . . [it's] hard science."

By putting to use some of the techniques I've suggested in this chapter, you will be well-equipped to expand your powers of concentration farther than you ever thought possible. Moreover, with your mind and body healthy and relaxed, you will be ready to attempt yet another mind-managing technique that can help you reach your peak. In the next chapter, memory functioning and enhancing techniques will be discussed. And in the final chapter of this book, you'll find the latest information about *visualization.* Used by some of the world's greatest athletes, it's one more tool that can help you reach your own personal level of total concentration.

CHAPTER XIX

Memory: The Black Hole of Neurobiology

"The art of memory is the art of attention."

Samuel Johnson

Your brain contains a far greater number of neurons than all the stars in our galaxy. One expert's modest estimate of your memory's total capacity figures it at one hundred billion bits of information. Even if we assume only one percent of it remains subject to recall, this still means each of us is walking around with more data in our heads than the most advanced research computer. And you can't remember where you put your car keys?

In this chapter, we will delve into the mysteries of memory, the elusive component of intelligence that is intertwined with our ability to concentrate and to learn. What is known about memory? How does memory work? Can it really be improved? Let's begin to find the answers.

YOUR ASTONISHING MEMORY

We all tend to focus on, and worry about, what we forget rather than what we remember, because we are constantly frustrated by the former and take the latter for granted. But it is our power of recall, not our lapses, that is the truly astonishing thing about our memory. Who was president of the United States before Franklin Roosevelt? What was the name of Dorothy's dog in *The Wizard of Oz*? How many home runs did Babe Ruth hit, and who finally broke his record? What is the make and model year of that huge car with the pointy tailfins?

When your answers don't pop up like pieces of toast from the toaster, your brain also has very sophisticated techniques available for coaxing them forth. Let's see, the president that preceded Roosevelt; well, why was Roosevelt elected? . . . the Great Depression . . . who was blamed for that? . . . Herbert Hoover, of course.

But your mind and memory is far more than a giant filing cabinet. Suppose you are presented with an anagram, a familiar word that has been scrambled: SNETIBAC. It so happens that there are 40,320 different ways that those eight letters could be sequenced, and if you laboriously set out to run through all of them (which is what a computer would do), at the rate of one new combination every five seconds, it could take as long as fifty-six hours before you stumbled on the correct one. But that's not what you do: you look at the whole word, and instantly your mind discards such possibilities as all the vowels coming first, and consonants last—AEIBCNST. Words aren't constructed that way. Vowels are usually sprinkled among consonants to make the word pronounceable. So without quite knowing what process is taking place in your head, you let the letters flow about while you stare at them, until they arrange themselves in a sensible pattern—usually within a few seconds. Of course, if I gave you a less familiar word, KKJVEIYRA, it might take you a little longer.
(Answers: CABINETS, REYKJAVIK)

THE BRAIN: NOT JUST A LUMP OF PROTOPLASM

Do you want to know how your brain works? Here's how one scientist describes the process[1]:

"Most neuroscientists think of the brain as a biological computer, a vast network of tens of billions of neurons that commu-

---

[1]From *Memory: Learning How it Works,* by George Johnson, *New York Times Magazine,* August 9, 1987.

nicate in a code of electrical impulses. Each neuron receives information, from the body's sensory organs or from other neurons, through its dendrite, a treelike structure whose thousands of tiny branches funnel these signals into the cell.

"If a neuron accumulates enough signals, it fires, sending its own electrical pulse down a stalk called an axon, which feeds, through connections called synapses, into the dendrites of other cells. One neuron can receive signals from thousands of other neurons; its axon can branch repeatedly, transmitting signals to thousands more.

"Once an electrical signal reaches the end of one of the axon's branches, called a terminal, it is ferried across the synaptic gap by molecules known as neurotransmitters. On the other side of the synapse, a bump—or spine—on the dendrite of the next neuron contains structures called receptors that recognize these transmitting molecules. If enough neurotransmitter is detected this neuron fires, sending another electrical signal down the line.

"While the process neurons use to communicate is becoming clearer, how they store information is still a mystery. But it is assumed that when the brain registers a new event (the image of a face, the sound of laughter), a unique pattern of neurons is activated. Unless this neural configuration is to fade with whatever evoked it, we must have a means of retaining it—of solidifying the connections between the neurons, creating a new circuit that acts as a representation of a piece of the outside world. This might be done by creating new synapses between the neurons or by strengthening the synapses that are already there. In either event, by reactivating the circuit, the brain can retrieve the memory—rough and perhaps a bit faded, but a serviceable replica of the original perception."

Got it? Ready for the exam? Found your car keys yet? Unless you're pretty far along in your graduate studies, or at least a very bright science major, it's unlikely that you fully understood the above explanation, because it is filled with unfamiliar terms such as *dendrite* and *axon* and *neurotransmitter*, and because the underlying concept of the electrochemistry of the brain is also unfamiliar to you. But the interesting thing is that you probably *did* get the basic idea of impulses traveling along a circuit, because the concept is not unlike the way your house is wired, or the way current travels from your car's battery to the starter mechanism. Close enough, anyway, to allow *your* brain's circuitry to summon up a rough analogy that helps. What took place within your brain as you struggled through that difficult excerpt also helps demonstrate that memory is not just an inert lump of protoplasm, but an active, contributing component of all your thinking.

A HANDFUL OF THEORIES ABOUT MIND AND MEMORY

Philosophers and scientists have been trying to fathom how the human mind and its memory works ever since the dawn of recorded history, but all their explanations have fallen short of the mark. Plato thought of the brain as a blank tablet (*tabula rasa*) on which knowledge was inscribed, then etched and furrowed until it formed a permanent record. If it were as simple as that, yesterday's scribblings on the slate would at the very least tend to obscure the data underneath, but we all know old gaffers who can rattle off the starting lineup of the 1939 Boston Red Sox flawlessly yet can't remember who won the game they watched on TV yesterday.

Anyone who has suffered the rigors of an old-fashioned education can recall teachers who considered your mind to be a muscle, and who delighted in trying to make you strengthen it like a set of biceps through exhaustive memorizing. But a century ago, the pioneering psychologist William James put a dent in this theory with a demanding experiment where he memorized 158 lines of a poem by Victor Hugo, then spent more than a month memorizing all 798 lines of the first book of Milton's *Paradise Lost.* Next he went back to Victor Hugo, only to discover that it was taking him longer per line to memorize the next stanzas of the original poem. All those workouts were making his so-called mind muscle weaker, not stronger, because he was cluttering it up with rote learning without a meaningful frame of reference.

Another popular analogy is mind-as-reference-library: everything that enters is card-catalogued and filed on the proper shelf. But what about all the things you remember just long enough to do them (pick up the dog at the grooming parlor before 4:00 P.M.)? Or the things you have conveniently rearranged in your memory (what a great time you had at your senior prom, when actually you were a shy wallflower)? Or your total recall of what it looked and felt like that golden August afternoon you sailed into Nantucket Harbor on a following northwesterly breeze, coupled with a total inability to remember what happened the next day, or week? If your mind were a library, what would you say about an important volume that had been placed on the wrong shelf? Gone but not forgotten? No, quite the opposite: forgotten, but not gone. The mind is a mysterious place.

As man invents more and more complex mechanical devices, there seems always to be a tendency to equate them with the workings of the mind. Brain-as-telephone-switchboard was popular for a while, at least until direct dialing and answering machines came along. Recently it has been brain-as-computer, which gives short shrift to creative genius, metaphysical insights, and the madness of love, among other things. The very latest, and most daunting, assault on the mysteries of the mind is found in Roger Penrose's *The Emperor's New Mind, Concerning Computers, Minds and the Laws of Physics*, wherein he posits that the physics of thinking involves phenomena in which quantum effects play an important role.

I am content to settle—certainly for the purpose of this book—for a more modest view: although we know a great deal more than we ever have about the anatomy of the brain, its electrochemistry, and its neurobiology, we do not know, and may never know, everything about how the brain, let alone the mind, works. As more than one scientist has observed, it is presumptuous to hope that we will understand how ten billion brains work when the best tool we have at our disposal to deal with the question is a single brain at a time. Therefore, let us bemuse ourselves for a bit with mental inconsistencies and paradoxes, and then move on to deal with the practical ways to deal with practical problems of memory.

PRODIGIES, SAVANTS, AND ABSENT-MINDED PROFESSORS

Scientific literature is filled with stories of implausible mental prodigies: Thomas Fuller, an illiterate eighteenth-century slave who could multiply two nine-digit numbers in his head; Zerah Colburn, a Vermont schoolboy who could instantly figure out mentally that eight raised to the sixteenth power was 281,474,976,710,656; George Parker Bidder, an even younger lad who soon outmatched Colburn by answering questions like "How many jumps will it take for a flea to circumnavigate the earth at its 25,020-mile equator at 2 feet, 3 inches per hop, and how long will it take him if he jumps 60 times per minute?" (Answer: 58,713,600 hops and one year, 314 days, 13 hours, and 20 minutes, assuming no rest periods.)

What is one to make of such astonishing feats of mental prestidigitation? Very little, for there are just as many true stories of people known to science as idiot savants—certifiable mental defectives who nonetheless can instantly calculate on what day Christmas will fall in the year 2193, or who can play Tchaikovsky's first piano concerto start to finish, without error, after hearing it once.

More relevant, and easier to relate to, are the numerous stories of absent-minded professors, like the ichthyologist who complained that every time he had to learn the name of a new student he forgot the name of a fish. Or the scruffy-looking man picked up by the New York police years ago when they found him wandering about Manhattan unable to remember the name or location of his hotel—Albert Einstein, of course. Or the famous inventor who went to City Hall to pay his taxes, and when he got to the head of the line couldn't remember his name—Thomas Edison. Their lapses were akin to thine and mine: they had more important things on their mind at the moment.

There is another side to the coin, however—other genius-level talents with staggeringly good memories that they put to effective use: Mozart, who could write out the entire score of a symphony for every instrument on one pass; Arturo Toscanini, who committed to memory every note of every instrument for some 250 operas and symphonies. Once, before a concert, a bassoon player is said to have come to Toscanini and confessed, "Maestro, the bottom key on my instrument is broken and I will not be able to play." Toscanini looked at him witheringly and replied, "But you don't play that note in tonight's performance."

Toscanini had a powerful motivation for his prodigious memory: he was too nearsighted to read the score and conduct simultaneously. And that provides one vital clue to what the rest of us mere mortals retain and forget: we remember what is important to us, what we really want to know, by putting it in a meaningful framework and concentrating on it. But what about your car keys? Be patient, we will find them. First we must explore the phenomenon of forgetting a little more closely.

THE PHENOMENON OF FORGETTING

It may well be true that we never really forget anything our consciousness has absorbed. There have been interesting experiments that show a person can relearn something once memorized more quickly than new material, even if it was in a foreign language and even after a lapse of many years. But it is also demonstrable that even a bright college student can't remember four-fifths of what he or she has learned by graduation. Why? Because he or she is dealing with an enormous amount of material, so only what is reinforced through use or interest remains instantly accessible. If you're a math major you're unlikely to forget the formulas you constantly need, but you may very well have put the facts from the ancient history course you didn't really like into the "file and forget" drawer of your mind.

But there's more to it than that. Have you ever played trivia with a mixed age group? Grandpa may dazzle you with his encyclopedic recall of the events of World War II and even be able to sing all the lyrics of "Chattanooga Choo-Choo," only to fall slackjawed and silent at the mention of the Bee-Gees or Madonna. World War II was obviously important to him, and so possibly was "Chattanooga Choo-Choo," but it's a fair guess that if he's ever heard the Bee-Gees or Madonna he wasn't really listening. Under pain of death, or deep hypnosis, he might be able to croak "More Than a Woman to Me" or "Papa Don't Preach," but don't count on it—those songs never entered his biocultural history, never passed from immediate memory to short- or long-term memory—terms we will be coming back to in a moment.

Much is made of the supposed shortcomings of older people's minds and memories. But exhaustive testing by any number of cognitive researchers has demonstrated that older people are not only just as "intelligent" as younger ones, but just as capable of absorbing new information—unless they are handicapped by such afflictions as Alzheimer's disease or alcoholism, which destroy the brain cells that are the stuff of memory. However, older people tend to learn more slowly and in a different way than the young. Instead of ingesting unconnected facts like peanuts, they search for ways to put the information into context—to make meaningful sense of it. Then they can not only retain it but use it more intelligently than someone whose fragmentary data is only useful for TV game shows. Conversely, if the information isn't useful, they tend to discard it. If they didn't, their minds would be as cluttered and dusty as the family attic.

NOT ONE BRAIN, BUT THREE

If all these examples of long-term recollection, photographic memory, and idiot savants seem confusing, it is because the brain itself is as complex a piece of software as has ever been packaged in a three-pound box. Perhaps that is why, although it only has the energy potential of a 25-watt light bulb, the brain requires 20 percent of our blood and oxygen supply. So intricate are its processes that neurologists have come to agree humans really have not just one brain but three, each of which performs different vital functions. The oldest and most primitive is the so-called reptilian brain, which is responsible for much of our instinctive behavior. The second layer is the limbic system, which contains the hypothalamus, a sort of thermostat that governs such things as sex drive, adrenaline flow, and body temperature; the pituitary gland, controlling growth and sex hormones; and the hippocampus, which controls basic emotional responses, organizes recollections of where things are placed or stored, and may be responsible for converting short-term memory to long term (which is why it is sometimes likened to a mental switchboard). Finally, the newest and largest evolutionary portion of the brain, which we share with other higher orders of mammals such as monkeys, dogs, and dolphins, is the outer neocortex layer. It is this area, responsible for our rational, logical processes, that we generally think of as "the brain," because it is the repository of language and logic skills and other intelligent processes that distinguish us from the rest of the animal kingdom.

This three-layer theory of the brain was first propounded in 1972 by Dr. Paul MacLean of the National Institute of Mental Health, and has by now been generally accepted by the scientific community. Among other things, it provides us with a plausible explanation for how different modes of intelligence, from instinctive reactions to complex logic, can exist within one skull. As MacLean himself explains it, "The three brains amount to three interconnected biological computers, each having its own intelligence, its own subjectivity, its own sense of time and space, and its own memory and other functions."

Such a construct also helps explain why generations of scientists have been frustrated in their search for the site in the brain where memory is stored. The sources for the senses—smell, taste, hearing, vision—have all been pinpointed, but although these faculties help us to remember, they are basically signal receptors, not memory banks. Nothing so specific has ever been found, although brilliant researchers have devoted their professional lives to the attempt.[2]

---

[2]Psychologist Karl Lashley spent twenty-five years dissecting portions of the brains of living laboratory rats in search of what he called an "engram," or memory trace. He never succeeded, and finally wrote, "I sometimes feel, in reviewing the evidence on the localization of the memory trace, that the necessary conclusion is that learning just is not possible."

THREE KINDS OF MEMORY

Today, most experts concur with a holographic concept of memory: just as any portion of a hologram can reproduce the whole image, so all memories are stored in all parts of the brain, subject to a variety of recall mechanisms. As Dr. Patricia Churchland of the University of California at San Diego puts it, "Philosophers have to admit that they were wrong about certain things. We thought memory was a single kind of process, but we now see that there are probably four or five kinds of ways that memories get stored."

To thoroughly explain such intricacies of neurobiology would require many fat volumes, but mercifully they need not concern us here. For our purposes, we can be content to know that in our daily lives we are dealing with three different *kinds* of memory. The first is immediate memory: as we barrel along the highway, we are aware of an endless stream of Toyotas, Chevrolets, beat-up pickups, Fords, panel trucks, Hondas, eighteen-wheel semitrailers, Volkswagens, Plymouths, and Lincoln Town Cars going the other way. Our mind receives them and then discards them. Just as we see thousands of leaves and record only "tree," all we retain is "Gee, there's a lot of traffic going the other way today."

The second category is short-term memory. After much testing, psychologists agree that most people can store only seven items at a time in transitory short-term recall—which is why telephone numbers are limited to seven digits and why, when advertising people want you to remember a longer chain of digits, they resort to acronyms: 1-800-BUY-CARS. Sometimes you can only remember a phone number just long enough to get from the directory to the phone, although if a particularly attractive person invited you to call and supplied the home number, you might retain the information for as long as two days.

Finally, we have long-term memory, the perhaps one-hundred-billion-bit storage capacity whose duration is infinite if it has been properly indexed and filed. Finding ways to improve the efficiency of that miraculous mechanism will be our next concern.

But wait, you say; that stream of dimly remembered traffic—

what about the fire-engine red Chrysler LeBaron? The one with the 2.2-liter turbo engine that can accelerate from zero to sixty in 7.2 seconds? Ah, that one. You mean the one with the matched-grain mahogany dash and real Corinthian leather seats? Of course. You remembered it because it's been in your long-term memory for some time, ever since you drooled over the four-page color magazine ad and memorized every detail, including the fact that your checking account is several thousands of dollars short of the base sticker price. Nonetheless, you have just proved that you can successfully encode several bits of pretty sophisticated information in your long-term memory without conscious effort. Why can't everything be so simple?

If you accept the premise that anything you ever really learned remains encoded somewhere within your grey matter, there are still several factors that govern how much that adds up to. The LeBaron fan demonstrated the effectiveness of one of them: if you are really interested in something, your mind will absorb and retain the details, at least if you are reasonably intelligent. That raises the second crucial factor: each of us has a genetic intelligence quotient that has been pretty much preset by ancestry. Put more simply, some people are smarter than others. But don't worry about it—if you're smart enough to have gotten this far in this book, you're smart enough to tackle a lot of things.

EDUCATION, TRICKS, AND TOOLS

Still, the question remains: How can you transform your *perceived limitations* into your *unrealized potential?* One word for it is "education." That doesn't mean you have to have a Harvard diploma to remember things—recall Dr. Einstein and his memory problems. It does mean there are many tricks and tools to improve your skills at efficient collection, filing, and retrieval of data. The most important is to accumulate over time a foundation of information, so that new learning can be absorbed into a meaningful context. If you learn the definition of dendrite, axon, synapse, and neurotransmitter, and that's *all* you learn, the information will last about as long as an unfamiliar phone number. But if you learn these terms in the context of how the brain uses them, as in the passage on page 240, your retention will improve greatly—maybe even permanently, if you are interested in the subject.

Of course, there are a host of perils that stand between you and efficient fact absorption. If a Marine drill sergeant was standing with his face two inches from yours, screaming "All right, dogface, I want your dogtag serial number, your rifle serial number, the date of the Marine Corps' birthday, and the name of the first commandant of the corps, and I want them NOW," your chances of coming up with them would be seriously diminished by sheer terror. Even in more benign circumstances, such as being called on unexpectedly in class, tension is a severe deterrent to memory. A distinguished lady of my acquaintance, who happened to be the daughter of an Episcopal bishop, was once unexpectedly asked to say grace before a large community banquet. Although she had repeated grace before each meal for her entire life, the request caused her mind to go blank. After a long and ghastly pause, she salvaged the situation deftly by saying, "Since this is an interfaith gathering, I think it would be more appropriate if each of us prayed silently for a moment." There's more than one way to think on your feet!"[3]

DEALING WITH OVERLOAD

A more common obstacle to recall than tension comes from overload, an unmanageable torrent of information pouring in from your professor on the lecture podium, or the coach screaming directions from the sideline, or a cacophony of buy and sell orders on the floor of the stock exchange. If there is no way to control the flow—as there is when you are reading a book—the only hope is to concentrate on what is really important, which is why students take notes in class, and why the stock market floor is a blizzard of scribbled pieces of paper at the end of every session. The stock specialist, of course, is only dealing with short-term memory—he can forget the specifics of each order as soon as it's

[3]Note: Information related to stress can be found in Chapter Eighteen.

executed. But your lecture notes aren't going to do much good unless you review them in the context of the accompanying reading assignment, since your professor is presumably supplementing the written material with pertinent new information that must be integrated with it.

Another friend of mine recently described his boss, the executive editor of a major newspaper, who operates all day among a Babel of ringing phones, clattering word processors, shouted instructions, and half a dozen conversations going on at once all around him. His job is to know everything that has been said, or asked, or written, and by the end of the day to meld it into a logically organized, clearly presented, balanced, and accurate product. No one could possibly retain all that information in his head: his weapon is a pocket notebook and a ballpoint pen. If someone suggests the crime story reporter should know that the district attorney is going to make an announcement, the pen goes *click* and a note is jotted down. The film from the flood story is delayed and will miss the early edition but will be available for the late city. *Click*. The Central America story needs a rewrite because the president is having a press conference at 4:00 P.M. *Click*. At the end of the day, the editor retires to his desk, reads his notes, and starts barking orders, making requests, reminding forgetful colleagues, making sure that a hundred disparate details have not been forgotten. And God help the person who has told him something inaccurate when the pen went *click*.

Few of us have to operate under that kind of relentless pressure. For most of us, distractions are the cause of our forgetfulness. We read a book, look out the window from time to time at the twittering birds or passing joggers, and then realize we've been turning the pages but absorbing nothing. We labor away computing our taxes while listening to Mozart, and half an hour later realize we've been doing all our computations in column A rather than column B. We go upstairs to get our glasses, notice the bed is unmade, make it, go downstairs, and realize we've forgotten our glasses. These are the things that make us wonder if we're getting senile, while all that's happened is we've allowed ourselves to become distracted.

Another term for it is running on automatic pilot, and most of us spend half our time in that condition—dropping off clothes at the cleaners, making peanut-butter sandwiches, going to the grocery store or exercise class. What's to remember? That, of course, is how we wind up at the cleaners only to discover that the shirts are still draped over a chair in the front hall. It is also why professional airline pilots, who have made thousands of take-offs and landings, have their copilots read aloud a lengthy checklist of all the necessary steps before each one. Leaving your shirts behind is bad enough, but attempting to land a jet with the wheels up is considerably worse. It has happened more than once when pilots "forget" to go through the checklist.

"Habit diminishes the conscious attention with which our acts are performed," observed the redoubtable William James a century ago. This accounts for most of our witless acts of forgetfulness. More important, if you are droning along on automatic pilot, there is no way for new information to get into your skull unless something unexpected and alarming—an elephant crossing in front of your car on Main Street would suffice—shakes you out of your mental lethargy. As neurologist Richard Restak puts it, "The brain is best understood in terms of three functioning units: alertness, information processing, and action." Another memory expert, Dr. Joan Minninger, author of *Total Recall*, defines the three R's of remembering as Registration, Retention, and Retrieval. Please note that if you are running on automatic pilot, you are not even going to reach step one.

CONTROL THE PROCESS AND YOU CONTROL THE MEMORY

If you feel you are doing an inordinate number of senseless things in your daily rounds, begin by waking up and making a habit of being observant, keeping your eyes and ears open, taking an active interest in your surroundings. If you pass the stack of old newspapers and tomorrow is the day the trashmen come, don't say "I'll do it later"—bundle them up and put them out now. By training yourself to be alert, you can eliminate the annoying bits of forgetfulness that plague you. The famous behaviorist B. F. Skinner, in a recent essay on coping with the aging process, revealed that if he hears on the radio that it may rain later in the day, he immediately goes to the closet, gets his umbrella, and hangs it on the front door knob—a useful recognition of the simple fact that he will probably encounter many episodes of memory interference between the time he hears the weather report and the time he leaves the house.

Staying alert to your routine actions can even help you find those car keys—or prevent your losing them in the first place. Once they've disappeared, your only recourse is to retrace your steps through mental recall: Let's see, I came into the house carrying the newspaper and a bag of groceries, and I was just going to take off my coat and hang it up when the phone started ringing, so I put everything down and talked to my mother for ten minutes, and then I went back to pick up the groceries and put them in the refrigerator, so—of course—there are the keys, folded in the newspaper. Next time, ringing phone or not, put the keys down on the front hall table, and thereafter *always* put them on the front hall table. "Control the process and you control the memory," as another learning specialist puts it.

That's pretty basic stuff. More complex things, like remembering people's names after meeting them only once, or being able to apply a mathematical formula correctly, require delving more deeply into the workings of the mind.

RECALL AND RECOGNITION

There are really two distinct forms of retrieval, even if you have put a bit of information into long-term memory. One is recall, the other recognition. Recall covers the tens of thousands of items you can summon up at the snap of your fingers: all the words you can automatically spell, on which shelf in the pantry to find the baked beans, how the furniture was arranged in the family living room when you were a child; in short, the ability to retrieve and reproduce material that has been encountered previously. It is a very sophisticated level of memory.

Recognition, on the other hand, covers a far broader spectrum of information that you can recognize with a little stimulus. If I asked you to recite the opening lines of Keats' ode *"To Autumn,"* chances are you'd draw a blank. But if I said, who wrote "Season of mists and mellow fruitfulness,/Close bosom-friend of the maturing sun . . ." the chances are pretty good (assuming you'd ever studied it in English class) you'd be able to remember the author.

A classic recall/recognition test that psychologists like to give involves asking people who've been out of high school for years, even decades, to recall the names of as many classmates as they can. The results are usually meager. But when presented with a deck of photographs of high-school students, some of whom were classmates and some of whom are ringers, the percentage of face recognition is always astonishingly high, even after many years. No wonder "The face is familiar but I can't recall the name" is such a common utterance.

Let's add a couple more aspects to the mix, and then go on to see what use you can make of this information in improving your own memory's efficiency. First, we are all blessed with both verbal and visual memories, both of them most useful attributes. (A third memory form, kinesthetic or skill memory, will be discussed in Chapter Twenty.) Visualizers tend to be quick studies, since they grasp the overall generalities and "see the whole picture." The bad news is that they are prone to make errors, because they overlook the details. Verbalizers, on the other hand, are more methodical, building up their data base sequentially rather than intuitively. Since everyone possesses both skills in varying mixtures, everyone can use both to sharpen memory skills.

We should also bear in mind that we all possess an ability to retrieve information more flexibly and ingeniously than a super-computer through hierarchical inference. If I asked you "Does a parrot have feathers?" you would be able to answer yes because by hierarchical inference you know that the vast majority of birds do. If I asked you "How far can a kiwi fly?" you would in all likelihood be able to answer "not at all," because you have filed that creature under "flightless birds." But if I asked a computer to tell me where the phrase "sacred cow" came from, it would scan "sacred + cow," and unless some programmer had slipped the answer in, like a dictionary definition, it would not be able to supply the answer. But *you* know, because you remember a picture from an old geography book of Brahmin cattle browsing contentedly through a vegetable stand in Calcutta, and a caption that explained this amazing sight: "Hindus regard cows as sacred and refuse to interfere with them." Think how long that fragment of information has lain untapped in your mind, ready to be retrieved by the right stimulus.

PLAYING THE MNEMONICS GAME

Let's try to put some of this marvelous capacity to work, remembering that you are not truly "improving your memory," but applying techniques that help to reinforce and retain the information you have taken in. Organization is the name of the game, and you've been doing it for years. How do you think you learned to count?

> One, two, button my shoe;
> Three, four, shut the door;
> Five, six, pick up sticks, etc.

You also learned which months had how many days by memorizing "Thirty days hath September . . ." and which way to reset your clock with "Spring forward, fall back." Rhymes and word association tricks like these are known by the odd name "mnemonics." Here are three quick aids to get such a tongue-twister into long-term memory: (1) it is derived from Mnemosyne, mother of the muses and Greek goddess of memory (a lot of m's in there); (2) Mnemosyne and mnemonic(s) are the *only* words in Webster's New Collegiate Dictionary that begin with *mn*; and (3) the word is pronounced knee-monic—think of playing a harmonica with your knee and you've got it.

Everyone relies on mnemonics of one sort of another. Nautical channels are marked by green buoys down one side, and red ones on the other. But what if you're sailing in the fog and you only see one buoy—to which side do you leave it? "Red right returning" is the way you remember—if you're coming back into the harbor, leave red buoys on your right, green on your left; outward bound, the reverse.

You know there are nine planets, but do you know their order in distance from the sun? Nine items are tough to remember in sequence, so just memorize "My very excellent mother just sews undies, nighties, and panties" and you've got the first letters of each plant in proper order: Mercury, Venus, Earth, Mars, Jupiter, Saturn, Uranus, Neptune, and Pluto.

Take my word for it, medical students have to do a lot of rote memorization, much of it involving polysyllabic Latin-root words. Try this for size: the twelve cranial nerves are the olfactory, optic, oculomotor, trochlear, trigeminal, abducens, facial, auditory, glossopharyngeal, vagus, spinal accessory, and hypoglossal. How are you going to get that into the mental file? It's easier if you start with this mnemonic:

> On old Olympus' tiny top,
> A fat-assed German viewed some hops.

Not elegant, perhaps, but an off-color word sometimes helps to lodge things in the mind. So do startling images, which are particularly handy in memorizing foreign vocabularies. The Latin word for light is *lux*: think of a cake of soap with a light bulb screwed into it. The French word for water is *eau*, pronounced "oh": think of someone falling off a bridge into the water and shouting "Oh."

There is no end to the association tricks you can learn to sort out confusion. For instance, you know what stalagmites and stalactites are, but which hangs down from the cave roof, and which builds up from the floor? Easy—stala*C*tites hang from the *C*eiling, stala*G*mites grow up from the *G*round. I have my own pesky recall problem, which—after making any number of wrong turns—I've solved by using a pair of acronyms. The stores in my town are not clustered in a mall, but strung out along a highway which I approach midway from a back road. Which way to turn at the intersection if I'm headed for the Gas station, Post Office, Veterinarian, Shoe store, Hardware store, Appliance store, Drug store, Plant nursery, Fish store, Book store, or Supermarket? "GasPOVS" to the left, HADPFiBS to the right does it for me, although I concede it could use some improvement.

THE VISUALIZATION/ASSOCIATION CONNECTION

A far more nettlesome problem for most people is remembering names, and no wonder—you enter someone's front door for a party, ten people rise to their feet, and the hostess points to each in turn and rattles off their names: "This is Bill Fliegel, and over there his wife Myrtle. . . ." Everyone nods and smiles and your mind is a blank; you're dealing with overload and tension simultaneously. The best thing to do is to try and reconstruct them one by one as the party goes along, and the best way to do that is by word or visual association. If that man's name is Pfister, Mister Pfister will serve nicely, or you might want to visualize him with his fist in front of his face. But names are seldom so convenient. Suppose his name is Rodney Oglethorpe? You might want to visualize him with a fishing rod in his hand, ogling girls, but by the time you've tried a similar mind trick for all ten names you're skating on thin ice. The fat fellow's name is Parker, so you think of Porker, and when the party's over you say, "Nice to have met you, Mr. Hogg." He's not likely to be flattered.

Any number of so-called memory experts have devised complicated formulae for memorizing every name in a room, and there are supersalesmen and politicians who have used such techniques with dazzling effect. For most people, though, a more cautious approach serves better: if it is an important business meeting, there is usually a way to get a list of the participants and their affiliations and titles in advance. If you met someone at a social gathering that you really liked, you'll probably remember the name; if you don't at the end of the party, ask how you can get in touch again. If you're a teacher with a roomful of new students, you're within your rights to ask them to wear name tags for a few days until things sort themselves out.

HOW TO "CHUNK" INFORMATION

Association techniques are more helpful for here-and-now tasks. You want to go to the grocery store to get a whole roasting chicken, milk, bread, sugar, a head of lettuce, sweet potatoes, and marshmallows. Okay, stand the chicken on the loaf of bread surrounded by a bed of lettuce, balancing the containers of milk and sugar on its beak, and juggling the potatoes and marshmallows—the scene is unusual enough to hold in your mind until you get to the store. You have done two helpful things: you have "chunked" the information into one unit, and you have visualized it. Chunking is simply sweeping random bits of data into manageable piles, and you have been doing it all your life. When you learned the alphabet, your teacher had you break it into the following rhyming chunks:

> ABCDEFG
> HIJK L-M-N-O-P
> QRS, TUV,
> WX and Y and Z
> Now I've learned by ABC's
> What do you think of me?

When you see "1776" or "1492" you chunk them and think "Declaration of Independence" or "Columbus." In fact, for the most part, everything you read is chunked as you go along, so that you retain the gist but not the exact wording. Chunking things you want to remember into manageable groups is the same sort of process. Again, "memory experts" can carry this to absurd lengths, boasting of students who can recall strings of eighty meaningless numbers by breaking them into bite-sized units to which they can affix reminder-meanings. 5591 run backward is the year Ford first brought out the two-seater Thunderbird; 20735 becomes 2:07:35, excellent time for a marathon. Unless you are planning to join a circus sideshow, why would you want to do this? Similarly, why would you want to remember forty items you need at the grocery store by grouping them in the "method of loci," imagining them in groups of five in every room of your house? Why not just put things down on the grocery list by the refrigerator as you run low on items?

If you're getting the impression that I think memorization tricks are fine up to a point, but that there's no substitute for really learning something, you are quite correct.

TRICKS VERSUS TRUE LEARNING

Tricks such as mnemonics *can* help, but they are basically a preliminary step. True learning requires understanding, which is compounded from organization and association of related material in ways that make it meaningful. That requires—no getting around it—concentration. However, concentration need not mean that you are condemned to spend the rest of your life hunched over a book in the library with your fingers pressing into your temples.

☐ Take heart from the fact that a lot of learning takes place at a subconscious level. Remember learning a sonnet for English class? The teacher told you to read it aloud three times just before going to sleep, and lo and behold, when you woke up, the poem—or at least the structure of the poem—was right there. This technique can be particularly helpful for children with ADD, as well—as long as your youngster understands that memorizing sonnets or multiplication tables must occur *just before bedtime*—not just before Bill Cosby.

☐ Remember, too, that adults and children learn from *visual* stimuli and *verbal* stimuli. Which way is easier for you? If you're a visual learner, you may benefit from converting written text into diagrams or pictures that help you remember. This technique can be particularly useful for youngsters who have difficulty with subjects such as science or history. If verbal learning is more your style, try using a tape recorder to help keep information in your memory. When studying for exams, one of my patients "dictates" facts and information into his hand-held recorder, then plays it back at various times during the day. He gets the most memorable results, he says, when he plays it once before bedtime, and again before entering the exam room. He also tape-records lectures—that way, he can listen to his professors at any time, and as many times, as he pleases.

☐ Can't remember what you've read? Become actively involved in the material—underline or circle key words, scribble your comments in the margins or in a notebook, read it aloud. Then test yourself—what's the main point? who's the main character? To reinforce what you've learned, discuss it with a friend, and try to relate the new information to previously stored material.

☐ Many individuals, particularly those who have memory deficits due to ADD, have trouble remembering things when they're under time pressure. If you're a student with this problem, it may be worthwhile to discuss it with your teachers, or have your parents intercede on your behalf. A sympathetic instructor may be willing to let you take untimed tests, or allow you to break up tests into "chunks"—you do a certain number of problems, then take a break; do a few more, and take another break.

No matter what the task, everyone can benefit from taking an occasional break. Both body *and* mind need time to relax. After a quick nap or a half hour of exercise, you'll return to your job or assignment refreshed. You may even wind up with a special bonus: an insight that had previously eluded you, or a solution to a problem that had you stumped. Scholars and scientists tackle research problems by immersing themselves in the material, then backing away from it for a while to rest and recover, then plunging in again, then relaxing. Intellectual breakthroughs often follow such a process in a momentary flash of insight, as when the apple fell on Newton's head. A clearer example is the nineteenth-century discovery of the structure of the benzene molecule by a German chemist with the impressive name of Friedrich August Kekule von Stradonitz. He ceased his labors on the intractable problem one evening, and then . . .

"I turned myself toward the fire and sank in a reverie. Atoms danced before my eyes. Long chains were firmly joined, all winding and turning with snakelike motion. Suddenly, one of the serpents had caught its own tail and the ring thus formed danced before my eyes. I woke immediately and worked on the consequences the rest of the night."

He was able to prove this intuitive leap—that benzene molecules formed a loop of carbon atoms that bonded onto each other as well as onto other atoms—and this sudden, subconscious breakthrough allowed other discoveries in organic chemistry to flow in rapid order. We may not always understand how such leaps occur, but we do know that they flow from a process of concentration and mental absorption and organization, followed by relaxation and incubation.

AT LAST: THE SECRET OF MEMORY AND LEARNING

This leaves it up to you to discover your own best style for learning. How long can you study at a stretch before you tire? Do you work best in the morning, or at night? Should you tackle rigid disciplines like math and physics in the morning, when your mind is clear and uncluttered, leaving softer subjects like English literature for evening? Can you rely on underlining material to prepare for a business meeting, or had you better take notes and then reorganize them when you're finished? Remember that each of our minds is endowed with certain strengths we can utilize and weaknesses we must overcome. But remember, too, that we all have far more memory capacity than we will ever need, or use. Our task is to learn to utilize that capacity in our most effective organizational style. We will leave the last word on the subject to the protean William James:

"The more other facts a fact is associated with in the mind, the better possession of it our memory retains. Each of its associates becomes a hook to which it hangs, a means to fish it up by when sunk beneath the surface. Together, they form a network of attachments by which it is woven into the entire tissue of our thought. The 'secret of a good memory' is thus the secret of forming diverse and multiple associations with every fact we care to retain."

Chapter XX

Concentration and Visualization

"How can I hit and think at the same time?"

Yogi Berra

Every tennis hacker can remember an occasional glorious day when the ball seemed to float over the net big as a grapefruit, when every stoke felt sweet and true, when his body mysteriously was always at the right spot on the court at the right time.

So, too, can every golf duffer recall those miserable days when his tee shots sliced into the rough, he shanked his approach shots off the heel of his club, and even simple two-foot putts rimmed the cup and refused to drop.

Why do those rare, wonderful days—and more frequent nightmare afternoons—happen? Think about your own sports experiences for a moment: on good days, weren't you invariably loose and relaxed? Chances are the weather was sunny and cheerful, and probably you were out for an informal match with friends. Winning or losing didn't matter all that much, because you were just there for fun.

But on your bad days, wasn't there always something lurking around at the back of your mind? Maybe it was only that a cold and blustery wind was blowing; more likely, it was the specter of an upcoming exam or meeting. Worse yet, perhaps you were playing with your boss and a couple of clients it was important for you to impress. Whatever the reason, something was making you tense, and as every athlete in the world can tell you, tension is the great enemy of concentration. Because when you're tense you're thinking about everything except what you should be: the ball coming at you, the moment itself.

Athletes call this kind of tension "choking," and it's more than just a figure of speech. When you get nervous, your body starts pumping adrenaline into the bloodstream, an instinctive defensive reaction to prepare you to fight or to run for your life. This kind of adrenaline rush may be just what you need if you're a sprinter or a weight-lifter, both of whom require short bursts of intense energy. But in almost any sport that calls for longer periods of smooth coordination, such a reaction is disastrous: it constricts blood flow, blurs the vision, impedes deep breathing, and causes muscles to lose flexibility—everything an athlete doesn't want to happen.

Every skilled athlete must learn how to shake off these demons, to play his or her game with total concentration while staying loose and relaxed. Those who have attained this state call it being "in the zone," and their descriptions are lyrical, almost mystical. They have called it reverie, an insulated state, a sense of ecstasy and joy where awareness is heightened and actions are anticipated before they occur. Some describe it as being on automatic pilot, where their surroundings recede into the background and they become so focused that they are unaware of themselves.

In his biography, *My Life and the Beautiful Game*, the great Brazilian soccer player Pele recalls what such perfect days felt like: "It was a type of euphoria; I felt I could run all day without tiring, that I could dribble through any of their team or all of them, that I could almost pass through them physically. I felt I could not be hurt. . . . Perhaps it was merely confidence, but I have felt confident many times without that strange feeling of invincibility."

For some, time itself seems to slow down. Ted Williams, baseball's last .400 hitter, remembers days when he could see the seams on the ball whizzing toward him at ninety miles an hour. John Brodie, former quarterback for the San Francisco '49ers, once told an interviewer that there are even moments in the chaos of a football game when "time seems to slow way down, in an uncanny way, as if everyone were moving in slow motion. It seems as if I had all the time in the world to watch the receivers run their patterns, and yet I know the defensive line is coming at me just as fast as ever."

This paradox of total concentration coupled with total relaxation has become such a holy grail for athletes and coaches that over the past generation a whole science has grown up around it. The movement's first great impetus came in the wake of the 1956 Olympics, which were totally dominated by the Soviets and East Germans. In the aftermath, it was gradually learned that both teams had been trained in relaxation techniques, borrowing from various Oriental disciplines to dissipate tension. But more important, the Iron Curtain athletes had been rigorously schooled to visualize every detail of their event—in shotput, high jump, diving, track, whatever their specialty—rehearsing each step over and over in their minds until the sequences were totally implanted, memorized, automatic.

The concept of supplementing physical training with mental training spread like wildfire, until today there is scarcely a college in the United States that doesn't have its own sports psychologists, and not an event that hasn't been rigorously tape-recorded and analyzed over and over. Football coaches run concentration drills of ever-increasing complexity to teach their pass receivers how to focus on the axis of the approaching ball to the exclusion of all else; physicists have laboriously recorded thousands of basketball free throws to document why a high-arching rainbow has a better chance of dropping into the basket than a shallow toss; baseball players study films of an opposing pitcher for hours to find any tiny glitch in his delivery that might reveal whether he is about to unleash a fastball, or a curve or a slider.

Books have been written by the score, and magazine articles by the thousands, attempting to explain the mysteries of relaxed concentration. Some of them are excellent (one of them will be discussed in detail below), but many of them slide into a sort of Zen mumbo-jumbo; if only you can shake out your muscles and clear your mind, they imply, your skills will improve rapidly. Assume a certain aikido posture and visualize drawing the warmth of the sun into your navel, and your backhand will mysteriously improve.

This sort of mysticism may well be useful at the highest levels of some sports, but it overlooks a fundamental point: in order to be relaxed and concentrate at whatever you are trying to do, you must have the fundamentals pretty well under control. Consider some humble examples: If someone were shouting in your ear, "Lift your right foot off the pedal and place it poised over the middle one; now press your left foot down all the way on the left pedal and turn the wheel with your left hand while shifting the gear lever upward with your right," you would probably run off the road and into a tree. Yet that sequence of movements is precisely what you do, without thinking about it, every time you steer your car into a sharp turn. It was only when you were *learning* to drive that you actually were conscious of performing those steps in sequence.

The same thing is true of walking. You don't have to tell yourself to place one foot forward while swinging the opposite arm to maintain balance, but when you were two years old it took a lot of practice and not a few falls before you got the hang of it. If you know how to type, you are not even aware of your fingers automatically seeking out the correct sequence of keys unless you are in the hunt-and-peck learning stage. So it stands to reason that no amount of muscle relaxing, exercising, deep breathing, and Zen consciousness is going to do much for your tennis forehand until you have passed the point where you have to keep repeating to yourself, "Bring the racket back, now step into the ball, lead with the heel of the racket, and make your follow-through go forward." In short, you can't do anything very well until you know the mechanics and your body has automated this process.

Still, it doesn't take long to master the rudiments of visualization and relaxed concentration. Let me give you another everyday example. A young girl I know, like so many of us, had a terrible time of it her first time on skis. The day was cold, grey, and windy, the snow was icy and hardpacked, her rented boots hurt, getting on the lift scared her, and the other kids were mean to her. She came home in tears, vowing "never again."

But her father was a good skier and knew she could be, too. He waited until the next sunny day with good snow, and then took her out himself—just the two of them. Now riding the lift wasn't scary, and right away she learned to plant her skis in a snowplow so she could come down the hill as slowly as she wanted. Pretty soon she was leaning out, first on one ski and then on the other, to make slow, shaky S turns across the hill. Now it was time for some visualization.

Until skiers learn to sink their knees down a little, and then lift out and forward as they turn, they will never know the rhythmic joy that is the essence of the sport. That night, father and daughter practiced such turns in front of a mirror—pole out, sink and lift, other pole out, sink and lift—for an hour. Then he told her when she went to bed to think about the turns—pole out, sink and lift, now the other one—until she fell asleep.

You know how the story is going to come out. The next day she gingerly tried out the idea, first in an awkward series of little bunny hops, then with more and more authority. Soon her weight was out over her skis, and by the end of the day she had begun to link one turn to the next, three, four, five times before losing the rhythm. She was on her way, and suddenly she *loved* skiing. That night, no one had to remind her to practice her turns as she fell asleep. It will be months and years before she can float down an expert trail like a feather, but with every new step, as she hones her technique, she can speed the learning process—by visualizing it in her mind's eye.

So now we know that visualization isn't just daydreaming; it's using the mind to train the body in a repetitive skill pattern, going out and practicing, then closing your eyes and visualizing some more. Depending on your sport, there are dozens of ways to go at it. A friend of mine who is a superb, consistent, zero-handicap golfer told me the reason his game is so steady traces back to the way his father taught him to swing. Day after day, hour after hour, he had him practice his stroke, not only without a ball to distract him, but without even a club in his hand. Only when he had grooved his swing into a perfect, effortless arc was he allowed to pick up a club and hit a ball.

This interplay between mind and muscle, action and reaction, situation and response, can be seen at every level of human activity, even the most cerebral. Most people would assume that what enables chess masters—those people who can play forty or fifty opponents at one time and beat them all—to perform such astonishing feats is a superior IQ that allows them to think many moves ahead and sort out the consequences of thousands of steps simultaneously. But more than twenty years ago, a psychologist named Adriaan de Groot undertook a study of chess players with different levels of skill. The masters, he discovered, were no better than novices at memorizing random arrangements of chessmen on a board. But when shown a board with an actual game in progress, the experts could instantly memorize the placement of each piece because they understood the strategic implications for the game. Now, and only now, would they be able to think several moves ahead.

Building on these insights, two psychologists working at Carnegie-Mellon Institute in the 1970s demonstrated that so-called chess intuition is really superior pattern-recognition ability, the fruit of long experience. The implications of this for any skill—not only sports, but including them—are profound. In a recent book, *Mind over Machine*, University of California researchers Hubert and Stuart Dreyfus reported on studies of how airplane pilots, automobile drivers, and language experts, as well as chess players, learned their skills. In every case, they found, the progression was from novice, just following the rules without a clear sense of the overall undertaking, to competence, proficiency, and expertise—each step bringing a gradual widening of understanding that allowed them to organize the situation in their minds and begin making choices about what to do next.

As they attained proficiency, all these learners began to bypass the reasoning process and get "into the zone." As the Dreyfuses describe it, "No detached choice or deliberation occurs. . . . It just happens, apparently because the proficient performer has experienced similar situations in the past and memories of them trigger plans similar to those that worked in the past." Soon they will be doing what comes naturally, operating on intuition without any direct consciousness of their actions.

These same cognitive skills apply directly even to such fast-paced games as basketball. In a special issue of the *Canadian Journal of Psychology* devoted entirely to a discussion of skills, psychologists Neil Burnett and Fran Allard of the University of Waterloo, Ontario, reported on a study in which they showed photos of basketball games in progress to groups of players, then asked them to recall positions and chart the action. Where the scene was random, varsity players did no better than intramural ones, but when a breaking play was shown in progress the experts did far better because they instantly grasped the meaning and implication of the players' positions as shown on the screen. Had they themselves been on the court, their bodies would have reacted instinctively to what was happening.

What this means is that effective concentration requires an understanding of context, in order to give the facts meaning. If you're like most people watching a baseball game, you'll have to glance at your scorecard in order to remember what a given hitter did his last time at bat: because you're not involved in the action, your mind has only followed it superficially. But participants in a game can often remember things that happened to them months and years ago, because they were totally focused on the events. There is a well-known story of the great baseball manager Leo Durocher, who was renowned for his analytic ability. Once, a newspaperman bet him that he wouldn't be able to reconstruct the events of a double-header from memory after it was over. When he went to the locker room afterward, scorecards in hand, Durocher sat him down and rattled off the whole four-hour sequence of events, play by play. Clearly he had been concentrating, because he was intimately involved.

Could you ever do such a thing? Before examining sports concentration further, let's take a couple of examples from other walks of life, because what applies to sports applies everywhere. Suppose you have to give a speech. Like most people, you hate to stand up before a crowd: you feel embarrassed and unconfident. And if you just throw together a few notes and hope for the best, your talk is bound to be aimless and wandering. On the other hand, if you write the whole thing out and read it, you're probably going to bore everyone to death.

There is one good solution: Master your material. Decide what you want to say and why you want to say it, so that you'll be speaking with conviction. Now, if you are a beginner at public speaking, write out your address, carefully and in full. That way you will have all your material fixed in your mind, including your major points in logical sequence as well as your anecdotes, illustrations, and asides. Now take brief notes—just enough to remind yourself of what comes next—put them on file cards, and throw the speech away. You now know what you want to say, you'll be concentrating, and you may even enjoy yourself.

A friend of mine once told me about the only time he was tempted to cheat on an examination at school. The subject was ancient history, filled with pharaohs and unpronounceable names and countries that no longer existed. He was a good student, but he just couldn't get it all fixed in his mind. So he resolved to write down the facts on vocabulary cards, stick them in his sleeve, and then peek when he got stuck.

But there was a problem: There were so many names and dates and places that he couldn't fit them all on a few tiny cards. So he went over and over his textbook, winnowing down the facts, getting them in order, making sure he had all the important ones. Of course you know what happened: By the time he entered the exam room, he had every vital name and date clearly fixed in his mind and he never had to use his crib cards. Concentration depends, among other things, on knowing what you want to do or say.

What about *relaxed* concentration? Here is where the traditional way of approaching tense situations runs against all logic. Gotta cram for this exam; everyone's going to hate this speech, so I'll rush through it as fast as I can; I'm probably going to strike out, so I'll just close my eyes and swing as hard as I can and maybe I'll hit a home run. Oddly enough, many coaches (and not a few teachers) think that the way to get the best from their pupils is to keep them under pressure. Vince Lombardi, the legendary coach of the Green Bay Packers, will always be remembered for his motto, "Winning isn't the most important thing; it's the *only* thing."[1]

Such exhortations may be appropriate for 275-pound linemen whose job is to spend the afternoon butting heads like mountain

---

[1] I wonder if Lombardi ever knew what really happened in the Packers' first Super Bowl victory. Max McGee, who caught the two winning touchdowns, was a substitute who had not been scheduled to play. So the night before the game, he went out on a date and didn't return until dawn. When the first-string end was injured and McGee was rushed in to replace him, he may not have been in peak condition, but he was obviously loose and relaxed!

goats. But for most people it can only set up a destructive chain of thought: losing equals failure; failure equals disgrace; if I make mistakes I'll be a failure and a disgrace. A train of thought like that can only lead to pressure and tension. It's practically a formula for choking.

But if imagining all the bad things that might happen can lead you to fail, why can't imagining success lead you to succeed? If you think you can do something (ski down that hill without falling), the chances are that you can. If you think you're going to fall, you're almost bound to. So the trick is to eliminate the negatives and the obstacles by visualizing how you would like to do it, and going over it in your mind in a focused daydream whenever you get a relaxed opportunity to do so.

In his book, *Feeling Good: The New Mood Therapy*, Dr. David Burns summarizes the logic this way:

□ All our moods are created by our thoughts. "You feel the way you do right now because of the thoughts you have at the moment."
□ When you feel negative or depressed, it is because your thoughts are dominated by "pervasive negativity." The whole world looks dark and gloomy. What's worse, "you'll come to believe that things are really as bad as you imagined them to be."
□ Negative thoughts almost always contain gross distortions. "Twisted thinking is the exclusive cause of nearly all your suffering."
□ Therefore, isolate and eliminate those "inner saboteurs" by learning not to generalize about past shortcomings. Just as you can fail by imagining you will, so you can succeed by imagining you will.

Those are not just empty exhortations. The world of successful athletes is filled with examples. Someone once asked pro place kicker Frank Coral if he ever felt pressure when he came on the field to attempt a crucial field goal. "No," he answered. "When I walked on the field I started visualizing the ball going through the uprights. It never occurred to me that I might miss."

As Charles Garfield, Ph.D., puts it in one of his books, "Peak performers are not people with something added; rather, they are people with very little of their potential taken away. They develop an ability to achieve what they set out to do, and to cultivate within themselves the characteristics they value most. More than any other factor, the difference between them and any other performers is that they consciously, persistently, intelligently refine and develop those characteristics."

This observation touches on a profoundly important fact about the average person's life. Because most of us are seldom challenged to draw on the best within us, we never begin to realize our potential. It never occurs to us that we might possess some superior skill, because no one has ever taught us to test out that possibility and nurture it through disciplined development.

Almost a century ago, the pioneering American psychologist William James observed, "Most people live, whether physically, intellectually or morally, in a very restricted circle of their potential being. They *make use* of a very small portion of their possible consciousness, of their soul's resources in general, much like a man who, out of his whole bodily organism, should get into the habit of using and moving only his little finger. Great emergencies and crises show us how much greater our vital resources are than we had supposed."

In the 1960s these insights were christened "the human potential movement," and another psychologist named Abraham Maslow popularized the phrase "self-actualization." He undertook a lifelong study of people with exceptionally healthy psyches, and he, too, came to the realization that they were not people with an extra dimension, but normal people whose potential had never been weakened by negative thinking or a destructive outlook and self-image. The rest of us are, as Maslow put it, "fixated at lower levels," because someone or something has implanted a false notion of our limitations.

In the world of sports, the implications are obvious. Just remember that for years before Roger Bannister broke the four-minute mile, physiologists had written learnedly that the human body was simply incapable of breaking that barrier. Today the world record for the mile is 3:48. The potential, obviously, had always been there. The barrier was mental, and breaking *that* barrier can open extraordinary possibilities.

As long ago as the nineteenth-century, in a book entitled *Principles of Mental Physiology,* W.B. Carpenter proposed what he called the "ideo-motor principle": in essence, whatever idea occupies our minds finds expression in our muscles. When that insight is applied to real-life situations, truly astonishing things can occur. A few years ago a rifle champion named Robert Foster was called into military service and forced to interrupt his training for a year. At the end of that time he entered a meet and broke his own record. How? Every day that he was unable to practice, he had made it a point to go through ten minutes of mental rehearsal of his specialty.

An even more dramatic example concerns Chinese pianist Liu Chi Kung, who finished second to Van Cliburn in the famous 1958 Moscow Tchaikovsky competition. Shortly thereafter he was jailed for seven years during China's Cultural Revolution, deprived completely of access to a piano. Yet when he was finally freed and resumed his career, his concert performances were better than ever. How could this be, with no chance to practice for seven long years? "I did practice, every day," Liu explained. "I rehearsed every piece I had ever played, note by note, in my mind."

Clearly, anyone who can visualize rifle practice in his mind or play piano for seven years without the benefit of a piano understands the ideo-motor principle. But there is more to this phenomenon of concentration that must be mastered before any skilled performer can enter "the zone." Neuroscientists who have used a brain-scanning technology called the PET scan have uncovered the fact that during periods of intense concentration there is a marked decrease in the *overall* metabolic rate of brain activity. For most athletes, the only area where activity intensifies is the visual cortex, where visual images are processed. With the mind thus focused, other conscious areas of the brain in effect shut down to eliminate distractions. Some researchers speculate that when this phenomenon occurs, primitive regions of the brain called the basal ganglia and CVS take over to produce instinctive reactions, which would account for why so many athletes talk of playing on "automatic pilot."

In any event, it seems clear that the complex, sophisticated, reasoning portions of the brain are the ones that are bypassed to let the visual cortex and your body's motor memory react almost unconsciously. And once again we are back to the basic truth that the better you are at whatever your sport or skill, the easier it is to perform without thinking about it. Keep your cerebral cortex out of it. Or, as former St. Louis Cardinals catcher Tim McCarver puts it, "The mind's a great thing as long as you don't have to use it."

Now that we have reviewed the ingredients and elements that lead to effective concentration in sports and other skills, the question remains: how can you develop your own abilities in this direction? Torrents of words have been written on the subject over recent decades, but among the best books I have encountered is *Peak Performance, Mental Training Techniques of the World's Greatest Athletes*, by Charles A. Garfield, Ph.D. Garfield lays out a detailed, months-long relaxation-training program, but he also interweaves more simplified exercises for those who don't aspire to Olympian accomplishments but merely want to improve their own levels of calm competence. His book provides an excellent synthesis of other research and specialized sports-training programs that can be valuable to anyone interested in the field. With Dr. Garfield's permission, I have summarized its basic findings at some length.

To Garfield, sports accomplishments can serve as a metaphor for overall success. Excellence in one area becomes a way of life in every area, extending techniques such as goal-setting and visualization to other endeavors. And, he observes at the outset, "The process of conditioning the mind in this way is really no different from the process of conditioning the body." To do so, he sets out a six-stage course of action. Phase one is an orchestrated program to develop what he calls "volition"—that is, willpower—by analyzing your own motivations. The goal is to establish voluntary control over your body's autonomic (i.e., instinctive) functions by visualizing whatever it is you want to accomplish while in a relaxed and reflective state—sitting or lying down, eyes closed.

Remember the young girl who learned to get rhythm into her

ski turns by rehearsing them as she was going to sleep? Garfield recommends a more detailed approach that he calls "clustering": as you explore the experiences that strengthened your will and self-esteem in the past, jot down words and phrases that remind you of just what you did and what it felt like when things were going well. The technique is very similar to one presented in an enormously successful book on goal-setting called *What Color is Your Parachute?* In essence, write down, one by one, all the things you enjoy, everything you're good at, as well as all the things you dislike and find hard. Then sort them out into piles, and what will emerge is a pattern of what you like to do and therefore will do well. It is a method for identifying a goal—or a problem—so that you can brainstorm it by identifying any personal conflicts and by recalling what motivated you in positive ways so that you can recall and re-create them later. Like everything else in your peak performance training, it's not something you just do once, but every day, whenever you can steal some relaxed time alone. Soon the good thoughts and feelings will begin to flow automatically in a repetitive pattern.

Phase two requires that you define the ultimate goal you want to accomplish, and then subdivide that ambition into a series of smaller, *attainable* steps. If your ambition is to run a marathon, it won't do you much good to visualize the whole 26-mile, 385-yard event and let it go at that. How far can you run today? How much further could you push it tomorrow? Should you do wind sprints interspersed with stretches of more relaxed jogging? What is your real inner motivation for wanting to do it in the first place? You will need to seek out expert advice to help organize a sensible training regimen, whatever your hoped-for accomplishment. With that in hand, create a mental road map that will take you from here to there, and keep running through the exact physical movements required of you. Then memorize the required sequences precisely, repetitively, in an accurate timeframe, until your body has developed a conditioned reflex response. Keep visualizing your end goal and your interim goals, because heightening your mental and emotional state can elevate and enhance your physiological state. But remember: you are never going to get where you want to be until you've mastered the mechanics, be it chess, or driving, or basketball. Only then will you be able to attain a state of voluntary relaxation.

The heart of *Peak Performance* comes in chapters three and four, devoted to voluntary relaxation and mental rehearsal. Because the author is writing for serious athletes, he sets out a detailed, three-month-long program of learning to relax muscle groups one by one, mastering deep diaphragmatic breathing, and gradually attaining self-regulation of the autonomic functions in the CVS that no summary can do justice. But the underlying principles apply to anyone who wants to improve his or her level of accomplishment: relaxation feeds confidence, so to attain a state of mind-body unification we must suppress the logical, linear left brain that keeps distracting concentration on the moment at hand in favor of the intuitive, visualizing right brain and its possible access to the CVS. As Garfield puts it, "Blind, rigid determination is *not* the key that will allow you to develop your greatest strengths and maximize your human potential in sport. In fact it will limit you. . . ."

The goal is to create a "neuromuscular template"—precise, effortless repetition of athletic movements, a brain-muscle biofeedback loop. You are striving to create moving mental images in order to implant automatic physical response. Only when athletes have learned to repetitively rehearse each increment of movement mentally until memorized do they enter what Garfield calls "a cocoon of concentration" that releases energy reserves and accelerates reactions to a point where time actually seems to slow down.

Note that, in the long, patient course of mental training that leads to this state of grace, peak performers concentrate on recalling and reconstructing their own best performances, keeping the timing realistic so that they can synchronize mental rehearsal with actual performance. The whole process of successful visualization is the precise opposite of most people's destructive habit of dwelling on their own mistakes and failures. The end result is an instinctive confidence that they are destined to win, or at least to perform to the best of their ability.

How does it feel when you can actually perform like that? Timothy Gallway, in his book, *The Inner Game of Tennis*, describes it this way:

"When a tennis player is 'on his game,' he's not thinking about how, when or even where to hit the ball. He's not *trying* to hit the ball, and after the shot he doesn't think about how badly or how well he made contact. The ball seems to be hit through an automatic process that doesn't require thought. There may be an awareness of the sight, sound or feel of the ball, and even of the tactical situation, but the player just seems to *know* without thinking what to do."

That is the fruit of successful visualization: an optimistic attitude that expects success. With that kind of confidence, we usually accomplish what we set out to accomplish.

A Summary in Poetic Perspective

In the final analysis, only a poem seemed capable of adequately expressing the motivation and feelings which drive clinical researchers, patients, and parents to reach successful outcomes. Indeed, the following poem best symbolizes and summarizes the symptoms and frustrations of patients with ADD, and the emotional rewards and personal satisfaction physicians derive from relieving and eradication the pain and suffering of desperately struggling human beings.

CONSTANT MOTION, TIMELESS DAYS,
NO RHYME OR REASON TO MY WAYS,
EYES THAT READ THE WORDS ALL BLURRY
AS ACROSS THE PAGE THEY SCURRY.

FEAR OF HEIGHT AND CROWDS AND STORES,
ONLY ONE PERSON . . . PLEASE NO MORE!
SENSELESS HURRYING, FRANTIC FITS,
NO RELAXING, NO TIME TO SIT.

A SIX YEAR OLD DAUGHTER, JUST LIKE ME.
HOW COULD THIS HAPPEN, HOW COULD THIS BE?
WHERE IS THE JUSTICE, WHERE IS THE LIGHT?
I'VE NO MORE STRENGTH TO CONTINUE THE FIGHT.

THEN THE BOOK THAT CHANGED OUR LIVES.
NEW HOPE PERHAPS WE WERE ALRIGHT.
THE DECISION TO JOURNEY TO NEW YORK . . .
FROM THAT GREAT MOMENT OUR LIVES WOULD FORK
TO UNTOLD MOMENTS OF PEACE AND CALM,
AND NEW EXPECTATIONS AT EACH DAY'S DAWN.

A TREATMENT PROGRAM WHICH WORKED WITHIN DAYS . . .
AFTER 33 YEARS OF LIVING IN A HAZE!
HOW DO I THANK YOU DEAR LEVINSON
FOR MAKING LIFE EASIER AND EVEN FUN.

SO TO YOU I DEDICATE THIS POEM,
WITH RENEWED BELIEF MAN WALKS NOT ALONE.
THOUGH LIFE WAS ROUGH AND TIMES WERE DOWN,
WE'RE SO VERY THANKFUL YOU TURNED US AROUND!

CATHY A. LANNING (33)
JESSICA M. SWANSON (6)

References

Allard, Fran and Burnett, Neil:
  Skill in Sport.
  Canadian Journal of Psychology, Vol. 39 No. 2, 1985.
American Psychiatric Association:
  Diagnostic and Statistical Manual of Mental Disorders, Third Edition,
  Revised. Washington, D.C.: American Psychiatric Association, 1980.
American Psychiatric Association:
  Diagnostic and Statistical Manual of Mental Disorders, Third Edition,
  Revised. Washington, D.C.: American Psychiatric Association, 1987.
Ayres, A. J.:
  Sensory integration and learning disorders.
  Los Angeles, CA: Western Psychological Services, 1972.
Barany, R.:
  Some new methods for functional testing of the vestibular apparatus
  and cerebellum. In Nobel Lectures, Physiology and Medicine,
  1901–1921.
  Amsterdam, Elsevier, 1967, pp. 500–511.
Barkley R.A.:
  Guidelines for defining hyperactivity in children: Attention deficit dis-
  orders with hyperactivity, in Lahey BB, Kazdin AE (eds). Advances
  in Clinical Child Psychology, Vol. 5. New York, Plenum, 1982, pp.
  137–180.
Barkley R.A.:
  Hyperactive Children: A Handbook for Diagnosis and Treatment.
  New York, Guilford, 1981.
Bender, L.:
  A visual-motor Gestalt test and its clinical use.
  New York: American Orthopsychiatric Association Research, 1938.
Benson, Ron:
  Helping Pupils Overcome Homework Distractions
  Clearing House.
  Vol. 61, April, 1988.
Bloomingdale, L.M., Davies, R.K., & Gold, M.S.

Attention Deficit Disorder: Some Possible Neurological Substrates in Attention Deficit Disorder—Diagnostic, Cognitive, and Therapeutic Understanding.
Spectrum Publication, Inc., 1984.

Blythe, P., & McGlown, D.:
An organic basis for neuroses and educational difficulties.
Chester, Eng.: Insight, 1979, 93–94.

Bolles, Richard N.:
The 1989 What Color Is Your Parachute?
Ten Speed Press, Berkeley, CA, 1989.

Boniver, R.:
Influence du piracetam sur le fonctionnement du systeme vestibulaire.
Acta Oto-Rhino-Laryngologica Belgica, 1974, 28, 293–299.

Brackett, Sylvia:
The Concentration Box.
Elementary School Guidance and Counseling,
Vol. 14, No. 2, December, 1979.

Bradley, C.:
The behavior of children receiving benzedrine.
Am. J. Psychiat. 94: 577. 1937.

Brody, Robert:
Taking Better Aim.
Sport, August, 1987.

Brookler, K., & Pulec, J.:
Computer analysis of electrostagnomography records.
Trans. Amer. Acad. Ophthalmol. Otolaryngol.
May-June 1970, pp. 563–575.

Brookler, K.:
Simultaneous bilateral bithermal caloric stimulation in electronystagmography.
Laryngoscope, 1971, 4, 101–109.

Brown, R., & Sleator, E.:
Methylphenidate in hyperactive children: Differences in dose effects on impulsive behavior.
Pediatrics 64:408, 1979.

Bruner, J.:
The organization of early skilled action.
Child Development 44:1. 1973.

Burns, David D.:
Feeling Good: The New Mood Therapy.
Morrow, New York, 1980.

Cantwell DP:
The hyperactive child.
Hosp. Prac. 14:65–73, 1979.

Carey, Benedict:
  Playing Under Pressure.
  Hippocrates, Nov./Dec., 1988.
Carpenter, William B.:
  Principles of Mental Physiology.
  rev. ed., AMS Press, New York, 1978.
Charles, L., & Schain, R.:
  A four-year follow-up of study of the effects of methylphenidate on
  the behavior and academic achievement of hyperactive children.
  J. Abnorm. Child Psychol. 9:495, 1981.
Conners, C.K.:
  A teacher rating scale for use in drug studies with children.
  Am. J. Psychiatry. 126: 805–888, 1969.
Conners C.K.:
  Rating scales for use in drug studies with children: Pharmacotherapy
  of children. Special issue Psychopharmacol. Bull. 24–84, 1973.
Conners, C. K. & Eisenberg, L.:
  The effects of methylphenidate on symptomatology & learning in dis-
  turbed children. Am. J. Psychiat. 120: 458–464. 1963.
Creekmore, N.N. & Creekmore, W.N.:
  Effective use of classroom walls.
  Academic Therapy, 22(4), 341–348. 1987.
Davidson, Charles W. and Powell, Lou Anne:
  The Effects of Easy-Listening Background Music on the On-Task Per-
  formance of Fifth Grade Children.
  Journal of Education Research, Vol. 80, No. 1, Sep./Oct., 1986.
Denkla MB, Bemporad JR, & MacKay MC:
  Tics following methylphenidate administration: A report of 20 cases.
  JAMA 247: 1729–1731, 1982.
Dolowitz, D. A.:
  Testing vestibular spinal reflexes.
  In Specter, M. (ed.) Dizziness and Vertigo.
  New York, Grune & Stratton. 1967.
Douglas, VI:
  Attentional and cognitive problems, in Rutter M (ed.): Developmental
  Neuropsychiatry.
  New York, Guilford, 1983, pp 280–329.
Dow, R. S., & Moruzzi, G.:
  The physiology and pathology of the cerebellum.
  Minneapolis, MN: University of Minnesota Press, 1958.
Dreyfus, Hubert L., Stuart E. Dreyfus & Tom Athanasion:
  Mind Over Machine.
  Free Press, New York, 1986.
Eberle, Nancy:

Six Ways to Sharpen Your Memory.
McCall's, Aug., 1986.
Eccles, J.C.:
Learning in the motor system.
Progress in Brain Research, 1986, 64, 3–17.
Eccles, J. C., Ito, M., and Szentagothai, J.:
The Cerebellum as a Neuronal Machine.
New York, Springer-Verlag. 1967.
Evans, William H., Susan, S. E., Rex, E. S., Pennypacker, H.S.:
The Effects of Exercise on Selected Classroom Behaviors of Behaviorally Disordered Adolescents.
Behavioral Disorders, Vol. 11, Nov., 1985.
Feingold, B.F.:
Why Your Child is Hyperactive.
New York, Random House, 1975.
Fernandes, C. M., & Samuel, J.:
The use of piracetam in vertigo.
South African Medical Journal, 1985, 68, 806–808.
Final Report to the Nutrition Foundation.:
The National Advisory Committee on Hyperkinesis and Food Additives. Oct., 1980.
Fitzgerald, Gail, Landis, Fick, Millich, Richard.:
Computer-Assisted Instruction for Students with Attentional Difficulties.
Journal of Learning Disabilities, Vol. 19, No. 6, June/July, 1976.
Frank, J., & Levinson, H.N.:
Dysmetric dyslexia and dyspraxia: hypothesis and study.
Journal of the American Academy of Child Psychiatry, 1973, 12, 690–701.
Frank, J., & Levinson, H.N.:
Dysmetric dyslexia and dyspraxia: synopsis of a continuing research project.
Academic Therapy, 1975–1976, 11, 133–143.
Frank, J., & Levinson, H.N.:
Compensatory mechanism in cerebellar-vestibular dysfunction and dysmetric dyslexia and dyspraxia.
Academic Therapy, 1976, 12, 1–24.
Frank, J., & Levinson, H.N.:
Seasickness mechanisms and medications in dysmetric dyslexia and dyspraxia.
Academic Therapy, 1976–1977, 12, 133–149.
Frank, J., & Levinson, H.N.:
Antimotion-sickness medications in dysmetric dyslexia and dyspraxia.
Academic Therapy, 1977, 12, 411–425.

Furlong, William Barry:
   The Flow Experience: The Fun in Fun.
   Psychology Today, June, 1976.
Gallwey, Timothy W.:
   The Inner Game of Tennis.
   Random House, New York, 1974.
Garfield, Charles A.:
   Peak Performance: Mental Training Techniques of the World's Great-
   est Athletes.
   Jeremy P. Tarcher, Inc., 1984.
Goodenough, F.L.:
   Draw-a-Man Test: the measurement of intelligence by drawings.
   Yonkers-on-Hudson, NY: World Book, 1926.
Goyette, C.H., Conners, C.K., & Ulrich, R.F.:
   Normative data on revised Conners parent and teacher rating scales.
   J. Abnorm. Child Psychol. 6:221–236, 1978.
Gray, J. A.:
   The neuropsychology of anxiety: An inquiry into the functions of the
   septo-hippocampal system.
   New York: Oxford University Press, 1982.
Hagen, J. W., & Hale, G.A.:
   The development of attention in children. In A. Pick, Minnesota Sym-
   posia on Child Psychology, Vol. 7. Minneapolis: University of Min-
   nesota Press, 1973.
Halacy, D.S., Jr.:
   Man and Memory: Breakthroughs in the Science of the Human Mind.
   New York, Harper & Row, 1970.
Hallahan, Dr. Daniel
   Improving Attention & Self-Monitoring: A Manual for Teachers
   Learning Disabilities Research Institute, Charlottesville, VA.
Halliwell, J.W., & Solan, H. A.:
   The effects of a supplemental perceptual training program on reading
   achievement.
   Exceptional Children, 1972, 38, 613–619.
Helfgott, E., Rudel, R. G., & Kairam, R.:
   The effect of piracetam on short- and long-term verbal retrieval in
   dyslexic boys.
   International Journal of Psychophysiology, 1986, 4, 53–61.
Helfrich, Janet S., Ed.D.:
   Learn To Concentrate.
   Athletic Journal,
   Dec. 1986.
Herold, Mort:
   You Can Have a Near-Perfect Memory.

Contemporary Books, Chicago, 1982.

Higbee, Kenneth L.:
Your Memory: How It Works and How to Improve It.
Prentice Hall, Inc., 1977.

Hunt, Morton:
The Universe Within.
Simon & Schuster, New York, 1982.

Husain, A, Chapel, J, & Malek-Ahmakdi, P.:
Methylphenidate, neuroleptics and dyskinesia-dystonia.
Can. J. Psychiatry 25:254–258, 1980.

Irlen, H.:
Personal correspondence concerning the use of colored lenses in dyslexia or LD. 1988.

Johnson, George
Learning How it Works
New York Times Magazine, August 9, 1987.

Kaga, K., March, R. R., & Tanaka, Y.:
Influence of labyrinthine hypoactivity on gross motor development of infants. In B. Cohen, International meeting of the Barany Society. Annals of the New York Academy of Science. 1981, 374, 412–420.

Kahn, E., & Cohen, L.H.:
Organic drivenness.
NEJM 1934, 210: 748–756.

Kirby, E.A., & Grimley, L.K.:
Understanding and treating attention deficit disorder.
Psychology Practitioner Guidebooks.
New York, Pergamon Press. 1986.

Klein, D.R., & Gittelman-Klein, R.:
Problems in diagnosis of minimal brain dysfunction and the hyperkinetic syndrome.
International Journal of Mental Health. 4:45–60, 1975.

Koestler, A.:
The Ghost in the Machine.
New York, Macmillan. 1968.

Kohen-Raz, R.:
Learning disabilities and postural control.
London: Freund, 1988.

Korner, A.F., & Thoman, E. B.:
Visual alertness in neonates as evoked by maternal care.
Journal of Experimental Child Psychology, 1970, 10, 67–78.

LaVelle, J.P.:
Zeroing In On Concentration.
Athletic Journal, June, 1982.

Lambert, N., & Sandoval, J.:

The prevalence of learning disabilities in a sample of children considered hyperactive.
J. Abnorm. Child Psychol. 8:33–51, 1980.
Lane, John & Taylor, Ronald:
America on Drugs.
U.S. News & World Report, Vol. 101, No. 4, July 28, 1986.
Laufer, M.W. & Denhoff, E.:
Hyperkinetic behavior syndrome in children.
J. Pediat. 50: 463. 1957.
Leiner, H.C., Leiner, A. L., & Dow, R. S.:
Does the cerebellum contribute to mental skills?
Behavioral Neuroscience, 1986, 100, 443–454.
Levine, M.D.:
Developmental Variation and Learning Disorders.
Educators Publishing Service, Inc., 1987.
Levine, M.D.:
Explaining Attention Deficits to Children; The Concentration Cockpit: Guidelines for its Utilization.
Distributed by Educators Publishing Service, Inc.,
Cambridge, MA, 02138. Copyright 1988.
Levinson, H. N.:
Smart but feeling dumb.
New York: Warner, 1984.
Levinson, H. N.:
A solution to the riddle dyslexia.
New York: Springer-Verlag, 1980.
Levinson, H. N.:
The cerebellar-vestibular basis of learning disabilities in children, adolescents, and adults: hypothesis and study.
Perceptual and Motor Skills, 1988, 67, 983–1006.
Levinson, H.N.:
Phobia Free.
New York: M. Evans, 1986.
Levinson, H.N.:
A cerebellar-vestibular explanation for fears/phobias.
Perceptual and Motor Skills, 1989 b, 68, 67–84.
Levinson, H.N.:
The cerebellar-vestibular predisposition to anxiety disorders.
Perceptual and Motor Skills, 68, 323–338.(c) 1989.
Levinson, H.N.:
The use & efficacy of the CV stabilizing medications in treating dyslexia, LD or ADD-clinical study.
Manuscript submitted for publication, 1989.
Levinson, H.N.:

Abnormal optokinetic and perceptual span parameters in cerebellar-vestibular dysfunction and learning disabilities or dyslexia.
Perceptual and Motor Skills, 1989 (a), 68, 35–54.

Levinson, H.N.:
The diagnostic efficacy of neurological, ENG, & optokinetic fixation, tracking & perceptual span parameters in dyslexia, LD or ADD.
Manuscript submitted for publication, 1990.

Levinson, H.N.:
Auditory hallucinations in a case of hysteria.
Br. J. Psychiat. 112:19–26.

Levinson, H.N.:
Abnormal optokinetic and perceptual span parameters in cerebellar-vestibular dysfunction and related anxiety disorders.
Perceptual and Motor Skills, 1989 (d), 68, 471–484.

Levinson, H.N:
The diagnostic value of cerebellar-vestibular tests in detecting learning disabilities, dyslexia and attention deficit disorders.
Perceptual and Motor Skills, Aug. 1990.

Llinas, R.:
The cortex of the cerebellum.
Scientific American 232:56–71. 1975.

Lowe, T.L., Cohen, D.J., Detior, J., Kremenitzer, M.W., et al.:
Stimulant medications precipitate Tourette's syndrome.
JAMA 247: 1729–1731, 1982.

Maranto, Gina:
The Mind Within the Brain.
Discover, May, 1984.

Martin, Rod A. and Lefcourt, Herbert M. :
Sense of humor as a moderator of the relation between stressors and moods.
Journal of Personality and Social Psychology, Vol. 45, 1983.

Martz, Larry:
Trying to Say No.
Newsweek, Vol. 108, No. 6, August 11, 1986.

McBee, Susanna & Peterson, Sarah:
How Drugs Sap The Nation's Strength.
U.S. News & World Report: Vol. 94, No. 19, May 16, 1983.

McKean, Kevin:
Memory.
Discover, November, 1983.

Millichap, J. G. & Fowler, G. W.:
Treatment of "minimal brain dysfunction" syndromes. Selection of drugs for children with hyperactivity and learning disabilities. Ped. Clin. N. Am. 14:767–77. 1967.

Minninger, Joan:
  Total Recall: How to Boost Your Memory Power.
  New York, Rodale Press, 1984.
National Association of Secondary School Principals:
  Learning Styles Profile.
  Tom Koerner, Editor & Publisher
North, A.F.:
  Screening in child health care: Where are we now and where are we going?
  Pediatrics 54:631–640, 1974.
Nutrition Foundation:
  The National Advisory Committee on Hyperkinesis and Food Additives. Final Report to the Nutrition Foundation, Oct., 1980.
Olney, Ross R. and Olney, Patricia J.:
  Imaging: Think Your Way to Success in Sports and Classroom.
  New York, Atheneum, 1985.
Owen, G.M.:
  The assessment and recording of measurements of growth of children: Report of a small conference.
  Pediatrics, 51: 461–466, 1973.
Palay, S. L., & Chan-Palay, V.:
  Cerebellar Cortex: Cytology and Organization.
  New York, Springer-Verlag, 1974.
Pele, with Robert L. Fish:
  My Life and the Beautiful Game.
  Garden City, Doubleday 1977.
Pelham, W.E., Atkins, M.S., Murphy, H.S., & Swanson, J.M.:
  A rating scale for the diagnosis of attention deficit disorders: Teacher norms, factor analyses, and reliability.
  Manuscript submitted for publication, 1985.
Pelham, W.E., Atkins, M.S., & Murphy, H.S.:
  ADD with and without hyperactivity: Parent, teacher, and peer rating correlates, in Pelham, W.E.: DSM-III Category of attention deficit disorder: Rationale, operational & correlates.
  Symposium presented at the annual meetings of APA, Los Angeles, Sept. 1981.
Pelham, W.E., & Bender, M.E.:
  Peer relationships in hyperactive children: Description and treatment, in Gadow, K., Bialer, I.(eds.): Advances in Learning and Behavior Disabilities., Vol. 1., Greenwich, Conn, JAI Press 1982, pp 365–436.
Pelham, W.E., Schnedler, R.W., Bender, M.E., et al.:
  The combination of behavior therapy and methylphenidate in the treatment of attention deficit disorders: A therapy outcome study, in Bloomingdale, L. (ed.): Attention Deficit Disorders, vol 1.

New York, Spectrum, in press.

Penrose, Roger:
The Emperor's New Mind, Concerning Computers, Minds and the Laws of Physics.
Oxford University Press, 1989.

Physicians Desk Reference:
PDP Edition 44, Edward R. Burnhart, 1990.

Piece, J.R.:
Optometric development vision therapy and academic achievement.
Review of Optometry. 114:48–63, 1977.

Powers, Melvin and Starrett, Robert S.:
A Practical Guide to Better Concentration.
Wilshire Book Co., North Hollywood, California, 1962.

Rapoport, J.L., Buchsbaum, M.S., Zahn, T.P., Weingartner, H., et al.:
Dextroamphetamine: Cognitive and behavioral effects in normal prepubertal boys. Science 199: 560–562, 1978.

Rappaport, J.:
Childhood behavior & learning problems treated with imipramine.
Int. J. Neuropsychiat. 1: 635–642. 1965.

Riddle, D., & Rapoport, J.:
A 2-year follow-up of 72 hyperactive boys.
J. Nerv. Ment. Dis. 162:126, 1976.

Robinson, D.P.:
Adaptive gain control of vestibulo-ocular reflex by the cerebellum.
J. Neurophysiol. 39:954–969. 1976.

Roche, A.F., Lipman, R.S., Overall, J.E., & Hung, W.:
The effects of stimulant medication on the growth of hyperkinetic children.
Pediatrics 63: 847–850, 1979.

Ross, A.O.:
Psychological Aspects of Learning Disabilities and REading Disorders.
New York, McGraw–Hill, 1976.

Safer, D.J. & Allen, R.P.:
Hyperactive Children: Diagnosis and Management.
Baltimore, University Park Press, 1976.

Satterfield, J.H., Hoppe, C.M., & Schell, A.M.:
A prospective study of delinquency in 110 adolescent boys with attention deficit disorder and 88 normal adolescent boys.
Amer. J. Psychiat. 139: 795, 1982.

Schommer, Nancy:
Stopping Scoliosis
Avery Publishing Group, New York.

Seiden, L., & Dykstra, L.:

Psychopharmacology.
New York, Wiley, 1971.

Shainberg, Lawrence:
Finding "The Zone."
The New York Times Magazine, April 9, 1989.

Shaywitz, S.E., Cohen, D.J., & Shaywitz, B.A.:
The biochemical basis of minimal brain dysfunction.
J. Pediat. 92:179–187, 1978.

Sleator, E.K., & Ullmann, R.K.:
Can the physician diagnose hyperactivity in the office?
Pediatrics 67: 13–17, 1981.

Sleator EK, Ullmann RK, & von Neumann A.:
How do hyperactive children feel about taking stimulants and will they tell the doctor?
Clin. Pediatr. 21:474–479, 1982.

Sleator, E.K., & Pelham, W.E.:
Attention Deficit Disorder, Dialogues in Pediatric Management.
Appleton-Century-Crofts/Norwalk, Connecticut, Vol.1, No.3, 1987.

Smith, Richard M. & Morganthau, Tom:
The Plague Among Us: Crack & Crime.
Newsweek, Vol. 107, No. 24, June 16, 1986.

Snider, R.:
The cerebellum.
Scientific American 174: 84–90. 1958.

Spitz, R.A.:
Hospitalism: An inquiry into the genesis of psychoanalytic conditions in early childhood. The Psychoanalytic Study of the Child, Vol. 1.
New York, International University Press. 1945.

Sprague, R., & Sleator, E.:
Methylphenidate in hyperkinetic children: Differences in dose effects on learning and social behavior.
Science 198: 1274, 1977.

Stephens, R.S., Pelham, W.E., & Skinner R.:
State-Dependent and Main Effects of Methylphenidate and Pemoline on Paired-Associate Learning and Spelling in Hyperactive Children.
Journal of Consulting and Clinical Psychology, 1984, 52:1, 104–113.

Swanson, J., Kinsbourne, M., Roberts, W., & Zucker, K.:
Time-response analysis of the effect of stimulant medication on the learning ability of children referred for hyperactivity.
Pediatrics 61:21, 1978.

Swanson, J.M., Sandman, C., Deutsch, C., & Baren, M.:
Methylphenidate (Ritalin) given with or before breakfast (part 1): Behavioral, cognitive and electrophysiological effects.
Pediatrics 72:49, 1983.

290

Time:
 The Enemy Within.
 Time, Vol. 128, No. 9, Sept. 15, 1986.
Trotter, Robert J.:
 The Mystery of Mastery.
 Psychology Today, July, 1986.
Uhes, Dr. M.:
 Learn How to Quantify Your Stress
 Human Performance Institute
 Lakewood, CO.
USA Today:
 The $110,000,000,000 Problem: Drugs.
 USA Today, Nov., 1988.
Ulman, R.K., Sleator, E.K., & Sprague, R.L.:
 A new rating scale for diagnosis and monitoring of ADD children.
 Psychopharm. Bull. 20:160, 1984.
Vinogradova, O.S.:
 Functional organization of the limbic system in the process of regis-
 tration of information: facts and hypotheses. In R. L. Isaacson and
 K.H. Pribram, The Hippocampus (Vol. S).
 New York, Plenum Press, 1975, pp. 3–60.
Von Uexkull, J.:
 A stroll through the worlds of animals and men. In Schiller, H. (ed.),
 Instinctive Behaviour.
 New York, International Universities Press, 1957.
Weiss, B., & Laties, V.G.:
 Enhancement of human performance by caffeine and the
 amphetamines.
 Pharmacol. Rev. 14: 1–36, 1962.
Weiss, G., Kruger, E., Danielson, U., & Elman, M.:
 Effects of long-term treatment of hyperactive children with
 methylphenidate.
 Canad. Med. Assn. J. 112: 159, 1975.
Wender, P.H.:
 Minimal brain dysfunction: An overview. In Lipton, M.A., DiMascio,
 A., Kilan, K.F.: Psychopharmacology: A Generation of Progress.
 New York, Raven, 1978.
Wender, P. H.:
 Minimal Brain Dysfunction in Children.
 John Wiley & Sons. New York, N.Y. 1971.
Wender, P.H.:
 The Hyperactive Child, Adolescent, and Adult: Attention Deficit Dis-
 order Through the Lifespan.
 New York, Oxford University Press, 1987.

Werner, Emmy E., Bierman, Jessie M., & French, Fern E.
   The Children of Kauai: Longitudinal Study from the Prenatal Period
   to Age Ten.
   Honolulu, University of Hawaii Press, 1971.
Werry, J.S., Minde, K., Weiss, G., Dogan, K., & Hoy, E.:
   Studies on the hyperactive child-VII: Neurological Status Compared
   With Neurotic and Normal Children.
   Amer. J. Orthopsychiat. 42(3), April 1972.
West, Robin Ph.D.:
   Memory Fitness Over 40.
   Triad Publishing Company, 1985.
Wolkenberg, Frank:
   Out of A Darkness.
   New York Times Magazine:62–83, October, 1987.
Wood, C. D., Cramer, B., & Graybiel, A.:
   Anti-motion sickness drug efficacy.
   Otolaryngology Head and Neck Surgery, 1981, 89, 1041–1044.
Wood, C. D., & Graybiel, A.:
   A theory of motion sickness based on pharmacological reactions.
   Clinical Pharmacology Therapeutics, 1970, 11, 621–624.
Wurtman, Judith J., & Margret Danbrot:
   Managing Your Mind and Mood Through Food.
   Rawson Associates, New York, 1986.

Index